A History of American Popular Music

A History of American Popular Music

FIRST EDITION

Philip Simon

Osher Life Long Learning Institute at Temple University

cognella
SAN DIEGO

Bassim Hamadeh, CEO and Publisher
John Remington, Executive Editor
Gem Rabanera, Senior Project Editor
Jeanine Rees, Production Editor
Emely Villavicencio, Senior Graphic Designer
JoHannah McDonald, Licensing Coordinator
Natalie Piccotti, Director of Marketing
Kassie Graves, Vice President of Editorial

Printed in the United States of America.

cognella® | ACADEMIC PUBLISHING
3970 Sorrento Valley Blvd., Ste. 500, San Diego, CA 92121

Brief Contents

Detailed Contents

Acknowledgments

Any author has a long list of people to thank for the inspiration and production of their book, and I am no exception, so I want to sincerely thank the following people and groups for their inspiration and help in writing *A History of American Popular Music.*

Lucinda (Cindy) Simon

My wife and partner for 33 years, who gave up so much of her time and who patiently provided so much love, support, and counsel during the writing of this book. She read, proofread, and offered content suggestions for most of the manuscript, and she cleaned up much of my erratic writing.

Marshall Kornblatt

My good friend and partner in musical crime, who also read much of the manuscript and offered suggestions for content. Marshall and I have played together (he is a wonderful jazz pianist) for 18 years, and he has spent dozens of hours with my Music 101 classes teaching the art of jazz and providing insight into how to listen to music.

Dr. Mark Johnson

Assistant Professor of Music and Associate Band Director at Christopher Newport University in Virginia, who became Director of Bands at Wilkes University after my retirement in 2019. Mark was originally going to be a co-writer on this book but instead opted to read and offer commentary on some of the chapters. Mark is a great friend and colleague.

Gem Rabanera

My Editor and champion, who went to bat for me and helped ensure my book made it to the finish line. Thanks Gem for believing in the project and being my constant advisor and support.

My Students

Since 1972, I have taught some form of American popular music history and performance at either the high school or college level. Every student I have engaged with has probably taught me as much or more than I taught them. I truly believe in two guiding principles of education: the teachable moment and the importance of engaging students face-to-face in the classroom.

My Teachers

Roger Dow, my senior high school English teacher, taught me to care about my writing.

Dr. Kenneth Melvin. Received his PhD under Bertrand Russell and introduced me to my lifelong passion for educational philosophy and the importance of education.

Dr. Artin Arslanian. The first great conductor and musical mentor in my life. He taught me compassion and passion for music.

Willis Traphagan. My tuba teacher at Boston University who gave me the confidence and musical knowledge to become a professional musician.

Willis Conover. The Voice of The Voice of America Radio Network, who introduced me to the study of American Popular Music in a summer class at the University of Maryland in 1971. Perhaps the most brilliant man I have ever known.

For all of the above, this book is dedicated to you!

Introduction

This book is the culmination of over fifty years of study, research, and teaching the history of American popular music. I do not consider myself an expert on the subject; there are numerous scholars—many of whom consulted for and are cited in this book—who can rightly be considered experts in one or more areas of APM.

This book is for you, the listener and student of American Popular Music. No matter what your age, you can become a more discerning consumer of music, popular or otherwise, by studying the music, learning to listen more deeply to it, and absorbing the fascinating history of it.

You owe it to yourself to be knowledgeable about the music you listen to on a daily basis. You will find that the more you understand what to listen for and how to evaluate it, the more your enjoyment of the music will grow. There is real pleasure in knowing how to describe, analyze, and deconstruct almost anything, and music is no exception. The best thing that can happen is for you to become familiar with a new style of music and add it to your daily listening.

I hope this book is stimulating to you and encourages you to broaden your musical interests.

Happy listening,
Dr. Philip G. Simon

Chapter 1

The Origins of American Popular Music

IMAGE 1.1

KEY TERMS

African retentions
European retentions
Two basic functions of music
Cost of slavery
Musical instrument classifications
Basic elements of music

Introduction

> Popular music ... is a lot easier to recognize than describe. We may define it as the result of a more than 400-year-old blending in the United States of two great music traditions, the European and the (West) African. It follows that, in a musical culture which began as predominantly European, the qualities that make popular music a little different and immediately recognizable probably have something to do with West Africa. (Stearns, 1958)

American popular music, in all its varied forms, is one of the most successful genres of music in human history. Music from North America, Central America, South America, and the Caribbean islands has dominated commercial music markets in much of the world for over 100 years.

It is doubtful that anyone in the first decade of the 20th century could have imagined that the folk music of Africa, brought by slaves to the Americas and blended with the European music tradition, would emerge as the preeminent folk and commercial music in the world during the 1920s and remain so to the present day. Louis Armstrong's second wife, Lil Hardin Armstrong, is quoted as saying, "We had no idea in the beginning that jazz was going to be that important, that somebody would want to know how we started, what we did, what records we made, and it's amusing to read in books telling why we did this. I'm glad they know because we didn't" (Ward & Burns, 2000, p. 129). Its popularity has eclipsed Western European concert music, commonly known as "classical music," which dominated Europe and America from the late 1700s to the early 20th century.

Purpose

Chapter 1 introduces the student to the major premise of the book—that the centuries old music and culture of West Africa blended with European music and cultural traditions on the plantations of the Southern United States, Central America, South America, and the Caribbean islands. In addition, the chapter provides definitions for, and descriptions of, the terminology and concepts used in the book. The reader will become familiar with and use this terminology as a working vocabulary to describe and understand the development of African American and European music into American popular music.

Outcomes

After reading Chapter 1, the student will have a thorough understanding of the following concepts and terms:

- The dual origins of American popular music
- Musical instrument classifications
- The basic elements of music
- African and European retentions
- The basic functions of music
- The importance of religion (especially Catholicism) to the development of American popular music

What Are African Retentions?

An **African retention** is a stylistic trait of African folk music or culture that has been passed on from generation to generation from the ancient origins of the culture to the present day. They are the African contributions to the building blocks of African American music and, especially, American popular music. For the purposes of this book, the study of American popular music history spans the time of the Middle Passage or Maafa (beginning of the slave trade) until the present day.

The following African retentions have the most profound influence on American popular music. They will be explained and discussed in detail in Chapter 2. Many others will also be examined throughout this book.

African pentatonic scale
The blues scale
Polyrhythm
Ring shout
Field hollers, shouts
Nonsense syllables
Call and response
The Trickster
Jure' (testifying shouts)
Ululating
Secret societies

What Are European Retentions?

European retentions are the musical and cultural traditions brought to the Western Hemisphere by the earliest settlers from Europe. The Spanish, Portuguese, Dutch, French, German, and English Colonists each brought their indigenous musical culture with them to the new world. They shared a common set of musical styles and traits, which collectively are called the European canon of musical tradition. When Africans were brought to the Americas as slaves, they learned these European traditions, and naturally, over time, added their own rhythmic and melodic patterns to the music to which they were exposed in church and the master's house. Some slaves, especially those trained as servants, learned to sing or play European instruments, such as violin, piano, organ, and guitar so that they could entertain the family and house guests at parties and dances.

The European retentions that blended with African elements and developed into American popular music are the following:

- major and minor scale system (often expressed as do, re, mi, fa, sol, la, ti, do)
- harmonic practices (chords)
- rhythm
- melody
- form

Other European retentions, such as stylistic features, will be discussed later in this book. The addition of African retentions, complex polyrhythms, and pentatonic melodic elements to these European retentions created American popular music during four centuries of blending.

The Two Basic Functions of Music

Whenever our lives include worship or entertainment, music is often part of the mix. Music is used both in sacred and secular settings.

Sacred (Religious)

Sacred music is used in most all religions as an accompaniment or at least a call to worship. It may be used in various ways: as simple melodies sung by one singer or multiple singers (chorus in unison); vocal soloists or groups accompanied by keyboard or instrumental groups, or harmonized melodies sung in parts, instrumental solos or ensembles. There are virtually unlimited combinations of voices and instruments.

Secular (Entertainment/Celebration)

Secular music is made for primarily social functions such as dancing, celebrations, and funerals (also sacred in nature). Secular music is made similarly to sacred music, either composed or improvised.

The list of musical techniques and cultural traits, collectively known as African and European retentions, combined musical and cultural influences from both continents and shaped almost all the genres of American popular music. They morphed into a cohesive whole over time, to form a new music unlike any before it. The mix has gone so far as to obscure many of the techniques unique to African folk music because we can more readily discern the European influences. However, some of the most prominent retentions are still in use and ubiquitous in contemporary popular music writing and performance.

Musical Instrument Classifications

- Idiophones, such as the xylophone, which produce sound by vibrating themselves
- Membranophones, such as drums or kazoos, which produce sound by a vibrating membrane
- Chordophones, such as the piano or cello, which produce sound by vibrating strings
- Aerophones, such as the pipe organ or oboe, which produce sound by vibrating columns of air
- Metallophones—metal instruments which are struck
- Electrophones, such as the electric guitar or electric bass, which produce sound through electricity and is required to be plugged in to an amplifier

Some connections between African music and culture and European music and culture, blended over more than four centuries of African American life in the southern United States, Central America, South America, and the Caribbean Islands:

- The Trickster, the African tradition of self-denigration and insults to others as entertainment
- Education of black house slaves in European music reading and performance on European classical musical instruments

- African secret societies, the typically all-male social unit (similar to the Masons or Knights of Columbus), which carry many of a tribe's cultural and musical traditions from generation to generation
- African pentatonic scale, the five-note melodic pattern in African music that is represented by the black notes on the piano
- African polyrhythm, the highly complex rhythmic structure of African folk music
- African musical instruments and vocal techniques, developed over centuries, taught by rote and handed down from generation to generation, carried in memory across the sea on slave ships and reconstructed from available materials in the New World
- Polytheistic African religions that allowed slaves to embrace Christianity (especially Catholicism with its many saints, the Virgin Mary, and the Holy Trinity, that seemed quite familiar to Africans used to worshipping many deities)

The Middle Passage, or Maafa, forcibly brought some 20 to 60 million people from the West Coast of Africa to the Western Hemisphere to be sold into slavery. The rich heritage of centuries of African culture traveled with them and, where allowed by the plantation owners, took root in the slave quarters and fields of the new world (Taylor, 2018, p. 55). Whether or not a slave was allowed to retain and practice his or her cultural and musical heritage was mostly a matter of the Christian religious practice of their owners. Slaves who were bought by Catholic plantation owners (most often Spanish, French, or Portuguese), were allowed to retain their culture and customs, including music, dance, religion, and language. When a slave ended up on a Protestant plantation (often smaller in size and number of slaves), there was often an expectation by the owner that the slaves would quickly adopt the faith, language, and "civilized manners" of their masters and renounce any outward African traits or retentions (Stearns, 1958).

In *The Story of Jazz*, Marshall Stearns discusses one stunning example of how the French–Catholic plantation owners in the Mississippi Delta region (the region near New Orleans that has a strong French heritage and tradition) likely contributed to the development of early Jazz in New Orleans. The French preferred slaves from Dahomey, who were bought in Haiti and whose religion, vodun, worshipped the snake god, Damballa, one of many deities. Slaves were forced to convert to Christianity on every plantation, whether Protestant or Catholic. But, newly converted Catholic slaves "... soon discovered that a great many Catholic saints bore resemblance to their own gods. The Church had pictures of the saints ... which suggested pointed parallels. St. Patrick, pictured driving the snakes out of Ireland (an Irish Catholic myth which persists to this day), reminded the slave of his own Damballa ... So, on St. Patrick's Day, the slaves played the drum rhythms sacred to Damballa, and worshipped both Damballa and St. Patrick at the same time ... on the same altar" (Stearns, 1958, p. 20).

Incidences such as the above multiplied many times over during the slave epoch, allowed the slaves on Catholic plantations to retain and practice significant portions of their indigenous religious, cultural, and musical heritage. On Protestant plantations, slaves were typically forced to worship only in the Christian way, but they adapted their worship, especially congregational singing in church, to the use of their traditional retentions—the African pentatonic scale (blended with the European major and minor scale system), call and response (also a European retention used in Protestant and Catholic religious services), and jure' or testifying (again, something familiar that they saw in White Protestant Church services).

Listen to and view these examples of African folk music, which use musical techniques that are African retentions.

Old African Polyrhythms

Watch at: https://www.youtube.com/watch?v=rrEqNTyMF_A

Butour Ngale—African Polyrhythm Demonstration

Watch at: https://www.youtube.com/watch?v=haGWi5lTibl

Key Takeaways

- American popular music is the result of over four centuries of blending African folk music and culture with European folk and classical music and culture.
- Retentions from both Europe and Africa contributed to the emergence of a new music, which was unlike any other on earth, around 1900.
- American popular music is one of the most long-lived and successful musics in world history.
- American popular music is known and enjoyed around the world.
- The Christian religion played an important role in shaping the retention of African music and culture.

Review Questions

Directions: Refer to what you learned in this chapter to help you respond completely and correctly to the questions and prompts below.

1. List and define the four basic elements of music.
2. In your own words, explain *secret societies* and their purpose. Give one example of a secret society.
3. What are some ramifications of the Maafa or Middle Passage on today's American society?
4. Why did slaves on Latin/French/Portuguese owned plantations have a better chance of passing their culture and music on to future generations?
5. Name five African or European retentions that remain important elements of our current popular music. Explain their importance.

Class Project

Build an African style percussion instrument from any materials found around your home or living space. Use one of the first five musical instrument classifications on page 3 as a template for constructing your instrument. Practice playing your instruments together in class using polyrhythms based on grouping of two, three, four, and six beats simultaneously. This will give you a feel for African style polyrhythmic drumming.

References

Stearns, M. (1958). *The story of jazz.* Oxford University Press.

Taylor, R. G. (2018). *The odyssey of an African American international educator in the field of modern world languages: An autoethnographic study.* Unpublished doctoral dissertation. Wilkes University.

Ward, J. C., & Burns, K. (2000). *Jazz: A history of America's music.* Alfred A. Knopf.

Credit

IMG 1.1: Copyright © 2014 Depositphotos/Mattz90.

From Africa to the Americas

Introduction

In Chapter 2, the reader will develop an understanding of the importance of European and African retentions to the development of American popular music. The chapter provides detailed definitions for the basic elements of music, European and African retentions, and discusses the role of Christian religions, especially Catholicism, in the continuation of centuries-old African retentions on the slave population of the Americas and Caribbean islands.

Purpose

This chapter provides the reader with detailed definitions of the terminology used throughout the book. The importance of African and European retentions and their gradual blending during the slave epoch in the southern United States is central to understanding the emergence of American popular music from before the Civic War into the 20th century.

Outcomes

- Students will be able to articulate the importance of European and African retentions to the emergence of American popular music in the United States and ultimately around the globe.
- Students will memorize and be able to articulate verbally and in writing the definitions in the chapter.
- Students will learn to use the definitions provided to describe the various ways in which American popular music progressed

KEY TERMS

Retentions
Basic elements of music
Folk music
European classical music
Maafa or Middle Passage
Pentatonic scale
Polyrhythm
Ring Shout
Field hollers
Call and response
The trickster
Jure
Ululating
Secret societies
Nonsense syllables
Form
Harmony
Melody
Rhythm
Major and minor scale

from the blending of African and European music, to slave life on the plantation, to African American music in the Post-Civil War Era.

- Students will be able to articulate the significant role that Christianity, especially Catholicism, played in the retention of African culture and music that led to the development of American popular music.

African and European Retentions That Shaped a New Music

The centuries of contact between African and European peoples (even before the advent of the slave trade) caused a blending of cultural traits known as retentions. Dozens of such retentions from both African and European sources resulted in a thorough blending of the melodic, rhythmic, harmonic, and formal elements of West African and European musical traditions.

Foli: A Stunning Example of the Depth of African Musical and Cultural Tradition

Watch at: https://www.youtube.com/watch?v=IVPLIuBy-9CY&list=RDrrEqNTyMF_A&index=4

In Chapter 1, we discussed **retention** as a trait that is transmitted from generation to generation within a culture and passed from one culture to another. African musical retentions, mostly in the form of melody and rhythm, are highly complex and many centuries old.

The video Foli provides a stunning example of the depth of African musical and cultural tradition. Although this video is a snapshot of one tribe, it exemplifies the total integration of music into daily tribal life, which is pervasive and consistent throughout the African continent.

Variations in the Basic Elements of Music

"Fantasia on 'In Dulci Jubilo,'" composed by Johann Sebastian Bach

Watch at: https://youtu.be/9tgUK4YGegM

The four basic elements of music are melody, harmony, rhythm, and form. African rhythm and melody are very complex, while European music, by comparison, is simple melodically and rhythmically. However, over many centuries European composers developed a complex harmonic language and sophisticated formal structures. European music uses very specific written symbols that do not allow a performer to deviate from the written page. For an example of European music from the mid-1700s (approximately the same time in the United States when slaves on American plantations began to meld African and European traditions into a new musical language), listen to "Fantasia on 'In Dulci Jubilo,'" composed by Johann Sebastian Bach.

Johann Sebastian Bach, considered to be one of the great composers of any era in Western European art music, wrote

FIGURE 2.1 European Performing Group (Orchestra)

music that was highly complex harmonically and structurally, but rhythmically and melodically less so. This recording of "In Dulci Jubilo," played on the organ, is powerful and deeply moving, especially in the context of a Christian worship service. Much of Bach's music was composed specifically for the church, but he also wrote what now is considered "art music"—music intended to intellectually challenge and emotionally uplift the listener.

It is important to understand that every note of most music of European composers is notated; that is, written down for each musician who plays the piece. Only occasionally is a performer, most often a soloist, allowed to improvise in a cadenza—a section in a piece for a solo instrument where, according to a prescribed set of rules, the soloist may create his or her own melodic material.

Not until the 20th century and the nexus of African American/European music blending is there any non-notated or extemporaneous (improvised) music. The one exception to this is the "experimental" 20th century music of some European and American composers who choose to eschew most traditional European music practices in favor of performance freedom and experimentation with "modern" musical techniques.

Here is an example of such a piece by the Italian contemporary composer Luciano Berio. It is "modern classical" music: *Ofanim (extraits)*.

By contrast, African folk music, even today, is utilitarian. It is used in daily living to accompany all manner of activities: pounding grain, washing clothes, chopping wood, celebrating harvest, birth, and death, and going to war. For the African tribesman, music flows from and accompanies every daily endeavor. In fact, there is no word in African languages for

Example of Modern Classical Music—*Ofanim (Extraits)* by Luciano Berio

Watch at: https://youtu.be/KfAGRunsgyA

art. Instead, what seems like art to Western eyes—sculpture, drawing, drumming, dancing, and singing—is the accumulation of centuries of culture and tradition used in daily life and passed on from generation to generation by rote.

Much of African cultural heritage was retained during the more than 400 years of African residence in the Americas. It is well documented that West Africans who were brought to the Americas as slaves brought no material possessions with them on the journey. In addition, when they arrived at one of the ports in the Caribbean, they were emaciated from months of below decks travel on a ship. They survived on almost no food, were scantily or completely unclothed, and unable to speak any language but their native tongue. These were the hearty souls who survived wretched shipboard conditions. Hundreds of thousands more perished along the way and were callously dumped overboard.

The survivors carried with them thousands of years of cultural traditions or retentions, handed down by their elders and retained in memory, which helped them to survive and build new cultural pathways in their new environment. Depending on the destination, whether a Catholic or Protestant plantation in the Southern United States, the Caribbean, Central American, or South America, they were more or less able to retain significant amounts of their musical and cultural heritage. A quick examination of this process, as described by Marshall Stearns, aids in an understanding of why so much of West Africa's tribal rituals and musical elements survived—most of them to this day.

The process of selecting slaves for a particular plantation evolved into a very specific set of choices, dependent on the preferences of a plantation owner. Stearns provides an overview of this:

> Beginning in the early 1600s, the search for slaves advanced down the West Coast of Africa, ... Portuguese traders, then Dutch, English and lastly French, dominated the trade. Each nation supplied its own colonies in the New World with slaves from the tribes it had plundered. ... Planters in each colony came to prefer the specific tribes supplied by the mother country. Thus, Brazilian planters continued to prefer the Senegalese slaves taken by Portuguese slavers, Spanish plantation owners preferred Yorubas, English, Ashantis, and French, the Dahomeans. Exceptions aside, the overall pattern continues to today: The African roots of Cuban (Spanish) music are Yoruban, Jamaican (British) is Ashanti, and in Haiti (French), Dahomean. (Stearns, 1958, p. 17)

Notice that three of the four major slave trading countries were predominantly Catholic. This provides a clue as to why so much of West African culture and tradition, as well as tribal ways survived in the often-brutal plantation environment of the New World. African tribal customs dictated that due to centuries of intertribal warfare and the consequent enslavement of the loosing tribe, the losers must adopt the customs and religion of the conquering tribe. Assimilation (and syncretism) became a way of life for enslaved tribesmen, long before the European slave traders arrived (Stearns, 1958).

The Cost of Slavery

"The Atlantic slave trade was itself a devastating but profitable capitalist venture for the West that trafficked in human cargo and spanned several centuries. It became a major factor in white domination and economic control of market forces. For the whole of humanity, the Middle Passage or **Maafa**—the African Holocaust— remains the largest and most callous mass migration imposed upon a people, transferring an estimated 20 to 60 million people across the globe to unknown lands.

The Nobel laureate Toni Morrison describes slavery as "the overweening, defining event of the modern world" because it was the "largest forced transfer of people in the history of the world." The Maafa provoked an unprecedented mass upheaval and uprooting of humanity never seen before or since. The consequences are still prevalent in life situations of individuals and communities to this day. Some of the modern-day consequences of the Maafa are apparent in the devaluing of Black life, in poverty, in the surge of stress-related health conditions, general miseducation, and the reification of white supremacist, neo-colonialist attitudes of white rule and privilege" (Taylor, 2018, p. 55).

Depending on where a slave ended up, he/she might be exposed to very different customs and musical and cultural traditions, and experience more or less horrifically violent treatment. Stearns suggests that slaves were treated very differently depending on whether they were sold to a Latin or French Catholic plantation or to a British/Protestant plantation (Stearns, 1958). "The general attitude ... of the Latin-Catholic planters, as contrasted to the attitude of the British-Protestant slave owners, permitted the survival of more West African traditions. If a planter was Portuguese, Spanish, or French, he didn't seem to care about what a slave thought or did in his spare time ... With a British owner, however, a slave was more likely to change his ways more quickly, discarding his own traditions and adopting the new" (Stearns, 1958, p. 18). The daily regimentation of slaves on Protestant plantations precluded them from practicing their indigenous cultural traditions, except in secret.

While all slaves in the southern U.S., Central America, and South America, and the Caribbean experienced cruel, violent, and exploitive conditions, those who lived and worked on Latin–Catholic plantations were more likely to retain, and outwardly practice, their indigenous culture and music than were their counterparts on British plantations. Typically, the British owned smaller plantations with fewer slaves. A slave might become more personally familiar with the "Massa" (plantation owner), perhaps even serving as a house slave and learning to sing or play a European musical instrument such as violin or piano in order to entertain the family and house guests. This acculturation into traditional European behaviors caused them to see White men as civilized and look to adopt that lifestyle, while concealing their own culture and traditions. This led to the need for recognition in White society on the part of freed African Americans before and after Emancipation. In particular, Protestant slave owners were insistent that their chattel renounce all vestiges of their polytheistic religion and convert to Christianity, specifically some form of Protestant worship (Stearns, 1958). This generated the importance of congregational church singing, which gave rise to the spirituals and gospel music of the black churches.

The Development of Distinct African American Music

As with almost all musical forms during recorded history, the earliest introductions of musical change proceed gradually, over hundreds of years. In Europe for example, the first form of standardized music, called plain chant, proceeded from simple one-line melodies to more complex multipart pieces over a period of almost 1,000 years.

In the United States, the first people to practice the transitional styles that contributed to the rise of American popular music will never be known to the world. They are the thousands of African American musicians whose names are lost in the dust of history, but who made important contributions to the early development of our popular music. Gunther Schuller, in his book, *Early Jazz*, relates a possible scenario by which this happened:

> We have to go back to the beginning of Negro music on this continent. During the seventeenth and eighteenth centuries slave ships brought thousands of Negroes to the Southern waterfront cities. Tribal groups were separated, and individuals shipped to different plantations." Once a slave was at his or her destination, they used their rich musical traditions, especially singing and drumming, to communicate with other slaves in a common musical and rhythmic language that baffled the slave masters. Slaves also appropriated ... some of the music he or she heard in their new surroundings: a fragment from a hymn, a scrap of music heard at a dance, and so on. Very gradually, Negroes all over the South, individually unaware of the totality of this process of musical acculturation, infused the white man's music with their own instinctual traits, leading to an astonishing array of musical expressions. Over many decades this accumulation of musical ideas began to crystalize into more specific modes of expression: the field holler, the spiritual, country blues, work songs, ring shouts and so many others ... all of them strongly related, overlapped and mixed with both African and European musical traits. (Schuller, 1986, p. 34–35)
>
> This "accumulation of musical ideas" is the blending of African and European retentions.

Types of African Musical Retentions

Let's look at African music retentions. We will consider the African pentatonic scale, polyrhythm, ring shout, field hollers and shouts, nonsense syllables, call and response, the trickster, jure' (testifying shouts), and ululating. In addition, we will consider the role of secret societies.

African Pentatonic Scale

A five-note scale forms the melodic basis of much African music. It can be heard as the five black notes (in any sequence) on the piano keyboard. The African thumb piano, called a kalimba, uses the notes of the pentatonic scale. Listen to this example of a kalimba. Only the notes of the pentatonic scale are used to create the melody, but there is also complex polyrhythm being played.

Example of a kalimba, an African Thumb Piano

Watch at: https://youtu.be/Yr-P5sWx-V0

Polyrhythm

Polyrhythm is the simultaneous use of two or more conflicting rhythms that are not derived from one another, or are simple manifestations of the same meter. The rhythmic conflict may be the basis of an entire piece of music. Polyrhythm requires at least two rhythms to be played concurrently. So, for instance, a rhythm in three and a simultaneous rhythm in four is polyrhythmic. Composers of European music seldom use complex polyrhythm. In African folk music,

FIGURE 2.2 The sound of polyrhythm

Example of African Polyrhythms

Watch at: https://youtu.be/rrEqNTyMF_A

polyrhythm is pervasive and constant. For a wonderful example of African polyrhythms watch the following video.

Ring Shout

A ring shout is a circle dance of African derivation used by slaves on southern Protestant owned plantations. Protestant plantation owners did not allow their slaves to practice most African retentions, including dancing (defined as crossing the feet), but the ring dance involved shuffling the feet, thus, according to religious leaders, it was not technically dancing. Modern popular dances, including square dancing, the stroll, and the bunny hop, can be traced to this African retention.

Field Hollers and Shouts

Used by Africans for centuries as communication between individuals over long distances, hollers and shouts became a way to communicate in the plantation fields, especially to signal when the guards were coming or to make fun of a particular guard. The shout/holler tradition continued on after the slave epoch in the performance of the blues, gospel music, and with African American street corner hucksters advertising their wares.

Nonsense Syllables

Nonsense syllables include the use of vocal sounds that are made up, usually improvised, and have no meaning, as part of African folk culture related to poetry, song, and the trickster. One can hear this tradition in the scat of African American jazz musicians, Doo Wop music of the 1950s and 60s, and contemporary rap and hip-hop.

Call and Response

An African song and chant component became important to the enculturation of slaves into the Christian faith. Both African music and Christian hymn singing include call and response—the lead singer or pastor sings a phrase and the congregants respond by singing back the phrase. The typical lead singer for a rock and roll group who asks the audience to sing a line of lyrics in response uses a further distillation of this technique.

The Trickster

The trickster is an ancient African cultural icon and mythological character who jokes with and/or harasses people until they give him a "treat" to go away. This morphed into minstrelsy end men, black comedians (think Eddie Murphy), and storied characters like Br'er Rabbit (in Disney's classic movie, *Song of the South*), Bugs Bunny, and rock and roll front men.

Jure' (Testifying Shouts)

Jure' (Testifying Shouts) is the African and Catholic custom, generally performed by European men during Lent. It includes dancing, singing, and clapping, while singing a short, repeated melody as part of a ring dance (African) or procession (European).

Ululating

Ululating is a high-pitched fluttering sound, made by women in both African and Middle Eastern cultures. It can be either a celebratory or mournful musical gesture, and it may be the model for the shake or lip trill used by jazz trumpet players beginning with Buddy Bolden and Louis Armstrong in New Orleans. It can be heard frequently in modern popular music, especially in rap and hip-hop. You can hear ululating in, "Mighty Mighty," by Earth Wind and Fire, at about the two-minute mark on the recording.

Example of Ululating, from "Mighty Mighty" by Earth Wind and Fire

Watch at: https://youtu.be/7hd-glyRj-A

Secret Societies

Secret societies describe an ancient African custom of male fraternal societies. It continued through African American culture to embody present-day organizations such as krewes in New Orleans, which sponsor marching bands and build floats for street parades such as Mardi Gras and funeral processions. Parallel European organizations include the Knights of Columbus and the Masons.

Types of European Musical Retentions

The European retentions which over time blended with African elements and developed into American popular music are the major and minor scale system, harmonic practices, steady rhythmic pulse, and form. Let's look at each retention individually.

The Major and Minor Scale System

The major and minor scale system of European music is one of many scale systems throughout the world. In the late 16th century, the major/minor scale system gradually emerged as the primary scale system used by European composers. The major scale is represented by the white notes from C to C on the piano keyboard, or the solfege syllables do, re, mi, fa, sol, la, ti, do.

Harmonic Practices (Chords/Harmonies)

The chords and harmonies of European music provide a major contribution to American popular music because African folk music has no purposeful system of chords or harmony. When one hears any harmonization in traditional African folk music, it is a two or three note chord, accidental and the result of singers or instrumental musicians improvising. That is, it occasionally deviates from a unison melody.

Steady Rhythmic Pulse

A steady rhythmic pulse is rhythms based on groupings of three or four beats per measure. European music is relatively simple rhythmically, and this simplicity and regular beat pattern allowed slaves to fit their much more complex polyrhythms into the steady 4/4 beat of a typical Christian hymn or European folk song or dance tune.

Form

Form is the musical structure or organization of a piece of music into distinct sections. A typical form in European music is **AABA**, commonly known as 32-bar song form. European songs of all kinds, when learned in church or on the plantation, gave slaves a simple, basic structure that allowed for the rhythmic and melodic flexibility inherent in African folk music.

The addition of African retentions, complex polyrhythms, and pentatonic melodic elements to these European retentions, over more than four centuries of syncretism (blending), is what ultimately led to modern American popular music.

Key Takeaways

- European and African retentions flow through both cultures.
- These retentions heavily influenced both cultures in America, and when blended together produced a hybrid culture that spawned a new and unique genre of music called American popular music.
- The adoption and adaptation of the Christian religion by African slaves during slavery is a major reason for the development of American popular music.
- It took over 400 years of syncretism (cultural bending) to reach the point where this new music was recognizable and embraced by people throughout the United States and the world.

Review Questions

Directions: Refer to what you learned in this chapter to help you respond completely and correctly to the questions and prompts below.

1. Explain the term *retention.*
2. How does Gunther Schuller describe the process of the blending of African and European music traits?
3. How was a slave affected who was bought by a Catholic rather than a Protestant plantation owner?

4. Discuss the ways in which music and culture were passed on in African tribal life.
5. Did African American musicians find it important to notate their music in order to pass it on to others? Why?
6. Name and describe four African retentions.
7. Name and describe four European retentions.

Extra Credit Project

View one of the videos listed in this chapter again. Take notes while viewing, and then write a one-page report on the use of African and European retentions by the performers in the video.

References

Schuller, G. *(1986). Early jazz: Its roots and musical development* (Rev. ed.). Oxford University Press.

Stearns, M. (1958). *The story of jazz.* Oxford University Press.

Taylor, R. G. (2018). *The odyssey of an African American international educator in the field of modern world languages: An autoethnographic study.* Unpublished doctoral dissertation. Wilkes University.

Credits

Fig. 2.1: Orchestra of the 18th Century, "European Performing Group (Orchestra)," https://commons.wikimedia.org/wiki/File:Orchestra.jpg, 2000.

Fig. 2.2: Copyright © by Emilio Labrador (CC BY 2.0) at https://commons.wikimedia.org/wiki/File:Dashiki_and_kufi.jpg.

Chapter 3

The Slave Experience in the Americas

Plantation Life, Music, Religion, and Syncretism

Introduction

In 1619, "20. and odd Negroes" arrived off the coast of Virginia, where they were "bought for victualle" by labor-hungry English colonists. The story of these captive Africans has set the stage for countless scholars and teachers interested in telling the story of slavery in English North America. "The focus on 1619 has led the general public and scholars alike to ignore more important issues and to silently accept unquestioned assumptions that continue to impact." The teaching of African American history in the United States (Guasco, 2017). There is evidence of a much longer history of African indentured servants and slaves in the Americas than is implied by the traditional story of Africans arriving at Jamestown, Virginia, in 1619.

In Chapter 3, we examine the development of slavery in the Americas and its ramifications for the development of a new music unlike anything heard before. The core ideas in this chapter are slave life on the plantation and the slaves' innate ability to adapt to their forced surroundings, including the replacement (or more precisely blending) of their polytheistic religious beliefs with monotheistic Christianity and the overwhelming importance of syncretism (the assimilation of two or more originally discrete traditions) to the survival of the African race in the Americas.

KEY TERMS

Syncretism
Middle Passage or Maafa
Plantation system
Field slave
House slave
Freed slaves
Emancipation
Ring Shout
Dance, drum, and song

Purpose

The purpose of Chapter 3 is to familiarize the reader with the multitude of adaptations and coping mechanisms used by Africans forcibly brought to the Western Hemisphere for the purpose of using them as slave labor. Their innate ability to adapt to new surroundings because

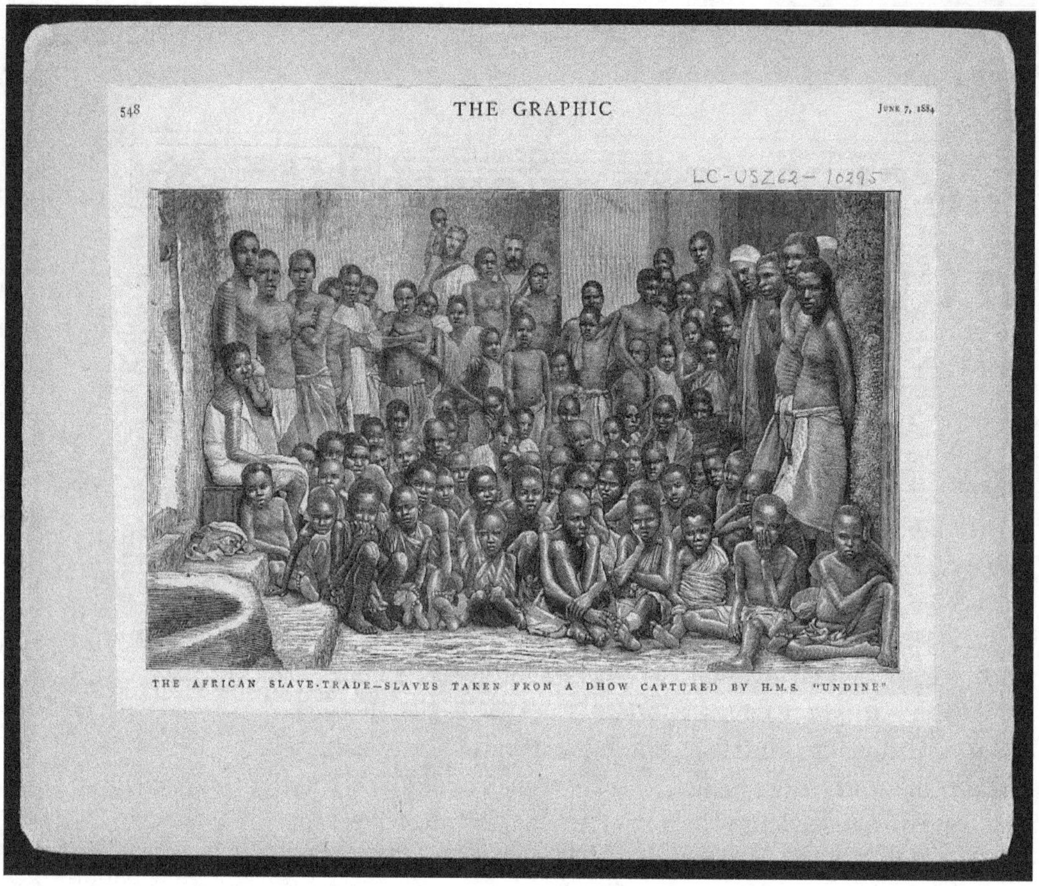

FIGURE 3.1 The African Slave Trade

of centuries of having to do so in Sub-Saharan Africa speaks to their resilience, fortitude, and tenacity.

Outcomes

After reading Chapter 3, the student will be able to:

- Describe and define *syncretism.*
- Articulate the reasons why the Middle Passage, or Maafa, *continues* to impact the lives of African Americans.
- Discuss the importance of African Retentions in American popular music.
- Describe slave life on the plantation.
- Define and give an example of polytheistic religion.
- Define and give an example of monotheistic religion.
- Articulate the importance of religious conversion for African Americans.
- Describe the ring as the transmission device for indigenous African culture.

The Arrival of African Slaves in the Americas

There is an overstated significance of 1619—still a common fixture in American history curriculum(s).

> 1619 was not the first time Africans could be found in an English Atlantic colony, and it certainly wasn't the first time people of African descent made their mark and imposed their will on the land that would someday be part of the United States. As early as May 1616, blacks from the West Indies were already at work in Bermuda providing expert knowledge about the cultivation of tobacco. There is also suggestive evidence that scores of Africans plundered from the Spanish were aboard a fleet under the command of Sir Francis Drake when he arrived at Roanoke Island in 1586.
>
> From the early 1500s forward, the Portuguese, Spanish, English, French, Dutch and others fought to control the resources of the emerging transatlantic world and worked together to facilitate the dislocation of the indigenous peoples of Africa and the Americas. In 1526, enslaved Africans were part of a Spanish expedition to establish an outpost on the North American coast in present-day South Carolina. ... Nearly 100 years before Jamestown, African actors enabled American colonies to survive. (Guasco, 2017)

It seems safe to say that 1500 is a more realistic date for the beginning of the slave trade between Africa and the New World. "By 1860, on the eve of the Civil War, there were almost 4 million slaves in the United States, out of a total population of 32 million," according to Leland (2004). Leland adds, this is remarkable considering that the importation of slaves was banned in the United States in 1808 (2004).

Much of the history of the Middle Passage, or Maafa, is lost to history because thousands of those who boarded ships at slave ports such as Bimbe, Cameroon, died during the trip, and their bodies were unceremoniously dumped overboard. This explains the wide range of numbers reported to have been taken from West Africa over the 400 + years of the slave trade. Whatever the exact numbers, they are staggering. As described by Rodney Taylor, the "African Holocaust" remains the largest and most callous mass migration imposed upon a people, transferring an estimated 20 to 60 million people across the globe to unknown lands (2018).

One of the most neglected, but insidious, historical narrative concerns the role of African tribal chiefs and kings in selling their own people to European slave traders. For centuries before the arrival of European slave ships at African ports, intertribal warfare throughout Africa produced conditions where the victorious tribe took slaves, often entire tribes, forcing the vanquished to adapt and assimilate into a new tribal culture. Over millennia, the ability of Africans to adapt to new surroundings, customs, religious beliefs, and daily living became so ingrained as to be an essential trait for survival. When the European slave ships arrived off the coast of West Africa, this **syncretism**, the ability to adapt, well served those who were sold into slavery by their tribal leadership.

The Nobel laureate Toni Morrison describes slavery as "the overweening, defining event of the modern world" because it was the "largest forced transfer of people in the history of the world." The Maafa provoked an unprecedented mass upheaval and uprooting of humanity never seen before or since, and the consequences are still prevalent in the life situations of individuals and communities to this day (Taylor, 2018).

So how does the Middle Passage, a multi-century crime against humanity, ultimately produce the most unique revolution in music in human history? It is through syncretism, the ability of a human being to adapt to and blend two or more different cultures that this takes form and flourishes.

Africans arrived in the New World, whether it was the islands of Hispaniola, Cuba, Puerto Rico, or a port on the southern coast of the United States, with nothing but possibly the barest of clothing. While they arrived with no possessions, they did possess, and use, the memories of how to build, create, and maintain their centuries old cultural pathways. The previously mentioned notion of African retentions, those cultural traditions and practices passed on from generation to generation over centuries, are what gave newly arrived African men and women the ability to remember and reconstruct all of their indigenous lifestyle, religion, music, and daily living—to the extent that plantation owners let the slaves maintain and practice these retentions.

As we saw in Chapter 2, there were significant differences in plantations owners' tolerance for and acceptance of, their slave's retention and practice of their indigenous cultural beliefs and skills, as well as their religion(s), music, dance, food, and many other traditions.

Enslaved Africans, drawing on centuries of remembered cultural traditions, managed to recreate their familiar tribal surroundings in a new, unfamiliar environment, that of slave camps in plantations all over the Americas. Music in particular, because of its importance to daily life, ranked high on the list of important activities to recreate and reimagine. Religion equally so, at least up to the point where plantation owners forced Christianity on slaves. At one point or another, each of the African retentions was used to fabricate this new life on the plantation.

The Ring Shout

The ring shout, an ancient retention of primary importance to the survival of the slaves, was the carrier of a multitude of musical traditions which became, "... foundational elements of African American music: calls, cries and hollers, call and response devices, polyrhythms, blue notes, elisions ..." and dozens of other musical retentions (Floyd, 1995, p. 6).

> In the world of the slaves, the ring shout fused the sacred and the secular, music and dance; it continued the African ... tendencies to eschew distinctions between religion and everyday life ... (Floyd, 1995, p. 6)

On Catholic owned plantations the ring shout and other indigenous activities were openly practiced during the slaves "off" hours. On the Protestant plantations the slave's musical and religious activities had to be practiced in secret. In both cases, enough of the old ways, traditions stretching back thousands of years, were remembered and retained. They flow through African American music to the present day. The ring shout, jubilee and spirituals, ragtime, blues, New Orleans jazz, rhythm and blues, all were shaped by black dance, drumming, and song, within and without the ring (Floyd, 1995).

Song

> Expressive of the plight of the transplanted African in a new land, black song helped the slaves bridge the newly created cultural gap by serving them in their daily activities. In Africa, men and women sang as they worked, and ... the practice carried over to the often-brutal toil of the African slave throughout the South. On the early plantations ... there were work songs, rhyme songs, songs of satire, derision and mimicry [indicative of the mythological trickster persona], children's songs and lullabies ... (Floyd, 1995, p. 50).

Their songs and vocalizations, shouts, hollers, and nonsense words and phrases accompanied their work in the fields, domestic chores in the "big house," and just about every aspect of daily life. Usually a lead singer set the pace for the group, which resulted in slaves working harder as they sang. At slave auctions singers with the "strongest voices" were likely to fetch the highest price from bidders (Floyd, 1995).

Musical Instruments

"African American song ... was accompanied by instruments, among which were some of African origin" (Floyd, 1995, p. 52). In order to organize their daily lives and give that life some meaning, newly arrived slaves had to design and build musical instruments—banjo (originally banza), reed and nose flute, xylophone, and especially percussion instruments such as log drums, rattles, sticks, bells, etc.—which could be used to accompany daily activities, ceremonies, dancing, and religious activities (Floyd, 1995).

In a previous chapter, the video "Foli" shows the making of a drum (djembe), metal bells, and the use of common household items like gourds, jars, and plastic gas cans to create percussive sounds. Imagine the same things happening, in much the same way, on a plantation during the era of slavery. It must have happened quickly so that traditional celebrations could proceed as soon after arrival as possible.

Consider that not all slaves on a plantation were from the same tribe or even region of West Africa. There had to be a spirit of cooperation and give-and-take within the slave community. The fundamental common purpose—survival—had to be a powerful motivator for them to work together to rebuild a culture similar to what they knew in Africa. This is another manifestation of syncretism that is inherent in the African psyche, borne of thousands of years of adaptation to circumstances beyond their control.

Religion

The first slaves to arrive in the Americas practiced some form of polytheistic religion. In fact, most of the first generation of slaves went to their graves believing in the indigenous tribal faith of their homeland. Each tribe had its own unique set of beliefs and customs. It is estimated that there were more than 3,000 African ethnic groups, each with its own religious system and practices. However, there were some shared basic principles, across all of sub-Saharan Africa, including a minimal and fundamental idea about God (singular) as a creator and provider (Floyd, 1995, p. 15).

While they believed in and worshipped many spirits, ancestors, animals, and mythological creatures, this common notion of a Supreme God bound the newly arrived slaves together so that they either openly or secretly practiced the ancient religious ways of their ancestors. In a previous chapter you read about the region of Africa that is now Dahomey, where the native religion was *Vodun*. They believed in the snake god, Damballa, among other deities. The Dahomians, and the other slaves brought to the Americas by Catholic plantation owners, saw and accepted the Catholic Saints, the Virgin Mary, and the Holy Trinity, which made it somewhat easier for slaves on French and Spanish Catholic plantations to adopt Catholicism. They found that the many lesser deities of Catholicism blended well with their belief in multiple gods and one Supreme God (Floyd, 1995).

In addition, Catholic plantation owners gave the slaves wide latitude in respect to the retention of their native religious beliefs. Thus, it was possible for the Dahomians to worship both their traditional Gods and Christ and the Saints, especially St. Patrick, who is always shown in paintings and icons as stepping on a snake (because he supposedly drove the snakes out of Ireland). Eventually this blending of Vodun and Catholicism morphed into a hybrid religion known today as Voodoo.

On Protestant plantations, the slaves were subjected to much more rigid control in every respect, including the expectation that they would totally renounce their indigenous religions and adopt the Protestant faith of their master. Many slaves continued to practice their native religion in secret, even after converting to Christianity, knowing that being discovered might lead to beatings, whippings, or even death.

Evangelical preachers from the North traveled to the southern plantations with the idea of converting the "heathen slaves" to Christianity. The younger generation of slaves born on the Protestant plantations were influenced by these evangelical preachers to accept the Christian faith. Many of these preachers were successful, and the plethora of evangelical Christian Black churches in the South today is a testament to both the preacher's commitment and the early slave's ability to adapt to a completely different religion and way of life. Both Catholic and Protestant clergy saw it as their mission to save the souls of the slaves.

FIGURE 3.2 Slaves worshipping with their master's family on the plantation

The following video details the assimilation of Christianity (evangelical Protestantism) by the slaves.

Assimilation of Evangelical Protestantism

Watch at: https://youtu.be/KmmTMg3e5Uo

The Beginnings of Minstrelsy on the Plantation

Chapter 5 will examine the Minstrel era. The origins of minstrelsy, however, can be found earlier, during slavery in the slave quarters and plantation houses of the southern United States.

In the fields and during their free time in the slave quarters, slaves often entertained each other with parodies, skits, and stories, some remembered from ancient tales handed down for centuries before the Middle Passage. Many of these stories were tales of the mythological trickster, or the signifying monkey. Over time they became symbols of the Black man's ability to triumph over more powerful, usually White, oppressors. They became heroes in Black culture. In the ancient tradition of the trickster, they made fun of themselves, their overseers, the master and his family, and visitors (Floyd, 1995). These traditions of storytelling, skits, dancing, making fun of self and others prefaced, and set the tone for, blackface minstrelsy in the early 19th century.

House slaves, those who were tasked with working in the plantation owner's family home, often were given big responsibilities caring for the home, feeding the children, and serving meals and entertainment to family and guests. They were cooks, butlers, nannies, mammies, and after learning European instruments, musicians. Learning to sing or play a musical instrument, such as piano, organ, or guitar, put a slave in a unique position. Once emancipated, either by their master or following the Civil War, house slaves had marketable skills in the world beyond the plantation. If they read music and sang or played in the European style, they might become professional musicians in the local city's opera house or theatre. In the early 1800s, some would join minstrel troupes as musicians or members of the cast. There were even Black composers such as W. C. Handy and James Bland who wrote minstrel songs.

For all of the reasons mentioned above, African American slaves set the stage for the first nationally popular entertainment, which oddly enough emerged from New York City in the early 1800s. Even though some Blacks contributed to the rise of blackface minstrelsy, its remarkable success is primarily attributed to White actors, musicians, and composers. The next chapter tells the story of the minstrel era.

Key Takeaways

- African slaves were imported to the Americas much earlier than 1619.
- Syncretism allowed slaves to quickly adapt to life on the plantation.
- African religions, although quite diverse, had enough commonalities with Christianity, including belief in one Supreme Being, to allow slaves to adopt the Christian faith or at least accommodate it within their traditional belief system.
- The ring shout was central to the perpetuation and continuation of African culture, music, and tradition.
- Whether a slave converted to Protestantism or Catholicism had a lot to do with how much of their indigenous culture was practiced and retained.
- Slaves, entertaining each other in their slave quarters, established the foundation upon which blackface minstrelsy grossly exaggerated slave life and culture throughout most of the 19th century.

Review Questions

Directions: Refer to what you learned in this chapter to help you respond completely and correctly to the questions and prompts below.

1. Define *syncretism* and describe the ways in which it helped Africans adapt to slave life on the plantation.

2. Explain why Catholicism is more responsible than Protestantism for the large number of surviving African retentions in African American culture.
3. Name some reasons why house slaves on the plantation were able to more easily transition to freedom after Emancipation than others.
4. Name some musical instruments slaves learned to play.
5. Describe how the slaves entertaining each other in the slave quarters prefaced the development of blackface minstrelsy in the early 1800s.

Extra Credit or Class Projects

1. Find a video of an authentic ring shout, and as you listen to and watch it, write down the African retentions used by the performers.
2. Seek out two or three other sources of information on the Maafa and write a short essay of the effects of the slave epoch on either 21st-century African American or African society.

References

Floyd, S. A. (1995). *The power of Black music.* Oxford University Press.

Guasco, M. (2017, September 4). The Fallacy of 1619: Rethinking the History of Africans in Early America. *Black Perspectives.* https://www.aaihs.org/the-fallacy-of-1619-rethinking-the-history-of-africans-in-early-america/

Leland, J. (2004). Hip: the history. Harper Collins Publishers.

Taylor, R. G. (2018). *The odyssey of an African American international educator in the field of modern world languages: An autoethnographic study.* Unpublished doctoral dissertation. Wilkes University.

Credits

Fig. 3.1: "The African Slave Trade," https://www.loc.gov/pictures/item/2007684717/, 1884.

Fig. 3.2: Frank Vizetelly and Mason Jackson, "Slaves worshiping with their master's family on the plantation," https://digital.tcl.sc.edu/digital/collection/civilwar/id/4381, 1863.

Chapter 4

The Blues

Introduction

This chapter on the blues will highlight the immense importance of the blues and its building blocks, the African pentatonic and European major and minor scales. The notion that the blues melodic patterns stem from and reflect the trials and tribulations of African Americans is mostly a myth. While blues lyrics often reflect those sentiments of the hardness of African American life, the melodies upon which the songs are constructed reflect thousands of years of African use of the pentatonic scale and other melodic techniques, blended in the new world with European scales, harmonies, and form.

KEY TERMS

Blues melody
Blues form
Blues chords
Chord progression
12-bar blues
16-bar blues
Mississippi Delta blues
Country blues
Chicago electric blues

Purpose

Chapter 4 introduces the student to another major premise of this book: the centuries old music of West Africa is built on the pentatonic scale and African singing techniques, blended with European scales and harmonies in the slave quarters of the plantations and Christian black churches of the southern United States. In addition, the chapter provides examples of the various scales from Africa and Europe to give the student a working vocabulary with which to read, sing, and hear the melodic patterns that make up the blues tradition.

Outcomes

After reading Chapter 4, the student will be able to:

- Identify by ear and musical notation the African pentatonic scale.

- Identify by ear and musical notation the European major and minor scales.
- Identify by ear and musical notation the traditional and modern blues scales.
- Describe the ways in which the blues developed over the 400 years of African American residence in the United States.
- Discuss the different regional styles of the blues.

FIGURE 4.1 B. B. King, icon of the blues

The Genesis of the Blues

The long-standing myth about the blues is that the music expresses the deep sadness and hopelessness of downtrodden Africans who were transplanted from their ancestral homeland, bound into slavery thousands of miles away from their home, and shamefully used and abused during slavery and after Emancipation. Further, the myth suggests that blues melody serves to articulate the pain expressed in the lyrics of the blues; that it bemoans life's harshest realities—loss of love, lack of money or a job, and other misfortunes. The lyrics of the blues may authentically articulate these and many of life's other most deeply felt moments, but blues melody (and its accompanying chord patterns) has a more pedestrian, but still interesting starting place.

As discussed in Chapters 1 and 2, the centuries of contact between African and European peoples (even before the advent of the slave trade) caused a blending of cultural traits, especially musical ones known as retentions. Dozens of such retentions from both African and European sources resulted in a thorough blending of melodic, rhythmic, harmonic, and formal elements. Once this blending was complete, somewhere toward the end of the 19th century, the style became known as the **blues.**

Those who coalesce a music into a definable style and make it popular (i.e., marketable to the general public) are the ones recognized as the originators of the style. African American blues performers, both male and female, emerged in the late 1800s and gained notoriety as the first generation of blues singers and musicians.

Before we identify those performers who brought the blues to prominence in American music, we should first know the ways in which the style came together. *Melody*, *harmony*, *rhythm*, and *form* are the technical terms that identify the fundamental elements of all music throughout the world. (Earlier in this book these were identified as European retentions, but they are really in use throughout the world.) The music known as the blues is a thorough blending of the African and European versions of these four elements. Each has a specific origin, either in West Africa, Europe, or both.

Gunther Schuller, in his landmark book, *Early Jazz,* says, "Exact proof of the origins of the blues has almost completely disappeared" (1986, p. 34). There is no way to know exactly when, or with whom, the blues styles and traditions became "The Blues." During the 400+ years that Africans and their music and culture have been in the Americas, a fully formed new style of music emerged gradually. Identified by its practitioners as the blues, its sound, performance style, lyrics, and instrumentation slowly revolutionized American popular song.

The Structure of Blues Melody

Melody is the formal name for a tune that one can sing, hum, or play and provides the most readily identifiable aspect of any piece of music. Even a musically untrained person is likely to be able to recognize and hear a tune such as the song "Happy Birthday," which is known and sung by children and adults all over the world. Although the song has a chordal pattern to accompany it, most of the time it is sung a cappella (without accompaniment) and in unison. Almost all humans can sing, that is, "carry a tune," well enough to be able to sing with others, sing on their own, and accurately repeat the melody of a song which they have heard more than once. It is also common for people with no formal training in music to adapt (improvise) their own musical background to the singing of a melody (such as "Happy Birthday," or a church hymn).

Blues melody comes from superimposing the African pentatonic (5-note) scale, represented by the black notes on the piano, on the major and minor scale patterns of European classical and folk music. The concept, called **blue tonality,** "can be heard in the field holler, work song, spirituals and gospel [songs], minstrelsy and ragtime, and most especially in the bittersweet mixture of the blues. ... Many songs, from Tin Pan Alley tunes to contemporary pop songs, are saturated with it. Blue tonality has colored America's musical life" (Stearns, 1958, p. 8).

The pentatonic scale is not unique to African folk music. Indigenous cultures around the world use various forms of it in their folk music. Many folk cultures, including Indian, Native American, Japanese, Chinese, and Korean developed pentatonic and more complicated scale patterns during centuries of musical development. It may be that if the early European slave traders had targeted another indigenous culture somewhere else in the world that culture's music would have become the basis for our modern American popular music.

Today's popular music takes advantage of the many musical cultures around the world. It is quite common for contemporary pop composers, musicians, and singers to use influences from Asian (K-Pop), East Indian (Bollywood), Latino (Tejano and Salsa), and Middle Eastern musical styles. Examples of such cross-cultural "borrowing" of music from other cultures include the following:

- Miles Davis's interpretation of Spanish flamenco style in his *Sketches of Spain* album in 1960
- Sting's use of Arabic rhythms and lyrics in "Desert Rose" in 1999
- Britney Spears's co-opting of elements from Bhangra (Indian popular music) in her 2003 song "Toxic"

Below is an example of the foundational European major and minor scales, the African pentatonic scale and the resulting blues scale.

FIGURE 4.2 The foundational European scales, African pentatonic scale and the blues scale

In addition to the pentatonic scale pattern inherent in West African folk music, there are a myriad of vocal and instrumental techniques that contribute to African influenced blue tonality, including bending tones, swooping up to and down from primary notes, ululating (described earlier in this book), shouts and hollers (also described earlier), and other pitch bending techniques.

It should be noted that there are other scale patterns from Europe that fit with and are used today in performing the blues, jazz, and most all forms of popular music. One example is the Dorian mode (D to D on the white notes of the piano) that has gained wide acceptance in modern popular music over the last 40 to 50 years.

The standard blues scale, shown above, is the basic scale, but most contemporary blues performers use a more modern version that utilizes another, more dissonant, "blue" note—the flat fifth-degree of the scale, shown below in Figure 4.3.

FIGURE 4.3 Modern version of standard blues scale

The "modern blues" scale and accompanying chords will be discussed more fully in a later chapter in conjunction with developments in mid-20th-century bop jazz and popular music.

Blues Chords

Blues harmony, made up of the chords that accompany the melody, is as basic as any in harmonized music. The simplest blues progression utilizes just three chords: I, IV, V (or V7) with regular returns to I. The Roman numeral system of designating a chord comes from European music theory. The chords correspond to the one (I) chord, four (IV) chord, and five (V) chord in the European harmonic system and can be expressed in the key of C, as C–E–G, F–A–C, G–B–D (F).

The chart below shows what a musician reads from sheet music, or plays by rote, when they play a chordal background (chord progression) to the 12-bar blues on an instrument such as piano or guitar, which is capable of playing three or more tones at one time.

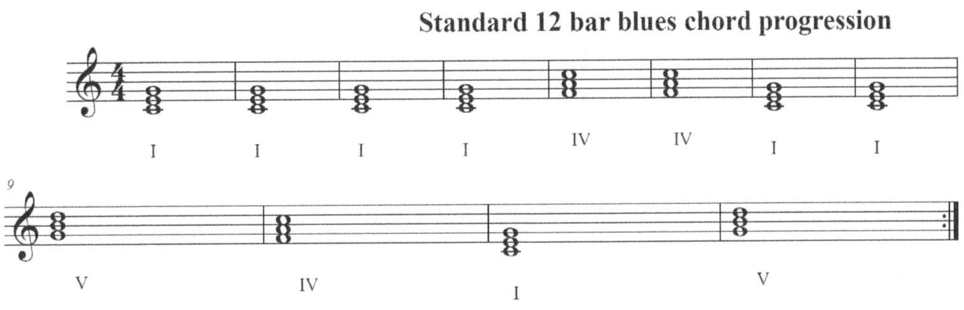

FIGURE 4.4 Twelve-bar blues chord progression

"In the beginning, Afro American music had no harmony" (Schuller, 1986, p. 38). There was no singing in parts, in the European sense, during slavery's early days (Schuller, 1986). With this as a basic understanding, any harmony which was added to the vocal/sung blues or played on a simple string instrument—such as the homemade banjo—had to have occurred after slaves on the plantations learned to play European instruments such as piano, organ, guitar, or mandolin. They would likely have learned to read European music notation, understand how chords line up with notes in the melody, and gradually incorporated the African pentatonic scale into the European scales to create the blues scale and European I, IV, V, I chords.

The formal structure of the blues takes two simple forms: 12 bars and 16 bars. The 12-bar version is used much more commonly today. The 16-bar version was played by African American and White street bands (marching bands) of the late 19th and early 20th centuries. It was common for them to play European and American marches in parades, and Christian hymns during funeral processions, both having an 8- or 16-bar formal structure, which is diagramed as AABA. This form is also common in ragtime (an even more complicated mix of African melodic and rhythmic techniques and European form), from which much of early New Orleans jazz is derived. The incredible creativity and flexibility of these early musicians allowed them to integrate African and European melodic harmonic, formal, and rhythmic traditions into the unified whole that emerged as New Orleans jazz in the early 20th century. New Orleans, or Dixieland jazz, remains primarily a blues-based music. Chapter 7 includes an extended discussion of the roots of Early Jazz.

Here is the chord pattern, or chord progression, of the 16-bar blues:

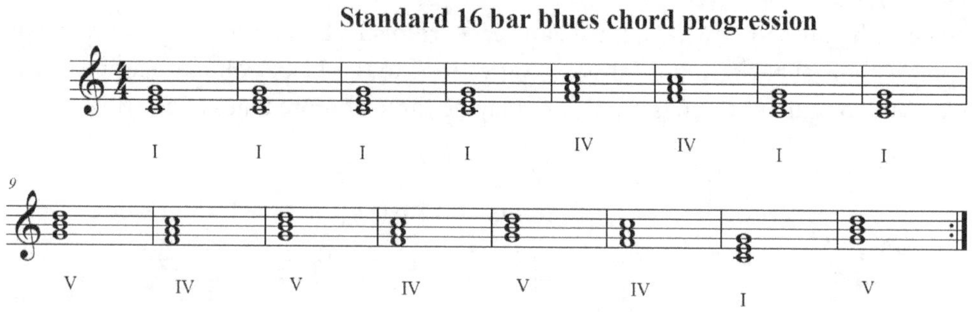

FIGURE 4.5 Sixteen-bar blues chord progression

Regional Styles

Following the Civil War, various styles of blues, all using either the 12- or 16-bar form and traditional blues chords, sprang up in predominantly Black, rural areas of the South, mostly between the Mississippi Delta region and East Texas. As with all African influenced music, the blues grew from the oral tradition of sharing, imitating, and reproducing music from one generation to the next. In the early 20th century, popular song composers like W. C. Handy (who could read and write music) composed and published written sheet music based on the blues. His music became exceedingly popular throughout the United States and was sung by the most well-known singers and musicians of the day, including Al Jolson, Bessie Smith, and Louis Armstrong.

It seems that the earliest African American blues singers were itinerant, much like the troubadours of Europe in the Middle Ages, and their names and many of their songs are lost to history. The next generation of blues performers, born in the late 1800s, grew up listening to the blues and became the first generation to sing and play the blues professionally. They made recordings (known at the time as race records and sold mostly in Black areas), and they performed for money in bars and clubs, at house rent parties, and virtually anywhere in the Black community where entertainment was needed.

Country Blues

The country blues tradition (also known as rural, down-home, or folk blues) also took shape in the Mississippi Delta during the era of reconstruction after the Civil War. The area between Memphis, Tennessee, and Vicksburg, Mississippi, running north to south, was home to one of the largest populations of slaves in the South. After the war, many former slaves became sharecroppers, working the same land on which they were once slaves. The blues emerged in this region as the music of poor, black tenant farmers, and levee, railroad and dock workers (Starr & Waterman, 2018).

The basic elements of the music (African and European retentions) resided in the slave communities from the beginnings of slavery. The new post-Civil War occupations of former slaves simply gave those who sang and played the blues a new set of individual experiences (along with the older, established song material) that they could recount in private or public social situations. The blues (as a part of the larger African tradition of music-making) was always a very personal style of musical expression, so it was not uncommon for bluesmen (and women) to recreate their own versions of traditional songs or create new songs using melodies and lyrics from parts of older tunes. Almost all followed the traditional 12-bar form (Starr & Waterman, 2018). The primary instruments used to accompany the blues include guitar, mouth harp (harmonica), and banjo—all instruments that were portable and inexpensive.

While the blues continued to develop through the early years of the 20th century in the rural South, it gradually became more formalized with the adoption of the blues style (melodic, chordal, and formal patterns) by Tin Pan Alley composers and recording companies interested in cashing in on the public's interest in blues music. For example, Bessie Smith's 1925 recording of W. C. Handy's "St. Louis Blues," a composed and notated blues in the Tin Pan Alley style, was sold as commercial sheet music. Other black singers, notably "Ma" Rainey, the "Mother of the Blues," became a star performing and recording the blues.

FIGURE 4.6 Blind Lemon Jefferson

Blind Lemon Jefferson

By the mid to late 1920s, more rural blues singers like Blind Lemon Jefferson (Figure 4.6) and Charley Patton found a stable audience through their recordings of various types of music—ragtime and church hymns in addition to the blues. Patton's style was associated with the Delta Blues tradition, while Jefferson reflected the East Texas style of his upbringing. Jefferson's guitar style used single note lines to respond to his singing (in the traditional call and response pattern of African Folk music), while Patton's voice and guitar style were rougher and heavier (Starr & Waterman, 2018).

Blind Lemon Jefferson, "Black Snake Moan"

https://www.youtube.com/watch?v=xzdJtsv1bqo

Early Blues Singers/Musicians/Composers

Blind Lemon Jefferson (West Texas Style)
Robert Johnson
Leadbelly (Huddie Ledbetter)
Mississippi John Hurt
Charley Patton (Delta Blues Style)
Gertrude "Ma" Rainey (The Mother of the Blues)
Bessie Smith (The Empress of the Blues)
W. C. Handy (Song Composer)

Chicago Electric Blues

As African Americans moved by the thousands from the South to northern cities in search of jobs, the blues moved with them. The migration of musicians from every southern city and rural county, particularly music towns like New Orleans, Memphis, St. Louis, and other cities along the Mississippi, guaranteed that the blues, ragtime, New Orleans Jazz, and the myriad of other African American musical styles would flourish in the North. In succeeding chapters, we will focus attention on ragtime, New Orleans Jazz, and more modern blues styles.

Chicago Blues was the first blues style to incorporate the amplified electric guitar and harmonica (played through guitar or PA speakers) as instruments used to accompany blues singers. Based on earlier blues idioms, such as the Delta Blues, Chicago blues was performed in an urban style and heavily influenced by Mississippi bluesmen who traveled to Chicago in the early 1940s. While the basic 12-bar form is retained, the subject matter of the lyrics and the more urban "industrial" sound of loudly amplified guitar, harmonica and vocals bring a more modern sound to the style.

Early bluesmen Big Bill Broonzy and Muddy Waters (who appeared in the Chicago-based *Blues Brothers* movie) migrated from the South to Chicago to escape harsh Jim Crow laws and poor working conditions.

The music of these early electric blues pioneers influenced rhythm and blues, and ultimately rock and roll musicians from the early 1950s on. Eric Clapton, Keith Richards, George Harrison, Stevie Ray Vaughn, John Mayer, and dozens of other rock and roll guitarists attributed their affinity for the blues to Chicago Blues style.

Long Live the Blues

The great thing about the blues is its flexibility and adaptability. You may have heard someone say that a particular blues performer, like Ma Rainey, never sings a song the same way twice, or that every blues singer or player has their own unique sound and style. This is certainly true, and the reason is that the simple format of the blues lends itself to endless permutations of the basic melody, harmony, and rhythm (within the context of the simple ABA blues form) with each successive repetition of the 12- or 16-bar pattern. For example, the performance of

"Black Snake Moan," recorded first by Blind Lemon Jefferson in 1926, will differ significantly when it is performed by other blues singers/guitarists.

The blues has been a primary influence, melodically, harmonically, and structurally in American popular music, from early New Orleans Jazz in the first decade of the 20th century to recent performers like ZZ Top, John Mayer, and H.E.R. in contemporary pop music.

Key Takeaways

- The blues is a prime example of the mix of African and European retentions.
- Blues lyrics reflect the travails of African American life in America, especially during and after the slave era.
- Most blues follows the 12- or 16-bar form.
- Early blues, known as country, rural, or down-home most likely originated in the Mississippi Delta region.
- More modern blues styles can be traced to Chicago and the Great Migration of African Americans from the South to northern cities, notably Chicago.

Extra Credit Project

Listen again to "That Black Snake Moan," performed by Blind Lemon Jefferson. Then search online for another recording with which to compare the Jefferson version. Note differences such as recording quality, tempo (speed of the performance), use of stylistic blues techniques such as shouts, hollers, swooping into or bending tones, and use of the standard blues chord progression.

Review Questions

1. From where does blues melody get its mournful, "soulful," feel?
2. Name some other indigenous cultures that use forms of the pentatonic scale.
3. Name and explain the two common chord progressions used in the blues.
4. Did the earliest blues have chordal accompaniment?
5. How did being a "house slave" on a plantation prepare some slaves to integrate themselves into White society?
6. Name five blues singers/performers.

References

Schuller, G. (1986). *Early jazz: Its roots and musical development* (Rev. ed.). Oxford University Press.

Starr, L., & Waterman, C. (2018). *American popular music* (5th ed.). Oxford University Press.

Stearns, M. (1958). *The story of jazz.* Oxford University Press.

Credits

Fig. 4.1: Copyright © by Tom Beetz (CC BY 2.0) at https://commons.wikimedia.org/wiki/File:B.B._King_in_2009.jpg.

Fig. 4.2: Generated with Finale. Copyright © by MakeMusic, Inc.

Fig. 4.3: Generated with Finale. Copyright © by MakeMusic, Inc.

Fig. 4.4: Generated with Finale. Copyright © by MakeMusic, Inc.

Fig. 4.5: Generated with Finale. Copyright © by MakeMusic, Inc.

Fig. 4.6: "Blind Lemon Jefferson," https://commons.wikimedia.org/wiki/File:Blindlemonjeffersoncirca1926.jpg.

Black Minstrelsy and Blackface (White) Minstrelsy

Black Invention and White Appropriation

Introduction

In this chapter, we turn our attention to the history of minstrelsy, or more precisely, blackface minstrelsy. **The intent of this chapter is to inform the reader, not present inflammatory or insensitive rhetoric.** The style and content of slave life on the plantation formed the basis for the content of the minstrel show. Before, during, and after the Civil War, African American speech, song, dance, and rhythms (all the indigenous African retentions) were gradually co-opted by white entertainers, song writers, and musicians from the 1820s through the early 20th century. White-produced songs, skits, and vignettes portrayed in an often cruel and denigrating way Negro life on the plantation and on the streets of the nation's towns and cities. Sadly, some of the minstrel performers and composers were African American. One such black composer, James A. Bland, wrote dozens of **"coon songs."** One became the original Virginia state song. By 1860, minstrel shows crisscrossed the entire country, entertaining hundreds of thousands of families.

KEY TERMS

Blackface minstrelsy

Ethiopian or coon songs

Black invention/White appropriation

Jim Crow

Zip Coon

Spiritual

In this chapter the reader will meet some of the most well-known composers, singers, actors and musicians of the minstrel era. The reader will also view a scene from a movie depicting a minstrel show, hear some **"coon songs"** (also known as **Ethiopian songs**), which is another name for a minstrel song, and read about the racist and tragic ways that African Americans were portrayed by White and some African American singers, song writers, actors, and musicians.

The minstrel performers used language and portrayals of African Americans as both slaves and freemen that is today considered racist, violent, misogynistic, cruel, and denigrating. Contemporary society no longer accepts these words and actions as appropriate in any

FIGURE 5.1 Sheet music cover for "Zip Coon," 1830s. Scanned from *Blacking Up: The Minstrel Show in Nineteenth-Century America*, by Robert Tol.

discourse. However, for the purpose of educating and informing those who are unaware, some racially charged words are necessarily used in this chapter.

Purpose

The purpose of this chapter is to provide the reader with frank information about one of the most unsavory periods in American popular music history. The reader will come to understand the institutional racism promoted and celebrated by the minstrel show from its humble and innocent beginnings in the slave quarters of southern plantations to the production of blackface minstrelsy by White entrepreneurs as the first nationally popular entertainment. The context of the time surrounding slavery and the Civil War era provides the lens through which one can come to terms with the attitudes of White America toward African Americans. "Today, blackface minstrelsy is quite reasonably regarded with embarrassment or anger" by White and African Americans (Starr & Waterman, 2018, p. 18).

Outcomes

After reading Chapter 5, the student will be able to:

- Discuss the blatantly racist content of Ethiopian or Coon Song lyrics.
- Detail the development of blackface minstrelsy from its origins on the plantations.
- Explain why African Americans performed in minstrel shows.
- Explain how Black invention/White appropriation applies to the minstrel show.
- Explain inherent, institutionalized racism in minstrelsy.
- Discuss the political and social atmosphere for African Americans in the Jim Crow era.
- Explain what African mythological character Zip Coon is meant to imitate.
- Diagram the format of the minstrel show.

Black Invention/White Appropriation

A phrase that aptly captures the notion of Whites co-opting (i.e., imitating) African American music and culture is, **Black invention/White appropriation**, or cultural appropriation. The adaptation and popularization of African American music by White singers, song writers, and musicians is pervasive throughout the history of American popular music, and it will be referenced numerous times in forthcoming chapters as the recurring theme of Black invention/White appropriation.

Today, due to a significant body of research into the contributions of African folk music and culture by ethnomusicologists who study folk music as their profession and other academic music scholars, there is a recognition that non-African American musicians emulated and or co-opted the style and cultural influences generated by centuries of African and African American musicians, dancers, poets, and singers.

Short History of Minstrelsy

Blackface minstrelsy is the first among many times that Whites copied or borrowed the music of Black Americans and refashioned it for the White consumer of music. It was the first distinctly American theatrical form. In the 1830s and 1840s, it was at the core of the rise of an American music industry, ultimately producing the first original American popular music styles and paving the way for the songs of Tin Pan Alley, vaudeville, and Broadway in the late 1800s. For several decades it provided the lens through which White America (especially in the northern states) perceived Black America. On the one hand, it had strong racist aspects; on the other, it afforded White Americans a singular and broad awareness of what some Whites considered significant aspects of Black American culture.

Why was minstrelsy so popular? The American public loved it because it reflected their point of view. Minstrel players acted the roles of people who were at that time referred to as *Negroes* (which was not a word of their own choosing), with an air of comic triumph, irreverent wisdom, and an underlying note of rebellion. It was no accident that minstrelsy was born during the era of Jacksonian Democracy and flourished at the same time as the abolitionist movement (Stearns, 1958).

With the invention of the **Zip Coon** character by George Washington Dixon, and the **Jim Crow** character of Thomas Dartmouth Rice, the eventual success of minstrelsy was assured. The accompanying song that Rice wrote, "Jump Jim Crow," in 1829 was an almost instant success. Minstrelsy experienced a growth in popularity that ultimately made it the most well-attended entertainment in the U.S. by 1840.

The minstrel show, or minstrelsy, consisted of comic skits, variety acts, dancing, and music performed by White people in blackface and occasionally Black people in blackface. It was also "... the first form of musical and theatrical entertainment to be regarded by European audiences as distinctively American in character ..." (Starr & Waterman, 2018, p. 46.)

Minstrel shows lampooned Black people as dim-witted, lazy, buffoonish, superstitious, happy-go-lucky, and musical. The minstrel show began with brief burlesques and comic entr'actes in the early 1830s and emerged as the full-fledged, three-act form during the next decade. By 1848, blackface minstrel shows were the national art of the time, translating formal art such

The spiritual "Deep River," sung by the Tuskegee Institute Choir

https://www.youtube.com/watch?v=xUSspIPQg_E

as opera and theatre into popular terms for their generally White, family-oriented audience.

Post-Civil War and emancipation saw a huge spike in minstrel show popularity. With freed Negroes available to perform and form all-Negro troupes such as the Georgia Minstrels in 1865, Black performers came into their own. Black minstrel performers like Horace Weston, Billy Kersands, Sam Lucas, and the composer James A. Bland (highlighted below), along with many others, enjoyed national and international success. They traveled to Europe with J.H. Haverly's European Mastodon Minstrels. They all performed in blackface, and most had White managers (Stearns, 1958, p. 115).

Spirituals (known as jubilees) entered the repertoire in the 1870s, marking the first undeniably black music to be used in minstrelsy.

By 1900, the minstrel show faded from its former popularity, and it was replaced for the most part by vaudeville. Minstrelsy survived as professional entertainment until about 1910, but some actors and singers, notably Al Jolson, started their careers in minstrelsy before moving on to vaudeville and silent movies. Jolson continued to perform in blackface throughout the 1920s. He became one of the biggest stars of early movies after performing the first song ever heard by a movie audience in the first talking picture, *The Jazz Singer*. This first "talkie" was actually completely silent, until the moment of Jolson's song performance. Suddenly the theatre came alive with the sound of his minstrel style voice, and the silent movie era was over.

Some minstrel troupes were still operating and traveling in the South as late as 1955. Amateur minstrel shows (generally without blackface) continued until the 1960s with high schools, church youth groups, and local theaters often staging them as fundraisers. During the 1960s, African American civil rights leaders like Martin Luther King Jr. began to score legal and social victories against racism, and they successfully used political power to advance the cause of justice and parity for African Americans. One fitting result of the civil rights movement was the final dissolution of minstrelsy as an American entertainment. Since then, it has completely disappeared from the American entertainment landscape.

Structure of the Minstrel Show

To prepare for a minstrel show performance, whether White or African American, men blackened their skin with shoe polish, coal dust, or burnt cork. The intent was to imitate the look of dark-skinned African men. They did not blacken the areas around the mouth and eyes, intending to highlight those areas of the face that were most expressive in Negro men. George Washington Dixon established the tradition of performing in blackface in 1828. Thomas Dartmouth Rice solidified the tradition by his blackface portrayal of Jim Crow as he sang his song "Jump Jim Crow" (originally a plantation slave song) in 1829 (p. 19).

A typical minstrel performance followed a three-act structure. The troupe first danced onto the stage, then exchanged wisecracks and sang songs. The second part featured a variety of entertainments, including the pun-filled stump speech. The final act consisted of a slapstick musical plantation skit or a send-up of a popular play. Minstrel songs and sketches featured several stock characters, most popularly the slave and the dandy (often a portrayal of the trickster character, such as Zip Coon). These were further divided into sub-archetypes, such as the mammy (a house slave who cared for the children of the "Massa"), her counterpart the old darky (usually portrayed as lazy or drunk), the provocative mulatto wench, and the Black soldier.

FIGURE 5.2 Al. G. Field Greater Minstrels: Doc Quigley's latest creation the "Dancing Professors"

Minstrelsy as Social and Political Controversy

Minstrel performers and impresarios defended their songs and portrayals of Blacks by claiming that the songs and dances were authentically Black, although the extent of the Black influence is less substantive and more wishful thinking. Thomas Dartmouth Rice claimed that his alter ego, the Jim Crow character, was derived from a black crippled stable groom he knew in Cincinnati (although there is no known authentication of this story). Rice claimed that he copied the stable groom's singing and dancing style, wore similar torn and tattered clothes, blackened his face, and presented his creation as the entr'acte during a play in which he performed. His persona caught on with audiences, and he became known around the world as "The Ethiopian Delineator" (Crawford, 2001, p. 200–201).

Minstrel shows were extremely popular from coast to coast in the United States and in Europe. They consistently drew families from all levels of society and every ethnic group, but to many they were also controversial. Racial integrationists decried them as falsely showing happy slaves on the plantation, while at the same time making fun of them; segregationists thought such shows were "disrespectful" of social norms, portrayed runaway slaves with sympathy, and would undermine the Southerners' "peculiar institution."

FIGURE 5.3 From the title page of *Uncle Remus, His Songs and His Sayings: The Folk-Lore of the Old Plantation*, by Joel Chandler Harris (1881). Illustrations by Frederick S. Church and James H. Moser. New York: D. Appleton and Company.

Example of Minstrel/Coon/Ethiopian Song Lyrics

Below is an example of lyrics using the "Uncle Remus American" dialect. The Uncle Remus character was first portrayed in Joel Chandler Harris's *Uncle Remus, his Songs and his Sayings: The Folklore of the Old Plantation* (Figure 5.3, using a Deep South Black dialect in storytelling. The character is more famously recognized in the Disney movie, *Song of the South*. This song, "Kingdom Comin," is by New England abolitionist, H. C. Work. The exaggerated dialect is most likely copied from the fictitious "Sambos and Topsies" of the minstrel stage:

Say, darkeys, hab you seen the massa
Wid de mufstas on his face
Go long de road some time dis morn'
Like he gwine to leab de place? (Martin, 1970, p. 40)

Notable Performers and Composers in Minstrelsy

Several early performers made a name for themselves by working in minstrelsy. Let's look at some who affected the future of entertainment.

Little-Known Black History Fact: Sambo

Read this article for an understanding of the derogatory term "Sambo," including its etymology and historical context.

Read at: https://blackamericaweb.com/2017/01/11/little-known-black-history-fact-sambo/

George Washington Dixon

"George Washington Dixon was the first white performer to establish a wide reputation as a 'Blackface' entertainer. He made his New York debut in 1828. Two of his earliest Ethiopian Songs to enjoy widespread popularity, 'Long Tail Blue' and 'Coal Black Rose,' were featured in his act" (Starr & Waterman, 2018, p. 19). Dixon was the inventor of the trickster style character Zip Coon, as well as the song of the same name. Dixon borrowed the boastful, self-important personality, garish clothing, and predilection for "the ladies" of his alter ego from the African trickster myth and those African American men he met growing up in Richmond, Virginia. He considered himself more of a journalist than an entertainer, and despite having a successful career as a singer and actor, by the late 1830s he was spending more time writing than performing.

Thomas Dartmouth Rice

Thomas Dartmouth (Daddy) Rice was born near the docks of the Seventh Ward of New York City, ostensibly ground zero for the beginnings of minstrelsy. Like Dixon, he invented a trickster-like character, **Jim Crow**, along with an accompanying song in 1829. Unlike Dixon's pompous character though, Jim Crow was more of a rural, country bumpkin. Rice sang the song in blackface while dancing an Africanized version of the European quadrille. The popularity of the character and the song shot him to instant popularity, and "Jump Jim Crow" became the first international American hit song. In 1832, he performed as Zip Coon in New York City, sparking "a veritable explosion of blackface performers all over the city" (Starr & Waterman, 2018, p. 19–20).

Rice toured England in the 1830s, and he was perceived by the English as, "The first native born American performer to export music thought to be quintessentially American in style and content" (Starr & Waterman, 2018, p. 21). It seems ironic that Rice's character soon became the most derogatory name for African Americans and surrounding almost 100 years of segregationist laws in most American states that barred Blacks from White schools, theatres, restaurants, hospitals, and most White owned businesses (Starr & Waterman, 2018).

Daniel Decatur Emmett

Daniel Decatur Emmett was born in 1815 in Mount Vernon, Ohio. In 1835, Emmett began his career as an entertainer when he joined a circus. He learned to write Black dialect (Ethiopian) songs while a circus performer in Cincinnati. His knowledge of African American music and culture most likely came from knowing a Black music-making family in his hometown. In addition to "Jump Jim Crow," his most popular song, he wrote a significant number of minstrel tunes including "Dixie" and "Old Dan Tucker." Evidence suggests that he probably borrowed the music from an old Negro tune, but used his own newly written lyrics.

Emmett, along with Frank Brower, appeared in blackface in theatres in New York City around 1842. Shortly after, they teamed up with fellow blackface minstrels William "Billy" Whitlock and Dick Pelham in the Virginia Minstrels.

Steven Foster

Steven Foster, who was born in Allegheny, Pennsylvania, is considered the first professional American composer and songwriter. He wrote more songs that won enduring popularity than any other tunesmith of the 19th century (Crawford, 2001). His music and the dozens of songs he wrote for minstrelsy or in the minstrel style are beloved by generations of Americans to this day. Many Americans learn his songs during childhood in elementary music class or singing in a school or community choir. His songs show the distinct influence of the African American camp meeting/spiritual style.

Foster was raised by a mulatto (half black–half white) nurse, and he learned to love Negro music as a young child. Stearns suggests that "His most enduring songs, which have become part

Listen to one of his most famous songs, "Camptown Races," which was one of his earliest minstrel show hits:

Watch at: https://www.youtube.com/watch?v=49_QHBR4OxE

of our folk music [certainly the rationale for teaching them in our schools], are of the minstrel type" (1958, p. 118.). They use the "Uncle Remus American" dialect so common in the songs of minstrelsy. "Swanee River," "Old Black Joe," "My Old Kentucky Home," "Massa's in the Cold, Cold Ground," and "Camptown Races" are all examples of his superb songwriting skills.

Foster was sympathetic to the abolitionist cause, and always wrote his lyrics to bring a sensitive, human portrayal to the mostly black characters used in his tunes.

James A. Bland

James A. Bland is one of the most famous and successful African American minstrel performers and composers of the minstrel era. His songs include many that are still used in the repertoire of singers, choruses, and string bands. Some of his most well-known include "In the Evening by the Moonlight," "Carry Me Back to Old Virginny," and "Oh, Dem Golden Slippers," which is performed by every marching string band in parades and concerts across the nation. Martin observes that along with Stephen Foster, Bland "wrote about negroes as humans, rather than creatures" (1970, p. 39).

This is a short list of songs commonly called Ethiopian or Coon Songs that either originated in blackface minstrelsy or are otherwise closely associated with that tradition. These songs, and even their titles, contain words that are today deeply offensive and completely unacceptable to readers of all races.

- "Babylon Is Fallen," Henry Clay Work (1863)
- "Billy Patterson," Dan Emmett (1860)
- "The Black Brigade," Dan Emmett (1863)
- "Blue Tail Fly" (a.k.a. "Jimmy Crack Corn") (c. 1846)
- "The Boatman's Dance," credited to Dan Emmett (1843)
- "Bonja Song" (c. 1820)
- "Bress Dat Lubly Yaller Gal"
- "Camptown Races," Stephen Foster, (1850)
- "Carry Me Back to Old Virginny," James A. Bland, original Virginia state song
- "Ching a Ring Chaw"
- "Claire de Kitchen," performed as early as 1832 by T. D. Rice and George Washington Dixon
- "Clar de Track," 1840s
- "Long Tail Blue," George Washington Dixon (1929)
- "My Coal Black Rose," George Washington Dixon (c. 1829)

See below to watch Ned Haverly perform a song and sand dance in blackface in a clip from the movie *Yes Sir, Mr. Bones* (Ormond, 1951). He was the son of J. H. Haverly, the owner of the largest minstrel troupe in the late 19th century—Haverly's United Mastodon Minstrels. Notice that some of his dance steps are reminiscent of the dance style of Michael Jackson. It is likely that Jackson, or one of his choreographers was familiar with this style of dance and used elements of it to choreograph Jackson's dances.

Watch a video of a scene from *Yes Sir, Mr. Bones*.

Watch at: https://www.youtube.com/watch?v=NT8yUhtZoXA

Also, the sand dance sequence shows Haverly's use of polyrhythm to create dance rhythms that conflict polyrhythmically with the basic rhythm played by the drummer in the band. His dress, reminiscent of the pompous clothing worn by the Zip Coon character, and his use of self-aggrandizing lyrics in the song, suggest his portrayal of the trickster persona in his stage character. This is consistent with the constant use of African retentions as parody and exaggeration in the minstrel show.

Key Takeaways

- The songs, skits, and dances of minstrelsy were loosely based on African and African American retentions and dialect, but the exaggerated and often racist nature of the content of minstrelsy made it controversial to some and completely unacceptable to others.
- Those who study or teach minstrelsy understand that the topic is sensitive and that it should be discussed with the utmost deference to those who may be offended by the language and descriptions presented in this chapter.
- While most minstrel entertainers were White, a significant number of African Americans performed in and composed songs for, minstrelsy.
- Both Black and White minstrels performed in blackface.
- Minstrelsy is the first of many examples of Black invention/White appropriation in American popular music history.

Extra Credit Project

View the video listed in this chapter again, taking notes while viewing, and then write a one-page report on the use of African and European retentions by the performers in the video.

Review Questions

Directions: Refer to what you learned in this chapter to help you respond completely and correctly to the questions and prompts below.

1. List and write a paragraph about each of four musicians, composers, or performers of minstrelsy.
2. In your own words, explain the structure of the minstrel show.
3. What are some of the main discussion points presented here around minstrelsy?
4. What reasons would African Americans have had for becoming performers in minstrel troupes?
5. Name four African retentions co-opted by minstrel musicians, singers, and composers.
6. Given the painful roots of minstrelsy, as well as the history of cultural appropriation around it, is there a positive way to acknowledge the ways minstrelsy influences music today?

References

Crawford, R. (2001). *America's musical life, A history*. W. W. Norton & Company.

Martin, Deac. (1970). *Deac Martin's book of musical Americana*. Prentice-Hall, Inc.

Ormond, R., Dir, (1951). *Yes Sir, Mr Bones*. UK: Exclusive Films.

Starr, L., & Waterman, C. (2018). *American popular music* (5th ed.). Oxford University Press.

Stearns, M. (1958). *The story of jazz*. Oxford University Press.

Credits

Fig. 5.1: "Sheet music cover for 'Zip Coon,' 1830s," https://commons.wikimedia.org/wiki/File:Zip_Coon_sheet_music.jpg, 1830.

Fig. 5.2: Courier Company, "Al. G. Field Greater Minstrels," https://commons.wikimedia.org/wiki/File:Al._G._Field_Greater_Minstrels_oldest,_biggest,_best._LCCN2014636972.jpg, 1900.

Fig. 5.3: Frederick S. Church and James H. Moser, "From the title page of Uncle Remus, His Songs and His Sayings," https://commons.wikimedia.org/wiki/File:Uncle_Remus_crop_1881_(high_res_transparent).png, 1881.

Chapter 6

Music in Post-Civil War America

Introduction

Between the end of the Civil War and 1900, many separate forms of African American and European American music combined to form a new music: jazz. At the same time, the sociopolitical events created by the emancipation of the slaves often held back the blending (syncretism) of White American and African American cultures. In this chapter, you will learn about the most significant musical styles that contributed to the birth of jazz and the creation of a post-slavery, free African American culture.

KEY TERMS

Sharecropper

Exodusters

Post-Civil War migration

Exoduster movement

Reconstruction

15th Amendment to the U.S. Constitution

Jim Crow laws

Congo Square

Secret societies

Pre-jazz musical genres (the building blocks of jazz)

Ragtime

Syncopation

Scott Joplin

Purpose

The purpose of Chapter 6 is to acquaint the reader with the main pre-jazz musical genres that ultimately blended together to produce New Orleans Jazz in the latter part of the 19th century. In addition, we will examine the sociopolitical events associated with the emancipation of the slaves at the end of the Civil War.

Outcomes

After reading Chapter 6, the student will have a thorough understanding of the following concepts:

- Emancipation of the slaves
- Post-Civil War migration of African Americans
- African American secret societies
- Pre-Jazz musical genres

Social and Political Ramifications of Emancipation

After Emancipation, former slaves had new opportunities. While some remained on the plantations where they lived as slaves, and became **sharecroppers**, others chose to move to new locations. Let's consider the effects of those changes on the musical landscape.

Post–Civil War Migration

During the tumultuous years at the end of the Civil War, former slaves were faced with significant decisions about their future. Should they stay on the plantation where they were born into slavery and accept the plantation owner's offer of land which they could farm as sharecroppers? Should they move to a northern state with the hope of getting a job in a big city? Should they relocate in or near one of the cities close to their former plantation?

The answer to those questions is all of the above. While many stayed close to their plantation homes and roots, others migrated relatively short distances to cities such as New Orleans, St. Louis, Memphis, Savannah, and Charleston. Still others became the first wave of freed African Americans to migrate from the South to northern cities.

The Library of Congress website offers some understanding of this initial movement of Blacks from the South in an article entitled "The African American Odyssey; A Quest for Full Citizenship." It reports, "After the Civil War there was a general exodus of blacks from the South. These migrants became known as 'Exodusters' and the migration became known as the 'Exoduster' movement. Some applied to be part of colonization projects to Liberia and locations outside the United States; others were willing to move north and west" (Library of Congress, n.d.).

An article in *USA Today* provides further insight into this first, historic migration:

> In the decade after the Civil War, former slaves in the South searched for a way out. They were sickened and exhausted by the racist terrorism that had followed emancipation. Though freed from slavery, African Americans were routinely cheated, attacked and killed by whites who tolerated them barely, if at all. ... So, they left. The so-called Exodusters moved west to Kansas. Some settled in cities like Topeka and Kansas City, and others established towns like Bogue and Nicodemus in the western part of the state. By 1880, thousands had taken part in what historians call the first major migration of former slaves. (Scruggs, 2019)

This little-known movement of former slaves to Kansas is just one aspect of recognition by former slaves that even with Reconstruction and federal laws passed to protect their rights, the South was inherently unsafe. Sadly, those who moved west and north found that the prospects for jobs and better living conditions were generally not much better than the places they fled. The towns in Kansas founded by Black Exodusters lost most of their initial population within 30 years of settlement (Library of Congress, n.d.).

Reconstruction

Reconstruction, implemented by Congress, lasted from 1866 to 1877. It supposedly reorganized the southern states after the Civil War, providing the means for readmitting them into the Union and defining the parameters by which Whites and Blacks could live together in a non-slave society. The South, however, saw Reconstruction as a humiliating and vengeful imposition and did not welcome it (Library of Congress, n.d.).

The U.S. Congress gave Black men the vote with the 15th Amendment to the U.S. Constitution, ratified March 30, 1870. It provided that all male citizens were entitled to vote, but the Black population was so large in many parts of the South that Whites were fearful of Black participation in the political process. Nevertheless, the Radical Republicans in the U.S. Congress were determined that African Americans be accorded all of the rights of citizenship (Library of Congress, n.d.). During this short period of time, Black men were elected to political office throughout the South. At one point there were more African American than White legislators in the South Carolina State Legislature.

Jim Crow Segregation

Jim Crow Laws, enacted throughout the South in the 1890s, were designed to rein in the federally mandated rights of Black citizens. In May of 1896, The U.S. Supreme Court upheld state-imposed Jim Crow laws with their "separate but equal" decision in *Plessy v. Ferguson.* It became the legal basis for racial segregation in the United States for the next 50 years. Jim Crow laws made every aspect of African American life difficult. Housing, travel, education, the arts, and almost every element of daily life were restricted by these repressive statutes. As you can see from the map below, even many northern states adopted laws designed to "keep the Black man in his place."

With so many States adopting repressive Jim Crow laws, African Americans were denied or had limited options for participation in politics, voting, access to upward mobility in employment, accessibility of affordable housing, access to transportation, and dozens of other aspects of daily life that White Americans took for granted. The previous chapter highlighted the reasons that minstrelsy fostered the development of negative attitudes of White Americans toward African American life during and after slavery. The effects of minstrelsy and Jim Crow on Black culture lasted well into the 20th century.

African American Secret Societies

The secret society is a centuries old African retention that has played an important part in the transmission of all aspects of African culture throughout the slave epoch and into the modern era. "In New Orleans, as in other cities, African Americans practiced ring ceremonies, accompanied funeral processions with marching bands, and organized secret societies" (Floyd, 1995, p. 81–82). It is clear from the historical record that the African American marching bands were organized and sponsored by and served an integral part of the culture of the secret society. Similar in organization to the European fraternal (singularly male) organizations such as the Masons or Odd Fellows, African American secret societies

FIGURE. 6.1 Visual representation of the states in the USA that used the Jim Crow Laws

were, and in some places like New Orleans still are, at the heart of the social structure of African American life.

Mardi Gras in New Orleans provides a good example of the importance of Secret Societies. Many of the floats and marching bands in the Mardi Gras parade, as well as peripheral celebrations around the city, are even today sponsored and funded by secret societies.

Congo Square

Place Congo, eventually known as Congo Square in New Orleans, was an active site for the practice of indigenous African dance, song, and religious rituals. In 1817, the New Orleans Municipal Council legalized such practices, "to act as a kind of safety valve to keep the slaves contented." (Stearns, 1958, p. 44). The dances also became a remunerative tourist attraction at which Vodun (Voodoo) music was played. "By the 1840s, the African dances of the old days had yielded to African-American hybrids, and by the 1850s performances in Place Congo had vanished" (Brothers, 2006, p. 139–140).

Pre-Jazz Musical Genres (The Building Blocks of Jazz)

Jazz developed from the blending of several types of music genres. Here we will consider march music, folk and classical music, minstrel music, the blues, and ragtime.

March Music

March music in America has its roots in the military march music of Europe. Throughout American history, European, and European inspired marches accompanied military men marching in parades and sometimes into battle. During the Revolutionary War, War of 1812, and American Civil War, military musical units (bands) on both sides of the conflicts marched with troops, often accompanying them into battle. By the end of the Civil War, a growing number of local town and traveling bands played marches, orchestral transcriptions, opera themes (often with vocal soloists), and original compositions. Many military bands transitioned from enlisted units to civilian bands.

FIGURE 6.2 Sign designating the site of Congo Square

One such example was the U.S. Army's 109th Field Artillery Battalion Band, stationed in Wilkes-Barre, Pennsylvania, which began as a fife and drum band during the Revolutionary War. The band served in the Spanish-American War, and World Wars I and II, and was decommissioned in 1943. In 1947, it was reorganized in Wilkes-Barre and became the Stegmaier Gold Medal Band, sponsored by the Stegmaier Brewing Company. Today, that band continues the tradition of playing live concert band music for local audiences, as the Wyoming Valley Concert Band (Pelton, 1985).

The golden era of marching/concert bands began shortly after the Civil War as former military band leaders and musicians formed civilian bands for the entertainment of their communities. Band leaders like Patrick Gilmore, Henry Fillmore, E. E. Bagley, and "The March King" John Philip Sousa, led post-Civil War professional bands that became highly popular ensembles with a broad following across the nation. Between 1880 and 1920, band music, which was usually played by seated concert ensembles rather than marching bands, was one of the most popular styles of entertainment in the nation. The most well-known musician of the period, John Philip Sousa, spent most of his adult life composing and conducting his own music, first as director of the U.S. Marine Band (The President's Own) and then as director of The Sousa Band, a professional band named after him. With his professional band, he made six world tours, appeared in every state in the union, and made numerous recordings.

African American marching bands in New Orleans and other southern cities followed the tradition of post-Civil war military bands by marching in parades, playing at social gatherings and most especially for funerals. "New Orleans had several black marching bands as early as 1860, all of which played parades for secret societies," as well as funerals (Floyd, 1995, p. 82). These bands played a mix of styles that were based on the European march form, but interjected slow tempo hymn songs on the way to the grave site, then picked up the tempo to a moderate march pace after the dear departed was laid to rest. The after-burial march back to the secret society lodge took on a celebratory tone marked by a technique known as "ragging the tune"—a euphemism for the up-tempo, lively use of ragtime rhythms, blues tonality with some improvisation. This is the immediate precursor of authentic New Orleans jazz, which emerges fully formed just before the turn to the 20th century.

American (European) Folk and Classical Music

For the first century of American independence, most of the music enjoyed in primarily White American homes was from—or at least inspired by—European folk and classical music. European style orchestras were formed in major cities throughout the colonies, and concertgoers enjoyed hearing the music of baroque and classical masters like Handel, Bach, Mozart, and Haydn. Even the popular folk and amateur music of the time was written in the style of European music.

Revolutionary war composers like William Billings wrote songs and hymns, mostly for singing. He composed six volumes of songs. His most well-known song, *Chester*, became the Revolutionary War's battle song, and its stirring lyrics inspired colonial soldiers to bravely fight against the British.

African music was cloistered on the plantations of the South and not yet an influence on American music, so African American/European hybrid music was yet to emerge. However, slaves did learn to sing and play European style musical instruments as part of their work on the plantation. Those who were brought into the house to look after the plantation owner's family were often taught to sing or play European instruments such as piano, violin, or flute for the entertainment of the family and their house guests. This began the long process of educating significant numbers of Blacks in European music performance and eventually leading to the syncretism (blending) of Black and European/American musical styles.

Minstrel Music

The discussion of minstrelsy in Chapter 5 provides ample evidence of its importance as a national entertainment between 1840 and 1910. Minstrelsy provided opportunities for African American musicians and composers to write songs, arrange music, and play in the bands of minstrel troupes. This was one way in which African American musicians advanced their musical skills, learned to read music, and became professional musicians.

Most importantly though, minstrelsy, as the first nationally popular entertainment form, gave rise to an ever-expanding music industry, including song publishing, concert and event promotion, and eventually recording, radio broadcasting, and movies. Many of minstrelsy's musicians and performers, both Black and White, transitioned to successful careers in the entertainment industry. For example, W. C. Handy, Bessie Smith, and Ma Rainey all began as minstrel performers who went on to significant careers in professional music and entertainment.

Al Jolson carried on the minstrel tradition of performing in blackface as a burlesque and vaudeville performer and into the first years of his movie career. In the first talking picture, *The Jazz Singer* (1927), Jolson sang "Mammy" in blackface, a clear indication that he felt his minstrel persona would resonate with and be accepted by his mostly White audience. Jolson became the highest paid and most popular entertainer of the 1920s.

Blues

Although we have already devoted an entire chapter to the blues, it bears repeating here that the blues tradition is at the core of all African American music. From its beginnings as the pentatonic scale (the primary melodic material of African folk music and an important African retention), the significance of the blues cannot be overstated. There is no African American music genre that does not use blues tonality. As we will see in Chapter 7, New Orleans Jazz is the first full flowering of the blending of European and African music—of which the blues is the most important.

Ragtime

Ragtime might be considered the final link in the chain that led to the emergence of New Orleans Jazz.

> Ragtime flourished for about twenty years-from 1896 to 1917. The general public first heard ragtime near the turn to the Twentieth Century at a series of World Fairs ... where itinerant pianists from the South and Midwest found employment along the midways (Stearns, 1958, p. 140).

Ragtime was composed and played by White and African American pianists who were well schooled in European classical music composition and performance. "It is a deeper and more complete blending of West African and European elements than anything that had gone on before," according to Stearns (1958). It is notated, highly complex in structure, and requires the skill of a well-trained, fine pianist.

Scott Joplin (c. 1868–April 1, 1917)

Ragtime's most well-known and prolific composer and performer was Scott Joplin. Known as the "King of Ragtime," he was a classically trained African American pianist and composer who was born and raised in Texarkana, Texas, and later moving to Sedalia, Missouri. He composed 40 rags, numerous songs, and two operas, the second of which, *Treemonisha*, is now considered a masterpiece of 20th century music and is performed by major opera companies throughout the world. Joplin's influence on other ragtime composers, New Orleans Jazz, and most styles of American popular music, is significant. He considered ragtime to be a classical style of music and wrote on the title page of each of his rags, "Ragtime should not be played fast."

Other notable ragtime composers and performers were Eubie Blake, James P. Johnson, and Tom Turpin. Ragtime's rhythmic complexity, rooted in its almost continuous use of syncopation, appealed to Black street musicians in New Orleans who co-opted and applied the syncopated feel to march rhythms. They created the concept of "ragging the tune," or swinging the beat, as they marched away from a grave site after a burial service. The syncopation and gregarious nature of ragtime perfectly suited the freewheeling, celebratory style of the New Orleans marching bands. Once ragtime music was firmly established as part of the New Orleans tradition, jazz was ready for prime time.

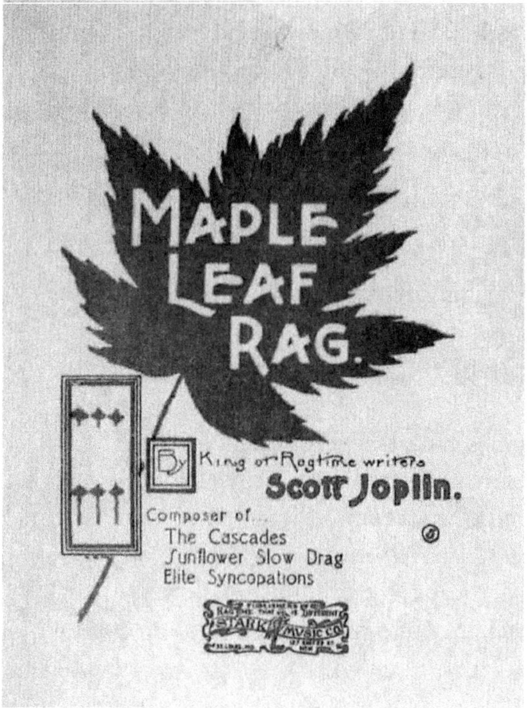

FIGURE 6.3 Title of the first score of Scott Joplin's *Maple Leaf Rag*. Published by John Stark in 1899.

The Maple Leaf Rag

https://www.youtube.com/watch?v=SGk7_Z9dfyw

Conclusion

It took more than 400 years for the full blending (syncretism) of African American and European music and culture to be complete. The first, and perhaps ultimate, expression of the formation of a completely new music is the New Orleans Jazz style, which emerged just before the turn to the 20th century. Early practitioners of the music—Bunk Johnson, Jelly Roll Morton, Buddy Bolden, Joe "King" Oliver, and dozens of others—probably had no idea that the music they pioneered would continue through the 20th century and well into the 21st. American popular music, first heard in and around New Orleans about 1900, is now a global music phenomenon that shows no signs of diminishing in popularity. Chapter 7 will closely examine the rise of New Orleans Jazz and its burgeoning popularity through the 1920s.

Review Questions

Directions: Refer to what you learned in this chapter to help you respond completely and correctly to the questions below.

1. In what ways did ragtime influence the development of New Orleans Jazz?
2. What decisions did former slaves need to make at the end of the Civil War?
3. How did those decisions relate to the development of New Orleans Jazz?

4. What part did march music play in shaping the style of New Orleans Jazz?
5. What was the purpose of Jim Crow laws?
6. Who was the most influential composer and performer of ragtime?

References

Brothers, T. (2006). *Louis Armstrong's New Orleans.* W. W. Norton & Company.

Floyd, S. A. (1995). *The power of Black music.* Oxford University Press.

Library of Congress Website. (n.d.). The African American Odyssey: A Quest for Full Citizenship. https://loc.gov/exhibits/african-american-odyssey/reconstruction.html#:~:text=After%20the%20Civil%20War%20there%20was%20a%20general,others%20were%20willing%20to%20move%20north%20and%20west

Pelton, R. (1985). *The story of the Wyoming Valley Band.* Unpublished article distributed to members of the Wyoming Valley Band by R. Pelton. Dallas, PA.

Scruggs, Afi-Odelia. (2019, March 6). Exodus: Blacks fled the South in droves more than a century ago, seeking true freedom. *USA Today.* https://www.usatoday.com/story/news/investigations/2019/03/06/black-migrations-black-history-slavery-freedom/2807813002/

Stearns, M. (1958). *The Story of Jazz.* Oxford university Press.

Credits

Chapter 7

African American Music Moves into the 20th Century

Introduction: Why New Orleans?

Southern Louisiana plantations were predominantly Catholic as a result of French and Spanish colonization of the region long before the United States was born. Catholicism in and around New Orleans encouraged the blending of African/European music and cultural traditions (retentions). Catholic plantation owners were much less concerned with their slaves' off-duty activities than were their Protestant counterparts. For example, Protestant plantations were generally smaller, and their owners held much tighter control over their slaves, not allowing them to practice any of their indigenous customs such as dancing. On Catholic plantations, owners allowed slaves to retain their musical and cultural traditions, including dancing, singing and making and playing drums and other musical instruments.

In most of the southern states, slaves on Protestant plantations learned to sing European hymns in European style, while slaves on Catholic owned plantations retained much of their African heritage by infusing their African folk music customs into their adopted and more loosely structured lifestyle (syncretism), including the hymns they sang in church and the traditional music they created. Thus, the region surrounding New Orleans produced a large number of catholic slaves who migrated to the city after emancipation at the end of the Civil War. Some were musicians who learned to play European music and instruments as slaves. They played in the brass marching bands, and in the clubs, dance halls, and bordellos that sprang up in the decade before 1900. Because of the African retentions they brought with them, they contributed to the style that became known as jass (eventually jazz) around 1900.

Purpose

Chapter 7 introduces the reader to the major factors which influenced music in New Orleans, and the reason it is considered the birthplace of jazz. It provides a basic terminology for New Orleans jazz style and encourages the reader to become familiar with the major contributors to the success of New Orleans jazz. The chapter also explains why an all-White jazz band, the Original Dixieland Jass (Jazz) Band, is important to the spread of New Orleans Jazz throughout the United States. The conclusion of the chapter explains the appeal of jazz music to a new generation of American young adults, both Black and White.

Outcomes

After reading Chapter 7, the student will have a thorough understanding of the following concepts and terms:

- Ragging the tune
- New Orleans Jazz Band instrumentation
- Group improvisation
- Storyville's place as the epicenter of New Orleans jazz
- The major contributors to the development of New Orleans jazz style
- The continuing importance of African retentions in African American music
- The importance of the brass (marching) band to the rise of New Orleans jazz

Key Terms

- New Orleans jazz—Music style first heard in New Orleans from 1897 on
- Ragging the tune—Term derived from the syncopated rhythms of ragtime
- Storyville—The legalized red-light District of New Orleans from 1897 to 1917
- Group improvisation—Signature style of improvisation of New Orleans jazz musicians before Louis Armstrong; the clarinet, trombone, and trumpet players improvise at the same time
- Jass—The original spelling of the word jazz

Music Along the Mississippi: From New Orleans to Chicago

Despite the thousands of pages written about the early years of New Orleans jazz, there is not much authentic, factual information about music in New Orleans before 1900. Much of what is written comes from first-person accounts and interviews, "a diverse collection of memories" (Brothers, 2006, p. ix), which are mostly anecdotal and first-person interviews. Often, they are accounts of incidences and informal discussions written down decades afterward. Many African American musicians who were active before 1900 could neither read nor write, and they grew up in a storytelling tradition (an enduring African retention), which could be unreliable, romanticized, or untrue. Black jazz musicians were known for their colorfully embellished, outrageously exaggerated descriptions of their and other's exploits.

One such example is the story of how the original spelling of the name jass became jazz, the permanent title of the music. It seems that the origin of the term *jass* is open to multiple interpretations. However, the most consistent story is that it derives from a word of African origin meaning to procreate. Paul Whiteman, the self-styled "King of Jazz," suggested in 1926 that it was a slang word meaning something "unmentionable" in polite society. "Most authorities believe that the term comes from New Orleans—from the Jasmine perfume favored by the city's prostitutes, or from "jezebel," the common word in 19th century New Orleans for a prostitute, or a synonym for intercourse in Storyville [the legal red-light district in New Orleans from 1897–1917]" (Ward & Burns, 2000, p. 65).

The transition to the traditional spelling of the word to jazz turns out to be a bit less titillating. The first white Dixieland group to use the term *jass* in their name, The Original Dixieland Jass Band, had to change their name rather abruptly from the original word *jass* to *jazz* during their first engagement in New York City. Their advertising posters were being defaced by young boys who scratched off the *j* in jass. Finally, the term *jazz* stuck and became the universal term for the style.

Storyville

There were a couple of hundred of bordellos (houses of prostitution) in New Orleans before Storyville was designated by the New Orleans City Council as the city's legal red-light district in 1897. "With the opening of Storyville ... things began to change. Playing jazz became a full-time profession ... and Storyville kept a dozen or so bands working every night" (Stearns, 1958, p. 71–72). Initially, most of the entertainment was provided by ragtime pianists like Jelly Roll Morton at Lulu White, where he made an astounding $18 a night. His piano style, playing ragtime rhythms but imitating the rolling rhythmic feel of the brass bands, stretched beyond ragtime style and contributed to the development of improvised jazz.

In 1917, the same year that the ODJB made their first recordings in New York City, the U.S. Navy closed down Storyville as a result of the United States entry into the First World War. With the bordellos closed and no work for the prostitutes, bartenders, staffs, and musicians, New Orleans fell into a depression, and musicians looked northward along the Mississippi, especially to Chicago, for jobs in the entertainment industry (Stearns, 1958).

Ragging the Tune

Although ragtime as a separate genre is discussed in Chapter 6, it will be treated here as one of the major influences in the development of New Orleans jazz, especially because of its rhythmic component known as syncopation. Ragtime, a very complex musical genre, demanded prodigious technique, stamina, and musicianship to play well. Pianists who could play an evening of ragtime music well were in high demand in the bars, dance halls, and bawdy houses of the late 19th and early 20th Century in New Orleans. The opening of Storyville in 1897 encouraged black and white ragtime piano players to migrate to New Orleans to find work in the newly expanded establishments of Storyville.

The ragtime craze, spurred on by the national success of Scott Joplin's published rags, live performances, and player piano roll sales, created intense interest among instrumental musicians, as well as pianists, for learning to play the ragtime style. Joplin wrote arrangements of his rags for winds, strings, and percussion that he published with the title *The Red Back Book*

Standard High-Class Rags. Thus, trained and skilled wind and string musicians who could read music learned to play Joplin's rags—and others—in the authentic style. In addition, the New Orleans street musicians, most who could not read, heard and began to imitate the syncopated feel of ragtime rhythm. They called it "ragging the tune." Any song, hymn, or folk melody could be made to sound "raggy" simply by playing syncopated rather than straight European style rhythms.

Major Contributors to New Orleans Jazz Style

No cultural phenomenon emerges as a fully formed, national influence in a day, week, year, or even a decade. New Orleans jazz developed over more than two centuries, percolating in the African American slave and freemen communities. It resulted from the syncretism of all of the African and European retentions. The mix was so thoroughly successful that the music that emerged in New Orleans around 1900 was new, unique, and highly infectious.

Hundreds of African American musicians, over many decades before 1900, played an integral part in creating jazz music. Most of their names, as with early blues musicians, are lost to history. Some of the most notable contributors, profiled in the following section, are a small sampling of those who found success in New Orleans and beyond.

Buddy Bolden

It is commonly acknowledged that Buddy Bolden is the first New Orleans cornetist and band leader to bring the street music of that city—already heavily influenced by the ragtime style (ragging the tune)—into the dance halls and blend it with the blues. His flamboyant personality and loud, aggressive playing style set the tone for cornetists who followed him, notably Joe King Oliver and Louis Armstrong. He was known for his loud, resonant tone, so much so that it was said when he played at dance halls outside of town, he could be heard in downtown New Orleans, a full 2 miles away. This may be one of those "exaggerated descriptions," possibly told by Louis Armstrong.

"He and his men performed everything demanding New Orleans audiences could want—waltzes, mazurkas, schottisches, polkas, rags, spirituals, blues ... all over town ... for black dancers, at places like Union Sons Hall—better known as Funky Butt Hall" (Ward & Burns, 2000, p. 21). Bolden was often known to play the blues there until dawn. There was not yet a name for the music Buddy Bolden and fellow musicians played at the start of the 20th century (some older players would call it ragtime for their entire lives), but the resulting new style, not blues or spirituals or ragtime alone, but a sum of its parts, was eventually known worldwide as New Orleans Jazz (Ward & Burns, 2000).

Jelly Roll Morton

Boisterous, and the consummate braggard and storyteller, Jelly Roll Morton is the epitome of the New Orleans musician who embodied the trickster persona. He told anyone who would listen that he invented jazz (in 1902 ... when he was just 12 years old). While he clearly did not invent the style, he was one of the first in the city to play jazz with authentic improvisation and to compose and write down tunes in the jazz style. His understanding of jazz as a style, distinct from, but using elements of blues and ragtime, came from his ability to reproduce in his playing the complex polyrhythms and collective improvisation of the New Orleans street bands.

Joe King Oliver

Central to the understanding of Louis Armstrong's primacy as the greatest cornetist, band leader, and jazz musician of the early 20th century is Armstrong's mentor and friend, Joe King Oliver. Oliver was cut from the same cloth as Bolden: brash, boisterous, and highly gifted as a jazz cornetist. He directly followed in the footsteps of Bolden, eventually becoming the most admired and sought-after cornetist and band leader in New Orleans. Only Freddie Keppard (the other highly regarded cornetist/band leader in New Orleans) was any match for Oliver's skill as an entertainer, band leader, and master of his instrument. "King Oliver" could play rough, sweet, fast, and high—all attributes the young Louis Armstrong admired. "Armstrong looked for any opportunity to be close to his idol" (Ward & Burns, 2000, p. 48). When he went "up the River" to Chicago, Oliver had great success with his Creole Jazz Band, and he very quickly sent for his protege, Louis Armstrong, who joined the band as the second cornetist.

With the three generations of New Orleans cornetists and band leaders—Bolden, Keppard, and Oliver—setting the standard for playing style, it is not too surprising that Louis Armstrong inherited not just their musical traits but also the mantle of leadership and innovation that made him the most beloved musician of the early 1900s.

Louis Armstrong

Louis Armstrong is undoubtedly one of the most famous and thoroughly documented musicians, in any style of music, of the 20th century. From his early days as an aspiring jazz cornetist in New Orleans to his preeminence as a world class entertainer for over 50 years, Armstrong maintained his position as "the most influential figure in American music" (Brothers, 2006). His fame spread around the world, and he received accolades and gifts from kings, presidents, and dignitaries. King George V of Great Britain gave him a Selmer K-modified trumpet. He toured internationally under the auspices of the U.S. State Department, "earning the nickname, 'Ambassador Satch'" (Wikipedia, 2022, Louis Armstrong).

FIGURE 7.1 Portrait of Louis Armstrong playing a Selmer K-modified trumpet given to him by the King of the United Kingdom.

Joe King Oliver and Louis Armstrong, "Dippermouth Blues"

https://www.youtube.com/watch?v=f2NNnepDLkc

Armstrong's mother, Mayann, was a prostitute, and he barely knew his father. His childhood was mostly played out on the streets of the city, chasing after the frequent parades as part of the "second line," riding on a rag pickers wagon to make a few pennies while learning to play a brass bugle from the driver. At age 12, he was sent to the Colored Waif's Home for 18 months for firing a gun in the city on New Year's Eve. At the home he discovered his life's calling. The band leader and music teacher at the home gave him a cornet, let him join the brass band, and he was set on the path for his life (Ward & Burns, 2000).

He met and took lessons with his idol, Joe King Oliver. Often, Oliver would recommend Louis for jobs, thus promoting Armstrong as one of the up and coming cornetists in the city. He developed quickly into a fine cornet player. By 1922, when he left New Orleans for Chicago, his reputation as a cornetist rivaled that of Buddy Bolden, Freddie Keppard, and Oliver. He had a big, powerful tone, fluid technique, and an exceptionally creative mind that allowed him to develop imaginative improvisations based on both the melody and chords of a song. It is this one aspect of his playing, the invention of a new style of improvisation based on the use of the background chords of a piece. For all of the 1920s until the mid-1930s, Armstrong was the most revered and well-known trumpet/cornet player and musician in popular music.

FIGURE 7.2 Poster advertisement for the Original Dixieland Jass Band

The Original Dixieland Jass (Jazz) Band

The Original Dixieland Jazz (Jass) Band (ODJB) was an all-White Dixieland (New Orleans) jazz band that made the first jazz recordings in early 1917. Their "Livery Stable Blues" became the first jazz record ever issued. The group recorded many jazz standards, the most famous being "Tiger Rag," which leader Nick LaRocca claims they composed as well (some Black New Orleans jazzmen argue against that claim). In late 1917, the original spelling of the band's name was changed to Original Dixieland Jazz Band (as described above). The band consisted of five White musicians playing the traditional New Orleans ensemble instruments: trumpet (leader Nick LaRocca), clarinet, trombone, drum set, and piano. "Other bands, both White and Negro, had preceded the Original Dixieland Jazz Band, but this band played the right spot, at the right time (Reisenweber's in New York City), and hit the headlines from coast to coast" (Stearns, 1958, p. 155).

The ODJB billed itself as the creator of Jazz, but, Louis Armstrong is quoted as saying, "They were the first to record the music I played" (Brothers, 2006, p. 245–246). This might be one of the clearest examples of Black Invention, White Appropriation in American popular music history. The ODJB was the first band to record jazz commercially and to have hit recordings in the genre. Band leader and cornetist Nick LaRocca argued that ODJB deserved recognition as the first band to record jazz commercially and the first band to establish jazz as a musical idiom or genre. While the first to record in the genre, they were by no means the creators of jazz. A careful listening to any of their recordings will reveal that they are not in the same league with any of the African American bands of the time, especially, King Oliver's Creole Jazz Band or Louis Armstrong's Hot Five or Hot Seven.

The Original Dixieland Jazz Band playing "Livery Stable Blues"

https://video.search.yahoo.com/search/video?fr=aaplw&ei=utf-8&p=Livery+Stable+Blues-Original+Dixieland+Jazz+Band#id=1&vid=0964654ef2412a60f1127190c4d98774&action=view

Other Notable Early New Orleans Jazz Musicians (Through the 1920s)

- Sidney Bechet—clarinet and soprano sax
- Johnny Dodds—clarinet
- Alphonse Picou—clarinet
- Freddie Keppard—trumpet
- "Kid" Ory—trombone
- Honore Dutrey—trombone
- Lil' Hardin (Armstrong)—piano
- Baby Dodds—drum set

Traditional New Orleans Jazz Band Instrumentation

- 1 Trumpet (occasionally 2)
- 1 Clarinet and or saxophone (sometimes both)
- 1 Trombone
- 1 Banjo and or piano (sometimes both)
- 1 Tuba or bass
- 1 Drum set

Conclusion

Jazz, or "Hot Jazz," developed and first performed by African Americans, became the first nationally popular youth music in the 1920s. It spread quickly to most major cities. Chicago,

New York, Los Angeles, San Francisco, Washington D.C., and Philadelphia had many groups that would go on to be nationally known, thanks to the hugely successful recordings of the Original Dixieland Jazz Band. By 1924 the music caught on with both White musicians and White audiences.

The White form of the music is not really jazz, but a bland copy, known as "sweet music" played by sophisticated dance orchestras in hotel ballrooms and dance halls. At this time, most White musicians do not improvise well, if at all; they play written out solos, sometimes copied from the solos of Black musicians.

African American musicians, especially those from New Orleans and other East Coast cities, become popular with White audiences, and record companies seek to record the major Black bands such as Joe King Oliver's Creole Jazz Band (1923) and Louis Armstrong and his Hot Five and Hot Seven (1925).

Key Takeaways

- Music in New Orleans at the turn to the 20th century was a vibrant and exciting mix of styles from every ethnic group in the city.
- Black and White musicians played in bands (segregated by race) on the street, in clubs, dance halls, and bordellos, mixing polkas, marches, schottisches, ragtime, blues and even classical melodies.
- In 1897, the legalization of prostitution in Storyville, the red-light district of New Orleans, provided increased opportunities for pianists, singers, and band musicians to entertain patrons in those establishments. When Storyville was closed down in 1917 by the federal government, musicians were forced to find places to play in other cities along the Mississippi river. Many traveled as far north as Chicago to find work.
- Every separate music style eventually blended together to create a new genre of popular music, called jazz, which would sweep the nation and become the predominant popular music style by the mid-1920s.

Review Questions

1. In what ways did Catholic plantations encourage the retention and syncretism of African American music and culture?
2. List the instrumentation of the traditional New Orleans jazz band.
3. What role did Storyville play in the development of New Orleans jazz?
4. What are the reasons for the exodus of musicians from New Orleans in 1917?
5. Name five New Orleans musicians prominent from the 1890s through 1920.
6. What set Louis Armstrong apart from his contemporaries in regard to his musical brilliance?

Class Project

Collect and listen to recordings of five New Orleans jazz bands, both White and Black, and compare them in terms of quality of the ensemble playing, quality of soloists, authenticity of the band's style, and overall jazz (swing) feel. Use a recording of Louis Armstrong's Hot Five or Hot Seven as one of the five for your template (comparison) recording.

References

Brothers, Thomas. (2006). *Louis Armstrong's New Orleans.* W.W. Norton & Company.

Stearns M. (1958). *The story of jazz.* Oxford University Press.

Ward, J. C., & Burns, K. (2000). *Jazz: A history of America's music.* Alfred A. Knopf.

Wikipedia. (2022). Louis Armstrong. https://en.wikipedia.org/wiki/Louis Armstrong.

Credits

Fig. 7.1: "Image of portrait of Louis Armstrrong," https://commons.wikimedia.org/wiki/File:Louis_Armstrong_1947.JPG, 1947.

Fig. 7.2: "Image of the Original Dixieland Jazz Band," https://commons.wikimedia.org/wiki/File:Original_Dixieland_Jass_Band_-_A_Brass_Band_Gone_Crazy_1917.jpg, 1917.

Chapter 8

Popular Music Spreads Across the Nation and Beyond

Yiddish Theatre, Tin Pan Alley, and the Roaring Twenties

Introduction

In addition to the influences of African American and Western European music and culture, central and eastern European immigrants, especially of Jewish Heritage, influenced American popular music beginning in the late 19th century. As early as 1882, Yiddish (Jewish) theatres opened up in Jewish neighborhoods in New York City. Many of the sheet music publishers and composers who founded Tin Pan Alley during that same time period were Jewish as well. The combination of Jewish music and theatre and the emerging popularity of African American music styles provided much of the impetus for the worldwide popularity of American popular music during the first half of the 20th century.

Technology grew rapidly in the late 1800s, mostly based on the shift to electricity as the generator of power. Technological innovations provided multiple pathways for the new style of music to spread across the United States, and eventually the entire world. Recording and playback technologies and radio and moving pictures were rapidly embraced by significant portions of the population. People could enjoy a wide spectrum of entertainment options without leaving the comfort of their home.

Entertainment became a multimillion-dollar industry. Big name stars emerged who sang live on radio broadcasts and in theatres and made recordings of the latest Tin Pan Alley hits. By the mid-1920s, former minstrel, vaudeville, Jewish theater, and Broadway performers and singers starred in movies made in Hollywood. The technology fueled entertainment revolution, which began with minstrelsy, military style bands, vaudeville, and Yiddish theater, quickly morphed into Broadway musicals, live radio broadcasts, recordings, ballroom

KEY TERMS

Yiddish Theatre
Tin Pan Alley
Vaudeville
Prohibition
Music publisher
Gramophone
Radio
Wets
Dries
Mafia
AABA
Chord progression
Tempo
Melody
Lyrics

dancing, and moving pictures. All of this came about before the end of the Roaring Twenties and the Great Depression of 1929.

Purpose

Chapter 8 outlines the major developments in American popular music from the 1880s through the end of the 1920s. It introduces the reader to the technology revolution driven by advancements in the widespread use of electricity. The contributions of Jewish immigrants to American music and culture, coupled with the continuing progress and popularity of African American music, assures the widespread acceptance by the American public of the music composed, published, and promoted by Tin Pan Alley. The era of Prohibition (1920 to 1933) poses unique problems for musicians, band leaders, entertainers, club owners, and those who seek to control the sale and distribution of illegal alcohol.

Outcomes

- Students will be able to articulate the reasons for the rapid rise of African American influenced popular music during the first two decades of the 20th century.
- Students will memorize and be able to explain the key terms used in this chapter.
- Students will know and be able to discuss the most significant composers, musicians, and entertainers of the early 20th century.
- Students will be able to explain the reasons for Prohibition and the dramatic changes in American society brought on by the 18th Amendment.
- Students will understand and be able to articulate the significant role that Yiddish theatre, Tin Pan Alley, and emerging technologies had on music and entertainment in the early 20th century.

"HIS MASTER'S VOICE"
This trademark and the trademarked word "Victrola" identify all our products. Look under the lid! Look on the label!
VICTOR TALKING MACHINE CO., Camden, N. J.

FIGURE 8.1 Victrola Advertisement

Technology Opens the World to American Popular Music

By the mid-1880s, electricity was harnessed and being used to power streetlights and home lighting in major cities throughout the United States. In quick succession, the invention of the radio, gramophone, microphone, and advanced recording and broadcast technologies provided a pathway for the worldwide distribution of recorded music. By the early 1920s, one could enjoy music, and entertainment of all kinds, in their home by putting a record on the Victrola or tuning into a radio broadcast.

Movies provided another opportunity for mass distribution of popular music and created the first generation of nationally popular stars of stage, screen, and recordings. Watch a video of Al Jolson, the first person to be heard as well seen on the movie screen, in the first "talkie," by clicking on QR code correct page on page 8.

As we continue chapter by chapter through the 20th century, we will update technological progress with discussions of the latest innovations in music, broadcast, and recording technologies.

FIGURE 8.2 Al Jolson, one of the biggest stars of stage, screen, and radio in the early 20th century.

Yiddish Theatre

The United States's first Yiddish theater production was hosted in 1882 at the New York Turn-Verein, a gymnastic club at 66 East 4th Street in the Little Germany neighborhood of Manhattan (now considered part of the East Village). In 1903, the Grand Theatre was built—New York's first Yiddish theater, In addition to translated versions of classic plays, it featured vaudeville acts (vaudeville inherited much of the minstrelsy tradition without its racist content), musicals, and other entertainment. Second Avenue gained more prominence as a Yiddish theater destination in the 1910s with the opening of two theatres: the Second Avenue Theatre in 1911 and the National Theater in 1912.

In addition to Yiddish theaters, the district had related music stores, photography studios, flower shops, restaurants, and cafes (including Cafe Royal on East 12th Street and Second Avenue). Metro Music, on Second Avenue in the district, published most of the Yiddish and Hebrew sheet music for the American market until they went out of business in the 1970s. The Hebrew Actors Union was the first theatrical union in the U.S.

The childhood home of composer and pianist George Gershwin (originally, Gershwine) and his brother and lyricist, Ira, was in the center of the Yiddish Theatre District, on the second floor at 91 Second Avenue, between East 5th and 6th Streets. They frequented the local Yiddish theaters. Composer and lyricist Irving Berlin (born Israel Baline) also grew up in the district, in a Yiddish-speaking home. Both the Gershwin brothers and Irving Berlin were among those who started their careers in Tin Pan Alley publishing houses, George as a song or music plugger. The list of Jewish Tin Pan Alley composers later in this chapter is indicative of the extent to which Jewish American composers contributed to American popular music and culture.

Tin Pan Alley

There is a collection of thousands of songs commonly known as the "Great American Songbook," that were composed primarily by songwriters hired by song publishers to create songs for the commercial popular music market. These "Tin Pan Alley" composers got their start writing exclusively for the music publishing houses on 28th Street in New York City. Even today, these songs are revered as superb examples of song composition. They have been sung by generations of the greatest of our male and female popular singers. Louis Armstrong, Lady Gaga, Beyonce, Tony Bennett, Frank Sinatra, Michael Bublé, Sarah Vaughan, and dozens of others built their careers singing the songs of Tin Pan Alley composers. When you hear contemporary music by songwriters like Billy Joel, Elton John, Lennon and McCartney, Carol King, Linda Ronstadt, or Carly Simon, you hear music crafted in, and descended from, the Tin Pan Alley style.

As Tin Pan Alley influenced American music, American music, in turn, influenced the world. Pioneering African American composers such as Richard McPherson (aka Cecil Mack), the writer of "The Charleston," and W. C. Handy, who composed "St. Louis Blues," worked on Tin Pan Alley. Irving Berlin, George and Ira Gershwin, Cole Porter, and Albert Von Tilzer, who wrote "Take Me Out to the Ball Game," all got their start in Tin Pan Alley (Wikipedia, 2023, Tin Pan Alley).

The publishers who opened their businesses in Tin Pan Alley in the late 1800s pioneered both sheet music publishing and commercial songwriting. In these publishing houses, dozens of composers labored in small rooms equipped with a piano to hopefully compose the next big "top the Billboard charts" hit. All those composers, playing their pianos simultaneously in different keys, tempos, and volumes, created a din which to some on the street seemed like the banging together of a large number of tin pans. The remnants of one of America's greatest musical and cultural movements can still be seen on 28th Street between Broadway and Sixth Avenue in Manhattan.

The Tin Pan Alley publishers employed singers and pianists as "song pluggers" or "song demonstrators." They were also employed by department stores and music stores to promote and help sell new sheet music. Music publisher Frank Harding is credited with innovating the sales method. Typically, the pianist/vocalist sat on the mezzanine level of a store and played whatever music was sent up to him by the clerk selling the sheet music. Patrons could select any title, have it delivered to the song plugger, and get a preview of the tune before buying it. This was how hits were advertised before quality recordings were widely available.

Although the terms are often used interchangeably, those who worked in department and music stores were most often known as "song demonstrators," while those who worked directly for music publishers were called "song pluggers." Musicians and composers who had worked as song pluggers included George Gershwin, Jerome Kern, Irving Berlin, and Lil Hardin Armstrong (Wikipedia, 2023, Song plugger).

One of the secrets to the success of Tin Pan Alley composers was their use of formulaic chord progressions and formal structures. The European retention of formal song structure, especially 32-bar song form, or AABA, and common chord progressions, such as I, vi, ii, V, I and 1, IV, V, I dominated the songwriting craft. These techniques, combined with lyrics about love, produced song after song that seemed familiar and comfortable to the vast music listening public. The chord progressions and forms were incessantly consistent, and the lyrics were most often about one of six variations on the love theme:

- First love
- New love
- Unrequited love
- Lost love
- Familial love
- Unfulfilled love

What made some songs hits and others not? Often it was the creative melodic and lyric abilities of the composer. Songs which had more clear lyrics and well-crafted melodies stood a better chance of being recorded by one of the prominent singers of the era, and thus were more likely to move up the charts to become a hit for both the singer and the composer. Publishers counted on a successful song being recorded by a famous, currently popular singer to generate sales of tens of thousands of units of sheet music.

Tin Pan Alley Publishers and Composers

A sampling of the dozens of publishers and hundreds of composers the publishers hired to write songs for the publishing houses of Tin Pan Alley include the following:

- Publishers
  - Leo Feist
  - Sam Fox
  - Edward Marks
  - Isidore Witmark

- Composers
  - Harold Arlen
  - Irving Berlin
  - Sammy Cahn
  - Hoagy Carmichael
  - George M. Cohan
  - Buddy DeSylva
  - Al Dubin
  - Vernon Duke
  - Dorothy Fields
  - George Gershwin
  - Ira Gershwin
  - Oscar Hammerstein II
  - Lorenz Hart
  - James P. Johnson
  - Isham Jones
  - Scott Joplin
  - Gus Kahn
  - Jerome Kern
  - Frank Loesser
  - Jimmy McHugh
  - Johnny Mercer
  - Lew Pollack
  - Cole Porter
  - Richard Rodgers
  - Edward Teschemacher
  - Albert Von Tilzer
  - Harry Von Tilzer
  - Fats Waller
  - Harry Warren
  - Vincent Youmans

FIGURE 8.3 New York City Deputy Police Commissioner John A. Leach, right, watching agents pour liquor into sewer following a raid during the height of prohibition.

Prohibition

Prohibition in the United States was a national ban on the sale, manufacture, and transportation of alcohol in place from 1920 to 1933. Congress enacted into law the 18th Amendment to the Constitution, with the support and encouragement of prohibitionists from all over the country. The Volstead Act set down the rules for enforcing the ban and defined the types of alcoholic beverages that were prohibited. Private ownership and consumption of alcohol was not made illegal. Prohibition ended with the ratification of the 21st Amendment, which repealed the 18th Amendment, on December 5, 1933.

The introduction of alcohol prohibition and its subsequent enforcement in law was a hotly debated issue. The contemporary prohibitionists or "dries" were mostly woman, who despite not having the right to vote yet, constituted a formidable and successful lobby of Congress. They labeled this as the "noble experiment" and presented it as a victory for public morals and health. The consumption of alcohol overall went down by half in the 1920s, and it remained below pre-Prohibition levels until the 1940s.

Anti-prohibitionists, the "wets," felt that Prohibition was an imposition of mainly rural Protestant ideals on an important aspect of urban, immigrant, and Catholic everyday life. Enforcement of the law during the Prohibition era was compromised by graft and corruption among politicians, law enforcement, and criminal elements that controlled the flow of illegal alcohol. This led to widespread flouting of the law. Among the general population, there was a lack of popular consensus for the ban, which resulted in the growth of widespread criminal organizations, including Cosa Nostra Mafia (Wikipedia, 2023, Prohibition).

Prohibition had a profound effect on the music industry in the United States, specifically with jazz and popular music. Speakeasies (illegal private clubs where patrons could gamble, dance, and listen to music while having an illegal alcoholic beverage) became very popular. With the popularity of jazz in speakeasies and the emergence of advanced recording technology, jazz's popularity skyrocketed. Many of the best jazz bands of the era, such as Duke Ellington's, were supported and bankrolled by the Mafia. The Depression made it difficult for jazz and dance bands to travel and continue to play and record, but the Mafia saw prohibition as a way to control all aspects of both the entertainment industry and the illegal distribution and sale of alcohol (Wikipedia, 2023, Prohibition).

Musicians, Composers, and Performers of the "Roaring Twenties"

We have already discussed the most prominent of the New Orleans jazz musicians who influenced the rise of popular music throughout the United States and abroad. However, there were many adults over age 30 of primarily the White, middle and upper classes who frowned on jazz music. They thought of it as rough and low class. It took the genius of George Gershwin, the salesmanship of Paul Whiteman, and the popularity of Al Jolson to change the negative image of jazz among White Americans and encourage the mass sales of jazz and jazz influenced popular music to White America.

FIGURE 8.4 George Gershwin appears on *Time* magazine Cover, 1925

George Gershwin

George Gershwin is the quintessential American composer. Skilled in the classical, jazz, and popular styles of his era, he wrote for every medium available, including symphony orchestra, the Broadway stage, opera, and popular song. From 1919 until his premature death from a brain tumor at age 38, George Gershwin, and his brother Ira, enjoyed unparalleled success as a composer and lyricist for the Broadway stage, movies, and serious concert hall music. George's first hit song, "Swanee," written in 1919, "sold a million sheet music copies and an estimated two million records" (Wikipedia, 2023, Al Jolson). Al Jolson agreed to sing it in a show and record it, ensuring that it would become the most popular and successful song of Gershwin's career.

Gershwin is widely regarded as one of the great musical geniuses of the 20th century. His popular songs and his most well-known classical compositions (music composed in the European concert hall tradition) such as *Rhapsody in Blue, An American in Paris, Concerto in F* for Piano and Orchestra, and the folk opera, *Porgy and Bess,* "demonstrate a sophisticated incorporation of stylistic devices derived from African American sources, such as syncopation and blue notes ..." (Starr & Waterman, 2018, p. 121). It was Gershwin's collaboration with bandleader Paul Whiteman on the creation and performance of *Rhapsody in Blue* that drove the rapid acceptance of jazz and jazz-influenced music by the general public.

View the video of the first act of Gershwin's masterpiece, *Porgy and Bess:*

Watch at: https://www.youtube.com/watch?v=fO2114PmTl4

Paul Whiteman

Paul Whiteman, had one of the most popular dance bands in the United States during the 1920s. Whiteman produced recordings that were immensely successful, and press notices often referred to him as the "King of Jazz." Using a large ensemble including strings and exploring many styles of music, Whiteman is perhaps best known for his blending of symphonic music and jazz.

His 1924 commissioning and debut of George Gershwin's jazz-influenced *Rhapsody in Blue* is a watershed moment in the development of American popular music. He produced a concert at Aeolian Hall in New York, featuring the premier of *Rhapsody in Blue*, with Gershwin as piano soloist as well as composer. Within weeks, Americans across the nation caught the "jazz craze" and bought millions of records by Whiteman and many other White and Black jazz bands.

Later, Whiteman's promotion and recording of symphonic jazz music influenced many jazz greats, such as Gil Evans, Miles Davis, and Stan Kenton. Whiteman recorded many jazz and pop standards during his career. He successfully courted the "classical music crowd" and convinced them that jazz was respectable and had come of age.

Whiteman's place in the history of early jazz is somewhat controversial. Detractors suggest that Whiteman's ornately orchestrated music was jazz in name only (lacking the genre's improvisational and emotional depth), and that he co-opted the innovations of Black musicians. Although Whiteman intended to hire some Black musicians, his managers suggested that to do so would negatively impact his popularity. Defenders note that Whiteman's fondness for jazz was genuine (he worked with Black musicians behind the scenes and in recording sessions as much as was feasible during an era of racial segregation). His bands included many of the era's most esteemed White jazz musicians and many argue that his groups handled jazz admirably as part of a larger repertoire. In his autobiography, Duke Ellington declared, "Paul Whiteman was known as the King of Jazz, and no one as yet has come near carrying that title with more certainty and dignity" (Wikipedia, 2023, Paul Whiteman).

Al Jolson

Al Jolson was a Lithuanian American singer, comedian, actor, and vaudevillian. He was one of the most famous and highest paid American stars of the 1920s, and he promoted himself as "The World's Greatest Entertainer." Jolson was known for his "shamelessly sentimental, melodramatic approach" toward performing, as well as for popularizing many of the songs he sung (such as Gershwin's "Swanee River.") Because of his continued use of "blackface minstrel" style makeup long after minstrelsy was passe, Jolson has been referred to by modern critics as "the king of blackface performers." Jolson is most remembered today as the star of the first talking picture, *The Jazz Singer* (1927) (Wikipedia, 2023, Al Jolson).

Watch and hear Al Jolson sing "Mammy" from the first "talkie," *The Jazz Singer*:

Watch at: https://www.youtube.com/watch?v=PIaj7FNHnjQ&t=55s

Jolson, yet another example of Black invention, White appropriation, sang jazz and blues in an overblown, overly dramatic style. His approach took traditionally African American music and popularized it for White American audiences who were otherwise unwilling to listen to it when performed by Black artists. Despite his promotion and perpetuation of Black stereotypes (very much in the minstrel tradition), his work was often well-regarded by Black publications, and he was lauded for fighting against Black discrimination on Broadway as early as 1911. An essay written by music critic Ted Gioia suggested, "If blackface has its shameful poster boy, it is Al Jolson," to put a fine point on the Black invention, White appropriation argument. (Wikipedia, 2023, Al Jolson).

Other Prominent Musicians, Band Leaders, and Entertainers of the Early 20th Century

Bix Beiderbecke
Eubie Blake
Vernon and Irene Castle
Russ Columbo
Bing Crosby
Xavier Cugat
Duke Ellington
James Reese Europe
Fletcher Henderson
Guy Lombardo
Ethel Merman
Vaughn Monroe
Bennie Moten
Jimmie Rodgers
Noble Sissle
Rudy Vallee
Thomas "Fats" Waller

Key Takeaways

- Popular music in the early 20th century derived from African American and European influences, especially the jazz music of New Orleans, which became the popular youth music of the Roaring Twenties.
- Technology, including the radio, gramophone, and moving pictures drove the rapid popularization of all forms of music, creating a multimillion-dollar entertainment industry.
- George Gershwin (and his lyricist brother Ira), Paul Whiteman, and Al Jolson are representative of the major composers, musicians, and entertainers who dominated the 1920s.
- George Gershwin and Paul Whiteman's collaboration on *Rhapsody in Blue* is a major reason for the enthusiastic acceptance of jazz and popular music by White, middle and upper class Americans in the mid to late 1920s.

Class or Extra Credit Projects

1. Try your hand at composing a Tin Pan Alley type song. Choose a key and tempo for the song. Using AABA form, write a set of lyrics, establish a melody for the A theme, a contrasting melody for the B theme, and a chord progression such as I vi, ii, V, I. If you cannot read and write music, perhaps you can partner with someone in the class who has those skills.
2. Write a multipage report on George Gershwin's folk opera, *Porgy and Bess.*

Review Questions

Directions: Refer to what you learned in this chapter to help you respond completely and correctly to the questions and prompts below.

1. List five prominent musicians, Black or White, of the early 20th century.
2. Describe the collaboration of Paul Whiteman and George Gershwin that resulted in Gershwin's masterpiece, *Rhapsody in Blue.*
3. Describe the developments in the entertainment industry brought about by the technological innovations of the late 19th and early 20th centuries.
4. How did Tin Pan Alley music publishers impact the sale and distribution of popular songs?
5. What are the major structural forms and chord progressions used by Tin Pan Alley composers?
6. In what ways did Prohibition impact American popular music?

References

Starr, L., & Waterman, C. (2018). *American popular music* (5th ed.). Oxford University Press.

Stearns M. (1958). *The story of jazz.* Oxford University Press.

Wikipedia. (2023). Al Jolson. https://en.wikipedia.org/wiki/Al_Jolson

Wikipedia. (2023). Prohibition. https://en.wikipedia.org/wiki/Prohibition

Wikipedia. (2023). Song plugger. https://en.wikipedia.org/wiki/Song_plugger

Wikipedia. (2023). Tin Pan Alley. https://en.wikipedia.org/wiki/Tin_Pan_Alley

Wikipedia. (2023). Paul Whiteman. https://en.wikipedia.org/wiki/Paul_Whiteman

Credits

Fig. 8.1: Victor Talking Machine Company, "Image of His Master's Voice," https://commons.wikimedia.org/wiki/File:VictorTalkingLogo.jpg, 1921.

Fig. 8.2: Warner Bros. Pictures, "Al Jolson," https://commons.wikimedia.org/wiki/File:Al_Jolson_Jazz_Singer.JPG, 1927.

Fig. 8.3: "Prohibition," https://commons.wikimedia.org/wiki/File:5_Prohibition_Disposal(9).jpg, 1921.

Fig. 8.4: Time Magazine, "George Gershwin," https://commons.wikimedia.org/wiki/File:George_Gershwin-TIME-1925.jpg, 1925.

Chapter 9

Fletcher Henderson and the Rise of Big Bands

Introduction

Chapter 9 presents the meteoric rise and two-decade prominence of the big bands. Beginning in the mid-1920s, Fletcher Henderson, Paul Whiteman, Duke Ellington, and many other visionary band leaders expanded the typical New Orleans style instrumentation from the traditional five to seven, to as many as 15 to 24 players (Paul Whiteman's Ambassador Orchestra had a full string section). The increase in instrumentation required the musicians to transition from the New Orleans style of group and solo improvisation to arranged and notated music. Nonreading musicians simply could not play in such a band. Paul Whiteman's band had been playing precisely arranged music since the late teens, although no one in his all-White band could improvise and there was no "swing feel" to the music.

"This was a different kind of arranged music, which thanks to Fletcher Henderson, Don Redmond ... Duke Ellington, and all the other Negro bandleaders who had figured it out years ago, enabled the big bands to swing" (Ward & Burns, 2000, p. 240). Fletcher Henderson and the early pioneers of the big band style were 10 years ahead of their time. Henderson, in particular, made profound contributions to the development of the big band style, but he was mostly unknown to the general public during the big band era from 1934–1946.

As early as 1924, many dance and jazz band leaders saw the need to expand the number of instruments in their bands to accommodate the larger dance halls and ballrooms in which they were booked, a consequence of the overwhelming nationwide popularity of jazz and dance music of the late teens and early 20s. Band leaders like Henderson, Ellington, and Whiteman hired musicians who could read music and play swing style, but not necessarily improvise. Formed

KEY TERMS

Big band
Swing
Arrangement
Arranger
Niche music
Hot jazz
Sweet music
Rhythm section
Improvised solo
Musicians strike
DownBeat magazine
Metronome magazine

in 1924 as a dance band, the Fletcher Henderson Orchestra only evolved as a jazz group with the addition of Louis Armstrong as a featured soloist in 1925–1926.

The music of the big band era was known by several names: swing, big band, big band swing, big band jazz, and sweet. It was a mix of great songs from Tin Pan Alley, Broadway, and the movies, original instrumentals arranged by master musicians, sung by charismatic singers, and played by superb players. On the low side of the quality spectrum were bands and singers who performed saccharine, sweet music and novelty tunes that pandered to the pedestrian tastes of the average citizen. From 1934/35 on,

> Big band swing became a hundred-million-dollar industry. Between thirty ... and forty thousand musicians would find work playing swing music after 1935. Another eight thousand men and women were needed just to manage, book and promote their appearances. Swing rescued the recording industry; only six million records had been sold in the United States in 1933; by 1939, that number would grow to fifty million ... (Ward & Burns, 2000, p. 240).

Another section of this chapter highlights the concept of "niche music"—a popular style of music which is in favor with a large segment of the listening public for a finite period of time, then drops off in popularity as other music styles capture the public's fancy. From the 1920s on, the progression from peak popularity downward to modest acceptance as a niche music becomes the fate of virtually every popular music style.

Purpose

This chapter will familiarize the reader with the development of the big band style and era. Some writers on topic of popular music call the big band era the greatest period of exceptional musicianship and high-quality music performance in American popular music history. While that might be an overstatement, there is no question that the volume of excellent music, played live and recorded by both Black and White musicians during the years of its peak popularity, was as great as during any other stylistic period before or since.

Outcomes

- Students will become familiar with and be able to discuss the major band leaders and musicians of the big band era.
- Students will be able to explain the key terms used in this chapter.
- Students will be able to discuss the development of the big band style from its beginnings in the mid-1920s.
- Students will be able to articulate the demise of the big band era and the rise of the singers in the mid-1940s.

Some Major Leaders of the Big Band Era

The leading musicians and band leaders of the big band era left a lasting legacy. These include Fletcher Henderson, William "Count" Basie, Benny Goodman, Glenn Miller, and Edward Kennedy "Duke" Ellington. Let's consider each of these giants of the big band era individually.

Fletcher Henderson: The Originator of the Big Band Swing Style

FIGURE 9.1 Fletcher Henderson

Pianist, arranger, and bandleader Fletcher Henderson led the greatest and most important of the pioneering big bands. A college graduate from a sophisticated Black family, he did not plan to be a professional musician, piano player, and band leader. Sadly, he is the poster child for those pioneers of American popular music who were lost to history and never received the accolades they were due. Although his band had such extraordinary sidemen as Louis Armstrong, Coleman Hawkins, Buster Bailey, Rex Stewart, Ben Webster, Chu Berry, Benny Carter, Roy Eldridge, and Red Allen, his legend and contributions were eclipsed in the public's consciousness by the great bands of the later big band era, which include Duke Ellington, Count Basie, Glenn Miller, The Dorsey Brothers, Artie Shaw, and Benny Goodman (for whom Henderson eventually worked as chief arranger and pianist).

Formed in 1924 as a dance band, the Fletcher Henderson Orchestra only evolved as a jazz group with the addition of Louis Armstrong as a featured soloist in 1925–1926. The musicians who followed in Louis's footsteps made the group a feature for some of the new style's most exciting soloists, and the arrangements of orchestrator Don Redman helped define the standard forms for big band jazz, a form that Henderson helped extend with his many subsequent superb arrangements.

Click on this link to hear a recording of Fletcher Henderson's Band with Louis Armstrong as trumpet soloist.

Watch at: https://www.youtube.com/watch?v=b-EG8FpoRCw&t=38s

Duke Ellington, who achieved legendary stature as the greatest band leader, arranger, and pianist of the big band era said, "My big ambition was to sound like Fletcher. He had such a wonderful band" (Simon, 1971, p. 187). Many other band leaders of the era admired the Henderson band and modeled their bands after his.

Henderson's most enduring accomplishment is his intimate involvement with Benny Goodman. Starting in 1934, he began contributing versions of his better arrangements to Benny Goodman's new big band, including "King Porter Stomp," "Sometimes I'm Happy," and "Down South Camp Meeting." Ironically, Goodman's recordings were huge hits at a time when

Fletcher Henderson's name was not known to the general public. Henderson eventually joined the arranging staff of Goodman's organization and continued to contribute some of Goodman's most successful hits.

Goodman's appropriation of Henderson's material also disguised Henderson's contribution to jazz at a key point in its history—the emergence of swing onto a national stage. One of the Benny Goodman band's most-played pieces, "King Porter Stomp," was based heavily on a Henderson arrangement.

In 1939, Henderson dissolved his band and joined Goodman's, first as pianist and arranger, and later working full-time as staff arranger. He re-formed bands of his own several times in the 1940s and toured with Ethel Waters again in 1948–1949. Then he suffered a stroke in 1950, resulting in partial paralysis that ended his days as a pianist. Fletcher Henderson, the father of the big band style, died in New York City in 1952.

William "Count" Basie

Count Basie was, "the leader of one of the most consistently swinging bands in history" (Simon, 1971, p. 79). Initially from Red Bank, New Jersey, where there is a performing arts center named after him, he gave himself the title "Count" to emulate other leaders like Paul Whiteman, the self-titled King of Jazz and Duke Ellington. In his late teen years, Basie lived in Manhattan, where he learned from the stride pianists such as James P. Johnson, Willie "The Lion" Smith, and Fats Waller. After seven years on the road, he ended up in Kansas City, playing for the Bennie Moten Band.

In 1935, Basie's career as a leader took off when Moten suddenly died and Basie formed his first band, a nine-piece unit which quickly became popular in New York. The band caught the attention of John Hammond, perhaps the most influential writer and producer in the history of jazz (Ward & Burns, 2000, p. 249). Basie's most famous tune, "*One O'Clock Jump*," which you can hear by scanning the QR code below, is in the quintessential Basie style—hard driving swing, exciting solos and section work, large changes of dynamics from very soft to roaring loud, and the sparse, but always perfectly timed interjections of Basie's piano. The Basie Band played "One O'Clock Jump" as its closing number for more than 50 years.

"One O'Clock Jump" by Count Basie and his Orchestra

Watch this video of the Count Basie Orchestra playing "**One O'Clock Jump**" in 1943.

Watch at: https://www.youtube.com/watch?v=WUPsGGZ-vbY&t=10s

"If Benny Goodman became the King of Swing in 1935, reaping the publicity and profits, the man behind the throne was Count Basie. It was the Basie band that gave depth and momentum to the whole swing era while planting the seeds that later gave birth to bop and the 'cool' school of jazz" (Stearns, 1958, p. 211).

Benny Goodman

Benny Goodman is credited with popularizing big band music, especially with White teenagers in the early 1930s. Much of his success however is more the result of his collaboration with

Benny Goodman and his Orchestra play "Let's Dance"

Listen at: https://www.youtube.com/watch?v=kp4FA7re3x8

Fletcher Henderson, Goodman's long-time trusted arranger and pianist. There is ample evidence that Henderson, as arranger of some of Benny's most successful hits, rehearsed the band for his arrangements and likely taught them the swing style for which Henderson's bands were famous. Goodman became one of the most successful and wealthy big band leaders of the era, while Henderson, who had difficulty keeping and managing a band for more than a year or two at a time, was relegated to the back history of big band swing.

In the early days of radio, live broadcasts of all types, including plays, variety shows, and recorded music played by disc jockeys made up much of the programming on radio. Benny Goodman's "Let's Dance" broadcasts from New York City are an example of the earliest live broadcasts of big band music. His broadcast first aired in December of 1934 and was heard across the U.S. as far away as California. His was the final of several music features each night, making it a late broadcast on the East Coast, and consequently, after most high school and college students went to bed. Thus, those who were more apt to like hot jazz music did not hear these broadcasts.

Following his popular "Let's Dance" broadcasts, Goodman took his band on a U.S. tour that ended in California. It was largely unsuccessful until he hit the West Coast. The band was met with a tremendous amount of ambivalence throughout the Midwest. The 3-hour time difference of his live broadcasts between coasts had allowed many youth in the western time zones to listen in nightly. When they heard that Goodman and the band were on a national tour, they were ready and eager to greet and meet the band bringing them this new hot jazz music.

The tour culminated with Goodman's performance at the Palomar Ballroom in Los Angeles. Although Oakland turnouts were said to have been good and crowds enthusiastic, the band did not expect what they were met with when they arrived in Southern California. What might have been the end of the road for the band (and an early demise for the big band sound), turned into a new era in American popular music: The kids at the Palomar Ballroom, in the summer of 1935, heard Benny and the band launch into a hot jazz number (fittingly, one of Fletcher Henderson's arrangements) and began crowding around the bandstand cheering and encouraging the group (much like the teenage fans of today idolize their favorite performers).

With the headlines talking about the success of the Benny Goodman band in California, magazines like *DownBeat* and *Metronome* began to print more articles about the music. John Hammond, while known to most for fostering the career of Louis Armstrong and discovering Count Basie and Billie Holiday, was writing about big bands in *DownBeat.* By 1936, when Benny Goodman was performing just blocks away from the magazine's Chicago offices, articles about the band filled its issues.

Jazz in the form of big band swing was now beginning to sweep the nation, and hundreds of regional and nationally known bands played to packed audiences at dances and concerts. Live radio remotes featured this new swing music from coast to coast. Most of the major hotels in large cities had a "wire," as it was called, meaning a line installed for broadcast transmission. Jukeboxes featured all the latest hits by Goodman, Miller, Basie, Ellington, and dozens of other famous bands. The new generation of youth of the 1930s and early 1940s embraced big band swing, just as the previous generation had New Orleans jazz and ragtime. Kids were dancing, record jockeys were spinning discs and talking about them, and the big band era had arrived.

Glenn Miller

Glenn Miller was an American big band leader, trombonist, arranger, and composer during the swing era. His band performed and recorded iconic hits including "In the Mood," "Moonlight Serenade," "Pennsylvania 6-5000," "Chattanooga Choo-Choo," "A String of Pearls," and over a dozen more, making him the best-selling recording artist from 1939 to 1942. In just four years, Miller scored 16 number-one records and 69 top-10 hits—more than Elvis Presley (40 top-10s) or the Beatles (33 top-10s) did in their careers.

In 1942, Miller volunteered to join the U.S. Army–Air Force to entertain troops during World War II. He formed an all-military big band, which traveled throughout Europe performing for civilians and men and women in uniform. On December 15, 1944, while flying to Paris to plan for the band's appearance there, Miller's aircraft went down in bad weather over the English Channel. The plane and its occupants were never found. He was posthumously awarded the Bronze Star Medal (Wikipedia, 2022).

When the war ended, the Glenn Miller legacy was perpetually secured by the installation of his wartime band as the Army Air Force Jazz Orchestra, now The Air Force Airmen of Note, in Washington, D.C. Today, the Airmen of Note play all over the world and are considered one of the greatest of all professional jazz ensembles.

Edward Kennedy "Duke" Ellington

"Benny Goodman's favorite orchestra was Duke Ellington's, he said, both because the flavor of Duke's music is entirely different than anything else in jazz ..." (246). For his part, Ellington is quoted as saying, "... Jazz is music ... Swing is business" (246).

Listen to "Diminuendo and Crescendo in Blue" by the Duke Ellington Orchestra:

Listen at: https://www.youtube.com/watch?v=PYgow060zOg

Duke Ellington is a good example of a successful band leader who adopted the Fletcher Henderson model. He, along with Henderson and other African American band leaders of the 20s, was one of the architects of the swing style. He began his career with a small New Orleans style group in Washington, D.C., moved to New York City, and eventually the Cotton Club in Harlem, where he expanded his band's instrumentation and wrote music specifically for the special shows that were a favorite feature at the Cotton Club.

These shows catered to the racist notions of a predominantly White, wealthy clientele. The scenes generally included Black actors, male and female in "jungle scenes," portraying them as savages only bent on carnal lust and pleasure. Ellington provided appropriate "jungle music," complete with bleats, squawks, moans, and other supposed jungle sounds. He tailored his arrangements especially to the individual sounds and styles of his highly skilled players. Ellington composed in such a way that his music told a story in an impressionist manner, much like the late 19th century French Impressionists Ravel or Debussy.

Major Big Band Leaders of the Swing Era

- ***Black bands and leaders***
  - Count Basie (hot)
  - Billy Eckstine (hot)
  - Duke Ellington (hot)
  - Lionel Hampton (hot)
  - Fletcher Henderson (hot)
  - Earl Hines (hot)
  - Jimmie Lunceford (hot)
  - Chick Webb (hot)

- ***White bands and leaders***
  - Jimmy Dorsey (hot and sweet)
  - Tommy Dorsey (hot and sweet)
  - Eddy Duchin (sweet)
  - Benny Goodman (hot and sweet)
  - Glen Gray and the Casa Loma Orchestra
  - Woody Herman (hot)
  - Harry James (hot and sweet)
  - Guy Lombardo (Sweet)
  - Glenn Miller (hot and sweet)
  - Artie Shaw (hot and sweet)
  - Lawrence Welk (sweet)
  - Paul Whiteman's Ambassador Orchestra (sweet/symphonic)

Why Are the Bands Listed as White or Black?

It should be noted that despite much progress in the integration of Black musicians into White bands and vice-versa, most bands performed in public as all White or all Black ensembles up until the end of the big band era. Thanks to John Hammond, Benny Goodman, Fletcher Henderson, and other socially conscious leaders, there was much Black/White collaboration behind the scenes: Black arrangers wrote and arranged tunes for White bands, Black musicians played on the recordings of White bands, and the famous Bennie Goodman quartet, quintet, and sextet were fully integrated. They performed regularly in concerts, at dances, and in clubs as a separate unit, and they made a historic and highly successful series of recordings for RCA Victor.

Hot vs. Sweet

By 1938 all of these bands and hundreds more played to packed ballrooms, dance halls, concert halls, and outdoor venues. All the bands, black and white, played a mix of hot jazz and sweet songs (almost always sung by a "boy" or "girl" singer), although some, like Goodman, Basie, Ellington, James, and Lunceford were more known as "hot" bands. By the start of WWII (1941), sweet music, sung by young crooners, overtook the popularity of hot jazz. With most men (including many of the big band musicians) off to war, dancing and up-tempo music lost popularity to slow, romantic ballads and novelty patriotic tunes.

The Decline and Demise of the Big Bands

The musicians' strike of August 1, 1942, forced on the industry by Musician's Union President James C. Petrillo, brought a complete halt to the recording of instrumental music for over a year. The result was that only singers such as Frank Sinatra, Dick Hayman, Doris Day, Ella Fitzgerald, and Lena Horne, backed by a chorus, continued to record and make money. By November 1944, the record companies capitulated, and agreed to pay the Musician's Union royalties on behalf of musicians who played on recordings. However, the damage was done.

The big bands, decimated by the war, high travel costs, and the strike, could not recover. The singers were now far more popular on their own. Some big bands broke up during the war because many of the musicians enlisted in the armed forces. A few of the big band era ensembles managed to continue on for many years, into the 50s, 60s, and 70s, or reinvent themselves playing new styles such as bebop, rhythm and blues, and funk rock.

Looking Ahead

During the big band era, African American and some White musicians continued to broaden their musical interests and experiment with improvisation techniques, especially in small groups. The big bands of Ellington, Basie, Calloway, Webb, Lunceford, and many others were fertile incubators for young, talented musicians who learned from the older generation, but were eager to push the boundaries of jazz by trying out new and innovative improvisations.

Clubs such as Minton's Playhouse in New York became meccas for young players eager to show each other what they could do. Improvisation battles known as "carving contests" were frequent and often lasted for hours. Musicians tried to outdo each other with long, intricate, and complex improvisations based upon modern chord progressions, but still based upon blues form and melody. This was the new, emerging hot jazz, called bebop. At the same time, other former big band musicians, mostly Black, went back to their roots and began to play rhythm and blues.

Niche Music

New Orleans jazz became the first nationally popular music in the early 20th Century. By 1924, Louis Armstrong, Joe "King" Oliver, The Original Dixieland Jazz Band, and many other

New Orleans based groups were performing and making recordings that brought jazz to a pinnacle of popularity. Armstrong, with his Hot Five and Hot Seven bands, perhaps more than any other musician of his generation, "crystallized a new idiom for jazz ... that quickly spread in popularity across the world" (Brothers, 2006, p. 276).

As the original style of jazz diminished in popularity in the late 20s and early 30s, a steady stream of new popular music styles took over, satisfying the public's fickle taste for new styles, dances, and performers. Typically, a new cycle begins every 10 years, sometimes even less. Once the general population no longer patronizes a popular musician or singer, or buys their recordings, the style becomes what this author describes as a "niche music"—a type of music which once enjoyed national or at least regional popularity but lost a significant part of its audience to a new, more appealing music style.

Older music styles never completely go away. A still loyal, but much smaller, group of fans continue to buy the records, attend the concerts and dances, and support the music and its groups. Niche music (and the performers who remain true to the style) continues to draw audiences, sell recordings, and remain active in the pop music universe. This includes styles such as New Orleans and Dixieland jazz, big band swing, bop jazz, rhythm and blues, early rock and roll, urban folk music, country and western swing, and doo-wop. Some styles, like New Orleans Jazz and Big Band Swing, have brief revivals of national or local popularity, briefly appealing to a new, younger generation. Others, like Doo Wop, continue to be wildly popular with the generation of people who grew up with that style.

Pop music is constantly reinventing itself, but with each change of style and performers, the older styles remain viable to the generation who grew up with it. It is safe to predict that every style of music with a reasonable period of popularity, right up to the present day, will continue to resonate with at least a small segment of the public for many years after its national popularity wanes. The author coined a phrase which captures this notion of the transitory nature of popular music (and culture): **Popular music is popular because it's popular ... until it's not (with a large segment of the population).** In upcoming chapters, the reader will see this niche music concept play out over and over again.

Key Takeaways

- The big band era was the youth music of the mid-1930s through mid-1940s.
- Fletcher Henderson, Duke Ellington, and Paul Whiteman were the first to expand the size of their bands and use written out arrangements rather than improvised music.
- While bands of the swing era were segregated on stage, behind the scenes there was much collaboration between White and Black musicians, arrangers, and composers.
- John Hammond, Benny Goodman, Fletcher Henderson, and Paul Whiteman believed in and worked to make integration a reality among White and Black bands.
- The decline of the big bands helped to usher in new and very different styles of music from 1946 through the 1960s.

- Every new generation of youth creates and embraces a new niche music that continues to enjoy limited popularity through succeeding musical eras.

Review Questions

Directions: Refer to what you learned in this chapter to help you respond completely and correctly to the questions and prompts below.

1. Name five White or Black big band leaders.
2. Describe the style of music known as hot jazz.
3. Describe the style of music known as sweet.
4. Listen to and compare two big band recordings—one by Duke Ellington and the other by Count Basie. Describe the differences you hear.
5. Explain the concept of niche music.

Class Project

Listen to and compare two big band recordings, one by a White swing (hot) band and one by a Black swing (hot) group. Write a one-page report on your reaction to the differences between the styles of the two ensembles. Answer questions such as the following:

- Which band swings more?
- Which band has more authentic jazz soloists?
- Which band plays better in tune and with more accuracy?

References

Brothers, T. (2006). *Louis Armstrong's New Orleans.* W.W. Norton & Company.

Simon, George T. (1971). *The big bands.* The Macmillan Company.

Stearns, M. (1958). *The story of jazz.* Oxford University Press.

Ward, J. C. & Burns, K. (2000). *Jazz: A history of America's music.* Alfred A. Knopf.

Wikipedia. (2022). Glenn Miller. https://en.wikipedia.org/wiki/Glenn_Miller. Accessed June 16, 2022.

Credit

Fig. 9.1: Maurice Seymour, "Slide 41, Henderson," https://commons.wikimedia.org/wiki/File:Fletcher_Henderson_(1943_publicity_photo).jpg, 1943.

Chapter 10

The War Years

Ascent of the Singers and Decline of the Big Bands

Introduction

In Chapter 9, you read about the meteoric rise and almost two-decade prominence of the big bands. The music of the big band era was known by several names: swing, big band, big band swing, big band jazz and sweet. Hundreds of bands and thousands of musicians and singers crisscrossed the nation by car, bus, train, and plane. They played for dances, live radio broadcasts, concerts, recordings, and movies. The jukebox became an important way for fans to "audition" a recording of a new song or instrumental before they spent their money to buy it. Sadly, for most of the big bands, it all came to an abrupt halt in 1942.

There were a number of factors that caused the decline of the big bands. By the start of World War II, sweet music, sung by young crooners and "girl singers," overtook the popularity of swing (hot) jazz. With most men off to war, dancing and up-tempo music lost popularity to slow, romantic ballads (preferred by lonely wives and girlfriends pining away for their absent men), and novelty patriotic tunes. Even the Count Basie Band made a recording called "For the Good of Your Country." Some big bands broke up because the musicians enlisted in the armed forces. High travel costs, a shrinking audience (mostly women supporting their families while the men were fighting the war in Europe or the Pacific Theatre), and limited engagements made it difficult for band leaders to keep their bands together.

Many big band musicians and leaders enlisted to play in the military bands or to fight on the front lines. Some bands, including the Glenn Miller Orchestra, enlisted en masse, with Miller becoming a captain and leader of the Army/Air Force Band, which entertained soldiers and civilians all over Europe. Many other leaders enlisted as well, including Claude Thornhill, Artie Shaw, Orrin Tucker, and Ted Weems.

KEY TERMS AND PEOPLE

Bop jazz
Rhythm and blues
Musician's strike
Minton's Playhouse
Royalties
James Caesar Petrillo
Frank Sinatra
Perry Como
Ella Fitzgerald
Sarah Vaughan
The jukebox
The microphone
American Federation of Musicians
Recording studios
G. I. Bill
Postwar baby boom
Niche music

This chapter will connect the dots from the end of the big band era during World War II, through the transition period, 1946–1954, when rhythm and blues and rock and roll become the preeminent styles of popular music.

Purpose

The purpose of Chapter 10 is to familiarize the reader with the reasons for the decline of the big bands, followed by the popularity of the former big band singers, bop jazz, rhythm and blues, and ultimately rock and roll.

Outcomes

- Readers will become familiar with and be able to discuss the reasons for the demise of the big band era and the ascending popularity of former big band singers.
- Readers will be able to explain the key terms used in this chapter.
- Readers will be able to discuss the styles of music that follow the end of the big band era.
- Readers will be able to name and write about the major performers in the years after big bands were no longer popular.
- Readers will gain further understanding of the concept of niche music as it pertains to the continued existence of swing music and big bands.

Changing Tastes and Attitudes of the American Public

The musical landscape of American popular music changed dramatically during and at the end of World War II. The big bands, which included dance bands, swing bands, sweet bands, novelty bands, and everything in between, lost their fan base during the period between 1942 and 1946. Basically, the reason the public turned away from the big bands and toward the singers was one of saturation. Fans grew weary of the big band sound and sought out new forms of entertainment, readily provided by the singers (Ewen, 1977, p. 499). Of all the reasons though, the Musicians Union strike likely played the most damning role in sealing the fate of the big bands.

Noted author and musician George T. Simon summarizes the dilemma of the recording strike facing the big bands during WWII in his book, *The Big Bands*:

> On August 1, 1942, Petrillo (James Caesar Petrillo, National President of the American Federation of Musicians) ... ordered his musicians to stop all recording ... If the recording companies could not devise some system whereby musicians were paid for the use of their recordings on radio programs and in jukeboxes,

> then he wouldn't let them record at all. The big band leaders almost to a man disagreed with Petrillo's actions. They recognized far better than he the importance of records to their future.
>
> For more than a year, no major company made any records with instrumentalists. They did record singers, however, usually with choral backgrounds. Finally, in September 1943, Decca capitulated and signed a new contract with the union, followed a month later by Capitol. Columbia and Victor, the two largest labels, which recorded most of the big-name bands, held out for another year. In November 1944, they recanted and agreed to pay the union a royalty for all records released. (1971)

Further explanation comes from David Ewen in his book *All the Years of American Popular Music:*

> While Petrillo was jubilant, his "victory" did not hit the record companies half as hard as it did the big bands. After more than a year of inactivity, they found that they were no longer the preeminent, favored music style of American audiences. "… within a few weeks' time in 1946, eight of the most popular big bands disbanded, including those of Benny Goodman, Harry James, Tommy Dorsey, Les Brown and Jack Teagarden." (1971, p. 460)

With all instrumental music silenced by the recording strike and other factors, the singers took over the recording industry and reinvented popular music for the next generation of listeners (Simon, 1971, p. 54). "The swing era had become the sing era" (Ewen, 1977, p. 455).

The big bands (and their musicians) did not go away completely. There were a number of avenues for both band leaders and their sidemen to continue making music and earning a living. Some band leaders reconstituted their bands in the late 1940s and early 1950s, taking advantage of the niche music concept introduced earlier in this book. Duke Ellington, Count Basie, Tommy and Jimmy Dorsey, Stan Kenton, Benny Goodman, Lawrence Welk, Guy Lombardo, and many others reconstituted their groups, playing one-nighters, extended engagements, recording albums, and touring internationally. (The Benny Goodman Band was the first American music ensemble to tour the U.S.S.R. in 1962.) The one thing they did not do was record number-one hits or top any of the charts. They all had their fan base, mostly their fans during the 1930s and 1940s, now adults in their 30s and 40s, who grew up listening and dancing to the music of their youth (which is the basic premise of the niche music concept). Even today, ghost bands of famous leaders like Glen Miller, Duke Ellington, and Count Basie travel around the nation, playing the original arrangements with young musicians who were yet to be born when the band's namesake was living.

Four Options for Ex-Big Band Musicians: The Studios, Bop Jazz, R&B, or Teaching

For the majority of band leaders and musicians, the way forward after the musicians' strike was in either retraining or reinventing themselves. They transitioned to working in the studios, playing bop jazz, or rhythm and blues, or teaching others.

The Studios

The dissolution of the big swing bands and their style of music afforded the singers the opportunity to take over the entertainment spotlight and begin a new era of popular music.

Songs, sung by former big band boy and girl vocalists, dominated the popular music charts from the mid-1940s until well into the 1950s. Every record was produced and recorded in a studio, generally with a large orchestra of former big band musicians (including string players), playing an arrangement written by a former big band arranger and conducted in some cases by former big band leaders.

As an example, former big band leader Sonny Burke transitioned to "a successful career as ... one of the West Coast's leading arranger–conductors in the recording and television fields. For several years, he produced all of Frank Sinatra's albums at Reprise Records" (Simon, 1971, p. 460). The major record companies, Decca, RCA, Columbia, and Capitol, had their pick of superb musicians from the now-defunct big bands, and they were paid handsomely as studio contract players for their experience and musicianship.

Hardened from years of playing for demanding leaders like Benny Goodman and Glenn Miller, these musicians set the standard for musicianship and work ethic in the studios for decades to come. It was not unusual for top singers like Sinatra, Tony Bennett, Ella Fitzgerald and Sarah Vaughan to request their own legendary sidemen like Sinatra's long-time drummer Irv Cottler, trumpet lead players Jimmy Maxwell and Conte Candoli, and bassist Ray Brown (who was also Ella Fitzgerald's husband). A studio contract player in Hollywood or New York during this period could earn a five-figure salary.

Bop Jazz

During the big band era, young black musicians experimented with advanced improvisation techniques and chords, especially in small groups. The big bands of Ellington, Basie, Calloway, Webb, Lunceford, Eckstine, and many others were fertile ground for young, talented Black musicians to learn from the older generation while experimenting with new and innovative chords, rhythms, and improvisations.

Clubs in major cities, such as Minton's Playhouse in New York City, became meccas for young players eager to show each other what they could do. Improvisation battles known as "carving contests" were frequent and often lasted for hours. Musicians tried to outdo each other with long, intricate and rhythmically complex improvisations based upon modern chord progressions, but still rooted in blues harmony, form, and melody. This form of jazz, generally played by a small group of three, four, or five musicians became known as bebop or bop. Its fan base was mostly urban, educated, Black and White young adults who saw bop as an art music, radically different from the pop music churned out for the general public. The Beatnik, or hipster of the era, saw themselves as sophisticated, hip, and cool, and part of that persona was invested in listening to and extolling the virtues of bop jazz. In Chapter 11 we will examine bop jazz in depth and unravel why it had a limited fan base.

Rhythm and Blues

African American (and some White), post-big band musicians were divided into two categories: Those who believed the future of their music career was in rhythm and blues, and those who saw their role in bop as the next important step in the evolution of popular music. Rhythm and blues, a fundamentally similar style to the riff big band style of Count Basie and other Midwestern Black bands, relied on simple up-tempo, riff based 12-bar blues, and uncomplicated solos and lyrics. Conversely, bop relied on increasingly complex harmonies, rhythms, and solos that often took up most of the side of a record.

R&B appealed to Black, working-class youngsters and young adults who enjoyed dancing to blues-based songs with uncomplicated, often sexually explicit lyrics. As the 1950s progressed, the music caught on with an increasingly large audience of White teenagers looking for an alternative music to call their own (much to the chagrin of their parents).

The demand for rhythm and blues meant that many ex-big band musicians who could not play bop or wanted to make more money than they could with bop jazz, saw their future in playing in an R&B band. In chapter 12 we will take an in-depth look at the rise and importance of rhythm and blues.

Teaching

The postwar baby boom meant many more children eventually enrolling in the nation's schools, and the need for teachers progressively followed the increase in student population. At the same time, school systems across the country expanded their curricular offerings, especially in the areas of arts education. Visual arts, music, dance, and theatre took a more important place in the public-school curriculum. There was a concomitant need for teachers to teach these newly added band, orchestra, chorus, art, dance, and drama classes. Many big band musicians attended college as music education majors and filled those jobs as public school music teachers, which was often made possible because the G. I. Bill provided college tuition money.

The G. I. Bill Changes Everything

> Officially the Servicemen's Readjustment Act of 1944, the G.I. Bill was created to help veterans of World War II. It established hospitals, made low-interest mortgages available and granted stipends covering tuition and expenses for

veterans attending college or trade schools. From 1944 to 1949, nearly 9 million veterans received close to $4 billion from the bill's unemployment compensation program. The education and training provisions existed until 1956, while the Veterans' Administration offered insured loans until 1962. The Readjustment Benefits Act of 1966 extended these benefits to all veterans of the armed forces, including those who had served during peacetime.

President Roosevelt signed the G. I. Bill into law on June 22, 1944. The G. I. Bill gave World War II servicemen and servicewomen many options. Those who wished to continue their education in college or vocational school could do so tuition free up to $500, while also receiving a cost-of-living stipend.

As a result of the G. I. Bill almost 49 percent of college admissions in 1947 were veterans. The G. I. Bill opened the door of higher education to the working class in a way never done before. Many of these newly enrolled college students were former big band musicians who enlisted in the military during the war years. As they returned to civilian life, the possibility of attending college as a way to learn a new skill or apply their musical training to becoming a music teacher was made a reality by the support of the G. I. Bill (history.com, G. I. bill).

Technology Update

Most of the advances in 20th century life were fueled by the developments in technology. Transportation, manufacturing, science and medicine, and the entertainment industry benefited from the industrial revolution of the late 19th century, the widespread development of a nationwide electrical grid, and research into all areas of human endeavor. This section highlights two technological developments that helped the entertainment industry to reach more of the population (especially the youth of America) during the early and middle 20th century.

The Microphone

In the pre-World War I era, music studios looked completely different—sound recording was still an entirely mechanical process involving no electricity ...

In the mid-1920s, the advent of electric microphones meant that for the first time, sound could be captured and amplified before being recorded. ... Microphones had existed since the invention of the telephone in the late-1800s, but they were too primitive to be used to record music. The development of crystal and condenser microphones, which began to be widely used in the music industry in 1925, opened up a whole new range of possibilities for recording ... the microphone put the singer at the center of popular music.

Singers like Billie Holiday and Frank Sinatra used the microphone to deliver highly subtle, emotive performances. The singer could personalize his or her singing style, creating a new intimacy with their audience. Holiday, in particular, developed a vocal style and microphone technique which made it feel like she was talking, rather than singing—giving her music an unmistakable air of familiarity and fun.

The microphone also gave rise to the era of the crooner—singers like Bing Crosby and Perry Como sung melodies featuring falsetto, vibrato and legato phrasing—whereby the singer smoothly glides between notes without pausing. Although not to everyone's taste, this singing style became the bedrock of love songs and romantic music for decades to come. Artists like Frank Sinatra got close to the microphone during quiet parts of a song to create a sense of closeness and intimacy.

While we take it for granted today, the microphone was undoubtedly a technology which irrevocably changed music, ushering in a new era that placed the singer center stage and helped to establish the era of the singers (Utopia Genesis Foundation, 2021).

The Jukebox

The jukebox is an important factor in the rapid development in the early 20th century of American popular music throughout the United States. "By the mid-1920s, recorded music was being heard not only in homes, but—thanks to the jukebox—also in bars, honky-tonks, ice cream parlors, restaurants, taverns and social halls." They offered dancing and listening pleasure through a coin-operated and activated phonograph in an elaborate and gaudy cabinet in which records could be played by inserting a coin into a slot and then pushing the appropriate button.

This machine was probably called *jukebox* because it was first used extensively in 'juke' houses," the Southern designation for a brothel (Ewen, 1977, p. 286). The word *juke* derives from the Gullah language and means bawdy.

> By 1939, 225,000 of these were in operation, and ... they were responsible for the sale of thirteen million records per year ... in the early 1940s, the war dried up the supply of live entertainment ... more and more jukeboxes were used to fill the void. (Ewen, 1977, p. 286)

FIGURE 10.1 The classic restaurant tabletop "wall box." Wall boxes were an important, and profitable, part of any jukebox installation. Serving as remote control, they enabled patrons to select tunes from their table or booth.

There were still some six hundred thousand of these machines in operation in 1974. The largest maker of jukeboxes, the Wurlitzer Company, "built 750,000 units over a forty-year span, but discontinued making them in 1974, ... convinced that the jukebox was becoming obsolete" (Ewen, 1977, p. 286).

The Singers

The four singers profiled in this section are among the most popular and iconic entertainers to come out of the big bands between the mid-1930s and early 1940s. Each enjoyed decades of popularity as A-list singers, movie and television stars, and in the case of Sinatra and Como, hosts of their own television shows.

Frank Sinatra

Francis Albert Sinatra, often known as "Old Blue Eyes" or "The Chairman of the Board," is frequently described as one of the most popular entertainers of the mid-20th century. Sinatra is among the world's best-selling music artists, with an estimated 150 million in lifetime record sales. Robert Thomas Christgau, an American music journalist and essayist, called Sinatra "the best singer of the 20th Century." His popularity is matched only by Bing Crosby, Elvis Presley, The Beatles, and Michael Jackson (Wikipedia, 2023, Frank Sinatra).

Sinatra "often commented on how much he learned merely by sitting on the same bandstand with Tommy Dorsey and watching him breathe as he blew his trombone" (Simon, 1971, p. 34). More than any other big band era singer, he was the most well-known entertainer of all time. Equally adept as a singer and movie actor, he remained a fixture in Hollywood and American homes from the mid-1930s until his death in 1998. He amassed numerous, significant awards, including an Oscar. He was a Kennedy Center Honoree in 1983, was awarded the Presidential Medal of Freedom by Ronald Reagan in 1985, and the Congressional Gold Medal in 1997. His recordings garnered him eleven Grammy Awards, including the Grammy Trustees Award, Grammy Legend Award, and the Grammy Lifetime Achievement Award. Sinatra was included in *Time* magazine's compilation of the 20th century's 100 most influential people (Wikipedia, 2023, Frank Sinatra).

FIGURE 10.2 Frank Sinatra sings a duet with Ella Fitzgerald

While Sinatra had the kind of success that most other entertainers could only imagine and hope for, he also had a dark side and secrets (eventually not so clandestine) that haunted him for most of his long career and continue to tarnish his image to this day.

For many years, the story of the mob in Havana (as well as its intimate connection to the entertainment industry) would be relegated to folklore and fictionalization. Now the rumors have been thoroughly researched and found to be fact.

In February of 1947, Frank Sinatra arrived in Havana, Cuba, holding a suitcase filled with $2 million in cash. He was flanked by two mobsters from Chicago, the Fischetti brothers, Rocco and Charlie. They were cousins of Al Capone, with long-standing reputations in the businesses of illegal gambling and killing. As bodyguards (for Sinatra) they were second to none—tough, loyal, and connected at the highest levels of the mob, which, at the time, was more robust and powerful than it had been since the glory days of Prohibition.

Sinatra knew all this—the singer had an affection for mafiosi that bordered on idolatry. They took care of him, and he took care of them. This was why, arriving in Havana with a heavy, undeclared fortune in his possession, Sinatra was not overly concerned. But no one was supposed to know that Sinatra would be staying there (he checked in under a false name), nor did they know the real name of the man to whom Sinatra was delivering his cash-laden suitcase: Charles "Lucky" Luciano. Luciano had helped Sinatra out by "settling" some old debts and, more importantly, helping him out of an onerous contract with a famous bandleader (Tommy Dorsey). Frank was forever after indebted to the honored society.

Weeks before Sinatra's arrival, a who's who of the American mob had gathered in Havana for a major conference, presided over by Luciano and his closest gangster associate, Meyer Lansky. Sinatra's cash delivery to Luciano constituted operational expenses for the mob. Some of it would grease the wheels of corruption in the Cuban government; some of it would cover Luciano's living expenses in Havana; and some would cover lavish meals for the mobsters, as well as choice rooms at the Hotel Nacional.

Sinatra was but a bit player in this saga. The cash he had delivered was seed money for one of the most grandiose ventures the American mob would ever undertake: establishing a base of operations in Cuba that would make it possible for organized crime to function as an international conglomerate. Fulfilling this plan would put the mob beyond the reach of U.S. law enforcement (English, 2019, Cigar Aficionado).

Listen to this recording of Frank Sinatra singing "I've Got You Under My Skin," live at the Sands Hotel, accompanied by the Count Basie Orchestra.

Listen at: https://www.youtube.com/watch?v=3IdIxi8kLzE&t=2s

Ella Fitzgerald

Of all the female singers to "graduate" from the big bands and develop a solo career, Ella Fitzgerald is undoubtedly the greatest. Her musicianship, ability to interpret a song, and jazz improvisation were unmatched by any other female vocalist during the big band era—and long after. As the greatest vocalist of her generation, she was the comparator by which all other female singers were measured, including Sarah Vaughan and Dinah Washington.

Watch Ella Fitzgerald live at the Montreux Jazz Festival with the Count Basie Orchestra:

Watch at: https://www.youtube.com/watch?v=Ablt3kaGtnY

Beginning in 1935, the early part of her career was spent entirely with the Chick Webb Band, with whom she recorded the biggest hit of her career, "A-Tisket, A-Tasket." When Chick Webb died of tuberculous in 1939, she took over the band, renamed it Ella Fitzgerald and Her Famous Orchestra, and ably led it until 1942 when she decided to become a solo act (Simon, 1971, p. 442–444).

Her timing was perfect in that the musician's strike began in mid-1942, just as she embarked on her own career as a solo vocalist. "She sang with the leading bands and jazz virtuosos, made extensive tours around the world, and became a prolific recording artist. Her records ... sold in excess of 30 million disks, and she made movies, beginning with a notable leading role in *Pete Kelly's Blues* in 1955" (Ewen, 1977, p. 352).

Perry Como

Perry Como had a relaxed and personable style both on and off stage. Although not a trained musician or singer, he possessed a naturally refined and pleasing voice. His quiet demeanor and good looks made him the heartthrob of post-WWII teenage girls. In 1946, he "was the first popular singer ever to sell two million records each of two releases issued simultaneously. Six more songs recorded by Como in the 1940s surpassed the million mark" (460).

As with most popular singers in the 1940s, he was an alumna of the big bands. And, like many of his contemporaries, he came from immigrant stock and a blue-collar family. He opened a barbershop at age 16, and for years was known as the "singing barber." His big break came in 1937 when Ted Weems, a very successful "sweet" band leader, asked Como to join his band. Como stayed with the band for 5 years until Weems was drafted into the military. What followed was a succession of radio and nightclub appearances, and then a recording contract with Victor, and a movie contract with 20th Century Fox, both in 1943. His two million selling records made him one of the top recording artists in America (461). Como's popularity remained strong throughout the 1950s and into the 1960s when he hosted a number of prime-time variety shows, eventually making him the highest paid television entertainer up to that point in time.

Watch Perry Como sing "Catch a Falling Star":

Watch at: https://www.youtube.com/watch?v=_VJlHWESyLI

Como received the 1959 Grammy Award for best vocal performance, male, five Emmys from 1955 to 1959, a Christopher Award (1956), and a Peabody Award shared with good friend Jackie Gleason in 1956. He was inducted into the Television Academy of Arts and Sciences Hall of Fame in 1990 and received a Kennedy Center Honor in 1987. Posthumously, Como received the Grammy Lifetime Achievement Award in 2002. Como has the distinction of having three stars on the Hollywood Walk of Fame for his work in radio, television, and music. (Wikipedia, 2023, Como)

FIGURE 10.3 Perry Como

Sarah Vaughan

Sarah Vaughan was one of the few singers of the post-big band era to have formal music training. She studied piano from age seven and played for school productions throughout her years in school. In 1943, she joined the Earl "Fatha" Hines Band during an engagement at the Apollo Theatre in Harlem. Her keyboard skills, combined with a beautifully rich and controlled voice, allowed her to develop both as a pop vocalist and jazz singer. The latter required a knowledge of, and ability to hear, a song's background chords so that she could improvise on both the melody and chords of a song, in much the same way as a jazz instrumentalist. Her voice and interpretive ability were often compared to that of trained opera singers like Leontyne Price. From 1946 on, she followed in the footsteps of other big band singers, embarking on a highly successful solo recording and live performance career that lasted until shortly before her death in 1990 (Ewen, 1977).

The album *Sarah Vaughan with Clifford Brown* and the single "If You Could See Me Now" were inducted into the Grammy Hall of Fame, an award established in 1973 to honor recordings that are at least 25 years old and have "qualitative or historical significance" In 1978, she was given an honorary doctorate of music by the Berklee College of Music. In 1985, she received a star on the Hollywood Walk of Fame, and in 1988 she was inducted into the American Jazz Hall of Fame. She was given the George and Ira Gershwin Award for Lifetime Musical Achievement by UCLA (Wikipedia, 2023, Sarah Vaughan).

FIGURE 10.4 Sarah (Sassy) Vaughan

Other Famous Singers of the Post-Big Band Era

Female

Ivie Anderson
June Christy
Rosemary Clooney
Doris Day
Helen Forrest
Billie Holiday
Lena Horne
Helen Humes
Peggy Lee
Helen O'Connell
Dinah Shore
Dinah Washington
Frances Wayne

Watch Sarah Vaughan:

Watch at: https://www.youtube.com/watch?v=5G7UIeYGq0k&t=115s

Male

Johnny Desmond
Mike Douglas
Bob Eberly
Ray Eberle
Billy Eckstine
Merv Griffin
Dick Haymes
Eddy Howard
Jack E. Leonard
Vaughn Monroe
Jimmy Rushing
Andy Russell
Mel Tormé
Eddie Fisher
Joe Williams

Key Takeaways

1. The big bands were supplanted by the former big band singers between 1942 and 1946.
2. Ex-big band musicians moved on to other career paths, either in music or in other professions; teaching, playing bop jazz or rhythm and blues, or studio contract playing were among the options available.
3. The jukebox helped to fuel, and expand the popularity of, all forms of American popular music from its widespread distribution in the 1920s until the mid-1970s.
4. Some singers, notably Frank Sinatra, Perry Como, Doris Day, Ella Fitzgerald, Sarah Vaughan, Merv Griffin, Peggy Lee, and Mel Tormé, became megastars, recording successful albums, appearing in movies, on television, and in nightclubs, and amassing huge fortunes as Hollywood royalty.

Review Questions

1. Name four male and four female singers who started their career during the big band era and became stars as solo vocalists after the demise of the swing era.
2. What is the major reason for the demise of the big bands? During what period of time did this occur?
3. Name three of the major record companies involved in the negotiations to resolve the musician's strike of 1942.
4. Who was in favor of the musician's strike, and who was not?
5. Besides the musician's strike, what were some of the other reasons for the demise of the swing era and the rise of the "sing era"?
6. Which was the most popular style during the post-big band era—bop jazz, country and western, rhythm and blues, or the singers.

Individual or Class Project

1. Write a one-page report or prepare a 5-minute lecture on the history of the jukebox.

References

English, T. J. (2019, July/August). When the mob ruled Havana. *Cigar Aficionado.* https://www.cigaraficionado.com/article/when-the-mob-ruled-havana. Accessed, July 2, 2023.

Ewen, David. (1977). *All the years of American popular music.* Prentice Hall, Inc.,

History.com eds. (2019, June 7). G. I. Bill. *History.* https://www.history.com/topics/world-war-ii/gi-bill, accessed July 2, 2023.

Simon, George T. (1971). *The Big Bands.* The Macmillan Company.

Utopia Genesis Foundation. (2021, March 18). Tech that transformed music—the microphone. *Medium.* https://utopiagenesis.medium.com/tech-that-transformed-music-the-microphone-793bb80dd512. Accessed, July 6, 2023.

Wikipedia. (2023). Perry Como. https://en.wikipedia.org/wiki/Perry_Como. accessed July 6, 2023.

Wikipedia. (2023). Frank Sinatra. https://en.wikipedia.org/wiki/Frank_Sinatra#Legacy and honors, accessed, July 2, 2023.

Wikipedia. (2023). Sarah Vaughan. https://en.wikipedia.org/wiki/Sarah_Vaughan. Accessed, July 6, 2023.

Credits

Fig. 10.1: Copyright © by Frederic Pasteleurs (CC BY-SA 3.0) at https://commons.wikimedia.org/wiki/File:Dscn2823-Wurlitzer-3500-Zodiac-On.jpg.

Fig. 10.2: ABC, https://commons.wikimedia.org/wiki/File:Frank_Sinatra_and_Ella_Fitzgerald_(1958).jpg, 1958.

Fig. 10.3: NBC Television, "Perry Como," https://commons.wikimedia.org/wiki/File:1968_Perry_Como_special.jpg, 1968.

Fig. 10.4: William P. Gotlieb, "Sarah Vaughan," https://commons.wikimedia.org/wiki/File:Sarah_Vaughan_-_William_P._Gottlieb_-_No._1.jpg , 1946.

Chapter 11

Bop Jazz

Popular Music Becomes Art

Introduction

One of the most consistent principles in the development of the high art (aesthetically significant art form) of any culture is that it begins as an expression of everyday folk life and culture (in music, think African and European folk music). Over time, it gradually gains in complexity until it reaches the highest expression of human artistic creation, abstract art. Some philosophers express this development by saying that art moves from the concrete (folk or popular art) to the

FIGURE 11.1 Portrait of Thelonious Monk, Howard Mc-Ghee, Roy Eldridge, and Teddy Hill, Minton's Playhouse, New York, N.Y., ca. Sept. 1947.

KEY TERMS

Rebob/bebop/bop
Cool jazz
Hard bop
Third Stream
Augmented 4th (flat 5)
Upper chord extensions
Substitute chord
Intro and chorus
Beat Generation (Beatniks)
Hipster
West Coast jazz
Horn section
Minton's Playhouse
Jam session
Gig
Narcotics
Nonet

abstract (high or aesthetically profound art). The process takes years, sometimes centuries, from the simplest art forms (created to accompany and enhance everyday tasks) of a primitive culture, to the loftiest creations of world-class artists, dancers, musicians, and actors. Another way of saying it is that art forms progress from the simple to the complex.

Bop jazz can be seen as the artistic high point of four centuries of blending African folk music and culture with European classical and folk music and culture. In Europe, it took over 1,000 years for the simple chants and songs of the early Christian Church to morph into the great European masterworks of Bach, Beethoven, Mozart, Haydn, Mahler, and many others. Likewise, the progress of African folk culture, mostly carried forward from the Maafa, through the slave quarters by music and storytelling, intersected with European music in the 1700s and blossomed by the mid-20th century into America's first art form—jazz.

> Bebop created a kind of Rubicon that many fans, critics and musicians of the 1940s could not cross. They had come to jazz in the years of swing, when it functioned as dance music and entertainment, and they dismissed the new way of playing as a fad; when it failed to fade, they lost interest in jazz. ... bop became so much the language of jazz that its influence proved retroactive: even young musicians who still played in swing or traditional styles adapted elements of the new harmonies, rhythms and melodies (Deveaux & Giddens, 2015, p. 259).

FIGURE 11.2 Poster produced by the New York Jazz Museum in conjunction with an exhibit that was presented at the Museum.

For this and numerous other reasons the most significant American musical art form, jazz (New Orleans, swing) produced bebop and never gained the popularity and recognition that would allow it to flourish and attract a long-term national following.

Bop jazz is the highest expression of that art form and the most significant development of art music (of any genre) in the 20th century. Every genre of music since 1950—rhythm & blues, rock and roll, country and western, pop, rap, modern classical music, and most other popular music styles—draw from the musical and social contributions made by bop jazz musicians. This chapter will make clear that the artistic significance and influence of bop jazz long outlived its brief popularity.

Purpose

The purpose of Chapter 11 is to familiarize the reader with the origins and importance of bop jazz to the ongoing development of modern popular music from the mid-1940s to the present day.

Outcomes

- The reader will be able to speak and write about the significant artistic accomplishments of bop jazz composers, arrangers, instrumentalists, and singers.
- The reader will be able to articulate the many different ways in which bop jazz contributed to the popular music genres that came after it.
- The reader will be familiar with and conversant in the terminology used in bop jazz.
- The reader will become familiar with the major performers of bop jazz and be able to differentiate between bop jazz and other forms of jazz, such as New Orleans (traditional) style, and Big Band swing.

The Origins of (and Trouble with) Bebop

The name of the jazz music style that was eventually known simply as bop originated as rebop, then bebop, and its origin is fairly straightforward. Dizzy Gillespie relates that, at an engagement in New York City, "For most tunes ... we just wrote an intro and a first chorus. I'd say, 'Dee-da-pa-da-n-de-bop.' And we'd go into it. People, when they'd want to ask for one of those numbers and didn't know the name, would ask for 'be-bop'" (Burns & Ward, 2000, p. 320). Another possible story of the name's origin is that it's from the Spanish expression, *Arriba* or *Riba*, which is the Afro-Cuban musician's equivalent for "Go!" (Stearns, 1958, p. 218). Whichever version is correct, the new style burst on the jazz scene with a sudden and very blunt impact. Almost overnight in 1945, top-tier veterans of the swing era bands were considered old-fashioned when they soloed.

Louis Armstrong was not shy about his feelings for the new style. He called it "that modern malice ..." and said, "Referring to 'Boppers' ... they want to carve everyone else, because they're full of malice ... So you get all them weird chords which don't mean nothing, ... and you got no melody to remember, and no beat to dance to" (Stearns, 1958, p. 219). Another big band era icon, Cab Calloway, called bop, "that Chinese music."

"The music of Parker and Gillespie and their peers was complex, sophisticated, exacting—only the most highly skilled musicians were capable of playing it" (Burns & Ward, 2000, p. 386). The music had been percolating among the younger musicians of the Black swing bands as an experimental, improvisational style since the late 1930s. After-hours jam sessions at small clubs like Minton's Playhouse in New York and in other cities allowed most anyone who "had the chops" to sit in, stretch out, and try new improvisations, chords, and rhythms. These "carving" or "cutting" contests pitted newcomers against the best of the seasoned pros, for instance, the young trumpet player Miles Davis against the master Dizzy Gillespie.

The first identifiable bop jazz combo, led by Dizzy Gillespie, opened at the Onyx Club on 52nd St. in New York, in late 1943. Members of the group included Oscar Pettiford (bass), Max Roach (drums), Lester Young (saxophone—one of the more progressive of the swing era saxophonists), and George Wallingford (piano—the only White member). Some of the most iconic jazz masterpieces debuted with this group during that engagement, including *A Night In Tunisia*, *Salt Peanuts*, *Round Midnight*, and *Be-Bop*, all still regarded as jazz masterworks and still performed all over the world (320).

Sadly, bop jazz, for all the reasons discussed in this chapter, could not financially sustain itself into the new decade of the 1950s. "'Bop is a flop, commercially,' *Variety* reported in 1949. The musical style is dying almost as fast as it began ..." Big band leaders such as Charlie Barnet and Woody Herman who switched to bop-based arrangements could not attract big crowds because the music was too fast and difficult for dancing. "For all his success, Dizzy Gillespie's payroll continued to outpace profits. ... "The big crowds of dancers the band needed to stay afloat stubbornly failed to materialize" (Ward & Burns, 2000, p. 358–359). In 1950, Dizzy's wife gave him an ultimatum: "100 musicians or me! Make up your mind." Gillespie let all of his men go (Ward & Burns, 2000, p. 358–359).

Instrumentation of the Bop Jazz Combo

Bop jazz is essentially chamber music in the improvisational jazz style. By definition, a chamber ensemble is small and plays in intimate settings like small nightclubs. The classic bop jazz combo is typically three to six players consisting of the following:

- **The rhythm section**—piano, upright bass and drum set (can function on its own as a complete group, for example in the Oscar Peterson Trio)
- **The horn section**—any combination of wind instruments including alto, tenor, or baritone saxophone, trumpet (fluegelhorn), trombone, clarinet (rarely), vibes.

The classic jazz quartet (the most common configuration for a bop jazz ensemble) includes piano, bass, drums, and saxophone (alto or tenor). Add a trumpet and the group becomes a quintet, such as the group which recorded *Salt Peanuts*.

Cool Jazz

In the 1950s, additional styles of jazz grew out of bop—cool jazz, hard bop, third stream (Avant-Garde), all sub-genres of bop, which jazz writers and musicians began to call schools, i.e., The Cool School. Miles Davis's *Birth of the Cool*, a nonet of 1948–1950, jump-started the Cool School movement. The nine musicians of the nonet included Davis, Gerry Mulligan (baritone saxophone), John Lewis (piano), Kenny Clarke and Max Roach (drums), Lee Konitz (alto saxophone), J. J. Johnson (trombone), Sandy Siegelstein, (horn), Bill Barber (tuba), and Nelson Boyd (bass). The group represented a who's who of jazz. Mulligan, Konitz, and Lewis epitomized the style and sound of cool jazz, and they were leading voices in jazz for decades to come.

When Mulligan moved to Los Angeles in 1951, he carried the cool sound with him and began to arrange for and play in groups that reflected this lighter, more elegant and sophisticated style of jazz. Other musicians, notably Chet Baker (trumpet), Dave Brubeck, pianist and leader of his own quartet (with alto saxophonist Paul Desmond), and Chico Hamilton (drums) adopted and refined the sound. By the mid-1950s, cool jazz was selling millions of recordings, and groups like Brubeck's Quartet appeared on college campuses across the nation (Deveaux & Giddins, 2015, p. 262–270).

Hard Bop

"The most profound counter statement to cool jazz was essentially a revival of bop, but with a harder edge. By the middle 1950s, the umbrella term **hard bop** was adopted by critics to describe a populous East Coast school of jazz that placed itself in direct opposition to the more arid precincts of cool. Ironically, Miles Davis helped pilot the turn. Put off by underfed, overly intellectual music that claimed to be derived from his nonet, he switched directions in 1954 with recordings that restored Jazz's earthy directness" (Devaux & Giddins, 2015, p. 271).

Many of the musicians who joined in playing and recording hard bop were from cities like Detroit and Philadelphia and reflected a more workingman's blue collar approach to making music than the lighter "stress-free" cool of West Coast jazz. "Hard bop preferred a sound that was heavy, dark, impassioned. The tenor replaced the alto as the saxophone of choice, and drummers worked in an assertive style that drove the soloists" (271).

Some hard bop bands cut back on bop's harmonic complexity in favor of more basic chords reminiscent of the sanctified church or rhythm and blues, creating a subset of hard bop called soul jazz. Notable players in the hard bop style were Miles Davis, Dizzy Gillespie, Sonny Clark and Hampton Hawes (piano), Sonny Rollins (tenor saxophone), Sonny Stitt (alto saxophone), and J. J. Johnson (trombone). Hard Bop, and those who continued to play in the bop tradition, lost much of its audience in the 1960s, as a result of the complacency of the musicians and competition from a widening variety of more popular music, including folk, country and western, rock and roll, Motown, funk and soul (271–272).

Third Stream

Third Stream was a short-lived collaboration between some bop and cool jazz musicians and modern classically oriented university/academic musicians. The group was principally led by pianist John Lewis (who had two music degrees) and Gunther Schuller. Schuller, who was as eclectic and brilliant as any musician alive, called the Third Stream, "a synthesis of elements in 'Western art music' with ethnic or vernacular" music (Deveaux & Giddins, 2015, p. 268).

Composers in both the modern classical (sometimes called the **Avant Garde**) and jazz worlds contributed works to the repertoire of some cool jazz ensembles (such as The Modern Jazz Quartet [MJQ] led by John Lewis).

One such piece, *Vendome*, by Lewis, was the impetus for the MJQ to become popular in and tour Europe, where reverence for classical music and jazz were on an equal footing (Burns & Ward, 2000, p. 377). "Although classical techniques would continue to figure in Jazz as sources of creative inspiration, the movement soon faded, and the term 'Third Stream' soon fell into disuse" (Deveaux & Giddins, 2015, p. 268).

The Architects of Modern Jazz

The following six musicians, Charlie Parker, Dizzy Gillespie, Charlie Christian, Bud Powell, Kenny Clarke, and Miles Davis are considered the architects of modern jazz. The following sections provide a thumbnail profile of each one.

Charlie (Bird) Parker

Charles Parker, Jr. (August 29, 1920–March 12, 1955), also known as "Yardbird" and "Bird," was an American jazz alto and tenor saxophonist and composer. His life was complex and traumatic. He was driven as a musician and tormented with multiple personality disorders and addictions. He is often compared, both for his level of genius and emotional disabilities, with European classical composers Mozart or Beethoven. He lived a short, chaotic life, punctuated by brief periods of musical brilliance and financial success. Much has been written about "Bird," both anecdotally by those who knew him and through interviews with him in national publications.

Parker was a highly influential jazz soloist and a leading figure in the development of bebop, a form of jazz characterized by fast tempos, virtuosic technique, and complex improvisation. He introduced the use of modern jazz harmonic ideas in his improvisations (much of it from the innovative compositional and piano legacy of Duke Ellington and Thelonious Monk), including rapid passing chords, new variants of altered chords, the use of the flat 5-scale degree (augmented 4th), and chord substitutions. His tone ranged from clean and penetrating to sweet and somber. Many of Parker's recordings featured his virtuoso playing style and complex melodic lines, sometimes combining jazz with other musical genres, including traditional blues, Latin, Broadway, and popular song.

Despite playing music from almost every popular music genre of the time, Parker seemed to want to obscure and even deny any connection to the styles and tunes of the previous 45 years. He intentionally took well-known tunes like "Cherokee," a big band flag waver for both White and Black swing era bands, and recomposed it for his blazing fast technique and advanced understanding of harmony, rhythm, and melody. The tune, which first appeared under the title "Ko Ko" in November 1945, was a wake-up call for traditional and swing era musicians to head back to the practice room or consider a new line of work.

Parker acquired the nickname "Yardbird" early in his career, along with its shortened form, "Bird," which was used for the rest of his life. The nickname inspired the titles of a number of his compositions, including "Yardbird Suite," "Ornithology," "Bird Gets the Worm," and "Bird of Paradise." There was even a club in New York City named The Bird's Nest. Parker was an icon for the hipster subculture and later the Beat Generation, personifying the jazz musician as an uncompromising artist and intellectual rather than just an entertainer.

Charlie Parker died on March 12, 1955, in the hotel room of the Baroness Pannonica de Koenigswarter at the Stanhope Hotel in New York. The official cause of death was pneumonia and an ulcer, but Parker had cirrhosis and had survived a heart attack. He was only 34 years old, but the coroner reportedly assumed, based on the autopsy, that Parker was between 50 and 60 years old (Deveaux & Giddens, 2015, p. 246).

Listen to this recording of Charlie Parker playing "Ko Ko" with Dizzy Gillespie on the original 1945 Savoy Recording of Charlie Parker and His Re Bop Boys:

https://www.youtube.com/watch?v=JmF7fv_mpDM

John Birks "Dizzy" Gillespie

Dizzy Gillespie was the polar opposite of Charlie Parker. Parker was "An erratic Bird in flight" (Collier, 1978, p. 362). Parker was undisciplined (except when it came to music), self-indulgent, sullen, and addicted to alcohol and heroin. Gillespie, despite his nickname, was astute, affable, and skillful in his management of a career, which lasted for decades beyond Parker's sad demise. In his later years, Gillespie was thought of with the same reverence accorded to Louis Armstrong as the elder statesman of jazz (Collier, 1978, p. 357).

The man who would become the major catalyst and most articulate spokesman for bop jazz was born in 1917 in Cheraw, South Carolina. He first took up trombone at age 14 and switched to trumpet the next year. In 1939, he joined the Cab Calloway band, where he established a reputation as a strong leader, exciting soloist, and the band prankster. He especially enjoyed playing jokes on Calloway and members of the trumpet section. His clownish antics quickly got him the nickname "Dizzy."

In 1943, he joined pianist Earl Hines' excellent progressive swing big band where he met Charlie Parker. Gillespie and Parker developed many of the musical characteristics they would soon apply to the fledgling rebop style beginning in 1944 with a new band formed by singer Billy Ekstine. This band was even more progressive and experimental and gave Parker and Gillespie the full latitude they needed to develop the new style. It is certain that the collaboration of the two in the Hines and Ekstine bands gave rise to the new style barely two years later (Ewen, 1977, p. 474).

Dizzy enjoyed the spotlight and entertaining people, welcoming the audience as an essential part of the performance process. His skill as an entertainer gave bop some audience accessibility to counteract, to some degree, the unwelcoming, disdainful demeanor of his counterparts on the bandstand. Dizzy was a musician's musician and a people person, but

Listen to this recording of Dizzy Gillespie:

Listen at: https://www.youtube.com/watch?v=I4c7SmAAiMg&t=160s

he fought an uphill battle in trying to convince his colleagues and the general public that bop could be both an admired art form and popular at the same time.

Charlie Christian

It's hard to imagine today that when 20-year-old Charlie Christian started playing amplified electric guitar professionally, the instrument was all but unknown and considered somewhat odd. He was born in Dallas, Texas, in 1919, and he came from a musical family. He was one of the first (along with Django Reinhardt) to bring the guitar out from the background role of accompaniment and rhythmic timekeeping. He established the guitar as a solo instrument while playing professionally in the Southwest and in 1939 was "discovered" by the great Black pianist Marylou Williams. She recommended him to John Hammond, who in turn suggested to Benny Goodman that he might want to audition him. Goodman, although not initially impressed, eventually recanted and put Christian in the mixed-race sextet that included Teddy Wilson on piano, Gene Krupa on drums, Lionel Hampton on vibes, Georgie Auld on tenor sax, and Goodman on clarinet (Collier, 1978, p. 342–345).

Christian is remembered for two major accomplishments during his short life: establishing the electric guitar as a solo jazz instrument worthy of the respect accorded to saxophone, trumpet, clarinet, and trombone and regularly using the flat 5 interval, C-F sharp in his solo improvisations. Others, notably Parker and Monk, followed his lead (Gehrke, 2011).

Listen to this YouTube recording of Charlie Christian. Note that many of his melodic patterns were copied and used extensively by other bop jazz players, including Charlie Parker.

Listen at: https://www.youtube.com/watch?v=Ce9Jtl9D-6FQ&list=PL4ypuAMic-GjrOrcdgiH-PnhN7jdSxJOgE&index=1

When not playing with Goodman, he was jamming with Thelonious Monk, Kenny Clarke, and other adventurous young, future be-boppers at the legendary Minton's Playhouse in Harlem. He died in 1942 at age 25, the result of persistent tuberculosis exacerbated by bouts of excessive drinking and late hours.

Earl "Bud" Powell

As mentioned above, many bop jazz musicians were in some way dysfunctional human beings, despite being highly intelligent and musically brilliant. Bud Powell, considered by many to be the greatest and most influential of the bop jazz pianists, was one of those who had serious emotional and psychological problems that affected both his personal and professional life. Born in New York City in 1924, he came from a musical family—his grandfather, father, and both brothers were pianists. He began to study piano at age 6 and developed classical technique through the study of European music. By age 15, he was already playing professional gigs around the city.

Listen to this recording of Bud Powell:

Listen at: https://www.youtube.com/watch?v=TaSDinL6pC8&t=129s

He frequented Minton's Playhouse and occasionally sat in with Gillespie and Parker when he was 17. His idol from this time on was Charlie Parker. He imitated, memorized, and incorporated Parker's linear solo style into his right-hand technique, eventually expanding phrases to lengths that even Parker could not accomplish in one breath. With his left hand, he developed sparse, dissonant chords that set the bar for other bop jazz pianists.

Although some writers consider him the lead pianist in the bop jazz movement, others point to Thelonious Monk and his even more dissonant and angular melodic and harmonic style. By the time Monk achieved some measure of success, Powell was already suffering with emotional difficulties that would plague him for the remainder of his life. In 1945, at only 21 years old, he spent 10 months in a mental hospital, and he spent more time in such institutions over the next several years. After a brief period of stability in which he was able to resume performing and recording, he was again committed to a hospital. This pattern continued, exacerbated by persistent heavy alcohol abuse, until his death in 1966 from the effects of alcoholism (Collier, 1978, p. 388–391).

Kenny Clarke

Bebop changed jazz drumming, and Kenny Clarke was at the center of the change. As with most of the musicians of that era, he started playing in the 1930s with Black swing bands, where the function of the drummer was mostly to keep time and provide a swing feel for dancing.

On one evening in the late 1930s, he was playing with the Teddy Hill Band. They started to play an exceptionally fast version of "Ol' Man River," and Clarke could not keep up to speed with the bass drum, which usually played four beats to the bar. He shifted the beat from bass drum to the ride cymbal, thus allowing him to create a propulsive, "shimmering cymbal sound that became the lighter, more flexible foundation for all of Modern Jazz ..." (Deveaux & Giddens, 2015, p. 232–233). The bass drum now became an accent and phrasing instrument, and his style of heavily accenting beats in unexpected places became known as "dropping bombs" (Deveaux & Giddens, 2015, p. 232–233). Clarke's simmering polyrhythms became the foundation of the modern jazz drumming style for younger drummers like Max Roach and Art Blakely (Deveaux & Giddens, 2015).

Listen to this recording of Kenny Clarke:

Listen at: https://www.youtube.com/watch?v=I4c7SmAAiMg&t=160s

FIGURE 11.3 Miles Davis at the Three Deuces in 1947, playing with Charlie Parker, Max Roach, and others (Photo taken by William P. Gotlieb).

Miles Davis

One of the many remarkable things about Miles Davis is that he managed to have a five-decade career as one of the most influential musicians of the 20th century despite addictions to heroin, alcohol, and cocaine. In addition, he suffered with two chronic illnesses: sickle cell anemia and diabetes. His life story fills the pages of dozens of books and articles; his recordings are revered by millions of fans and his music is played by jazz musicians all over the world. He was born in Alton, Illinois, in 1926 and died in 1991.

Each time there was a major shift in popular music—from 1945 through the end of his life—Davis was at the forefront of the change. He was in on the ground floor of bop jazz with Parker, Gillespie, and Powell. He ushered in the second phase of modern jazz, cool jazz, in 1948–50, with his **"Birth of the Cool" nonet** that influenced West Coast jazz musicians with a lighter, less technically forceful energy and more lyrical style of improvisation. A few years later, he migrated back to bop, which by then was being called hard bop. In succeeding years, he experimented with, and then embraced, electronic instruments (even electronically enhancing the sound of his trumpet and the drum set), migrated to rock-tinged jazz (using a rock drum feel and electric bass), then fully embraced the whole gamut of popular music styles called **Fusion** in his 1969 best-selling album, *Bitches Brew.* It was his most commercially successful album, selling over 400,000 copies the first year. During the next six years he made 13 albums, each one relying less and less on jazz influences. He told his pianist, Herbie Hancock, "We're not going to play the blues anymore" (Burns & Ward, 2000, p. 445–446).

He stayed relevant and commercially popular through the 50s, 60s, 70s, and 80s by changing his style and adopting a new musical persona with each change in popular tastes. He performed sold-out concerts worldwide, while branching out into visual arts, film, and television work before his death from the combined effects of a stroke, pneumonia and respiratory failure.

Listen to this recording of Miles Davis:

Listen at: https://www.youtube.com/watch?v=r-gOVGLe-dA

In 2006, Davis was inducted into the Rock and Roll Hall of Fame, where he was recognized as "one of the key figures in the history of jazz." *Rolling Stone* described him as "the most revered jazz trumpeter of all time, not to mention one of the most important musicians of the 20th century"—though some would argue with this description (Wikipedia, 2023, Miles Davis) Miles won eight Grammy Awards and received 32 nominations (Wikipedia, 2023, Miles Davis).

Other Important Musicians of Bop Jazz

Art Blakey—drums
Clifford Brown—trumpet
Ray Brown—upright bass
Dave Brubeck—piano
Serge Chaloff—baritone sax
Maynard Ferguson—trumpet
Stan Getz—tenor sax
Dexter Gordon—tenor sax
Roy Haynes—drums
Percy Heath—upright bass
Milt Hinton—upright bass
Milt Jackson—vibes
J. J. Johnson—trombone
Lee Konitz—alto sax
John Lewis—piano
Thelonious Monk—piano
Gerry Mulligan—baritone sax
Oscar Peterson—piano
Oscar Pettiford—upright bass
Bud Powell—piano
Buddy Rich—drums
Max Roach—drums
Sonny Rollins—tenor sax
Zoot Sims—tenor sax
Sonny Stitt—alto sax
Clark Terry—trumpet
Lennie Tristano—piano
Kai Winding—trombone
Phil Woods—alto sax

The Bop Mystique

The profile of the typical bop jazz musician was that of a man (only a few women played Bop) who took music and his instrument very seriously, was introspective, and did not seek the limelight. He shunned publicity and felt that the public should look upon his music as an art form, not entertainment. Bop jazz musicians mostly lived by the phrase, "Be cool, man, and most musicians sank into their own deep freeze" (Stearns, 1958, p. 221). Often high, drunk or so aloof as to completely ignore those who came to hear them, they desired to be judged on the merits of the music alone. Dizzy's affable nature aside, his bandmates, "overdid it, sometimes playing with his back to the audience, and walking off the stand at the end of his particular solo" (Stearns, 1958, p. 221–222).

Words like *cool, cat, man, hip*, and *groovy* came to prominence in the bop era, first used by the musicians among themselves, then by the fans of the music, who flocked to clubs around the country to hear their idols. The fan associated with bop was unflatteringly called a *hipster*, in the 1950s a *beatnik*, and although highly intelligent, they showed no visible emotion while listening to their idols.

> The hipster, who played no instrument, was ... A camp follower belonging to the fringe group following jazz ... he prided himself on his outsize musical integrity. He was desperately uncompromising, so much so that Louis Armstrong was seen as an "Uncle Tom," who had sold out to, "the man." The hipster was sophisticated in the sense that his emotions appeared to be anaesthetized. His face was a mask and few things moved him. The proper pose was one of despair when listening to Miles (Davis ... by now the high priest of cool ...) live or on

> recording. The hipster was the jitterbug of the thirties in a Brooks Brothers suit and a crewcut. ... narcotics were an inevitable part of such a pose ... he had come to desperate terms with a bewildering reality by rejecting everything (Stearns, 1958, p. 222–223).

By the early 1950s, the hipster morphed into the beatnik and, still infatuated with jazz (now entrenched as post-bop and cool jazz), they became the counterculture of the 1950s, represented in literature by the beat novelists—Jack Kerouac and William Burroughs—and poets—Allen Ginsberg and Gregory Corso.

Key Takeaways

- The short period of popularity of bop jazz belies the fact that it has influenced decades of American popular music of every genre and style.
- The five main architects of modern jazz were Charlie Parker, Dizzy Gillespie, Bud Powell, Kenny Clarke, Charlie Christian, and Miles Davis.
- Despite its beginnings in the Black swing bands of the 1930s and 1940s, bop jazz and its progeny attracted almost as many superb White musicians, singers, and arrangers as African American. Jazz music was 20 years ahead of its time in race relations and equality.
- The Beat Generation started with the hipsters of the bop years and morphed into the counterculture of the early 1950, which spawned Beat poets Alan Ginsburg and Gregory Corso and novelists Jack Kerouac and William Burroughs.

Review Questions

Directions: Refer to what you learned in this chapter to help you respond completely and correctly to the questions and prompts below.

- Name the three most iconic musicians of bop jazz. What was the main instrument of each?
- What did Charlie Parker and Charlie Christian have in common other than their first name?
- What was the typical instrumentation of the bop jazz combo?
- What was the secret to Miles Davis's success for more than 50 years?
- What was the name of the typical bop jazz fan?
- Name the literary style that arose and represented the counterculture movement during the bop, cool, and hard bop jazz years?

Class Project

Choose one of the bop jazz musicians profiled in the Architects of Modern Jazz section and write a synopsis of their life or identify their most highly regarded compositions or recordings.

References

Burns, K., & Ward, G. C. (2000). *Jazz: A history of America's music.* Alfred A. Knopf.

Collier, J. L. (1978). *The making of jazz.* Houghton Mifflin Company.

Deveaux, S., & Giddins, G. (2015). *Jazz* (2nd ed.). W. W. Norton & Company.

Ewen, D. (1977). *All the years of American popular music.* Prentice Hall, Inc.

Gehrke, K. (2011, October 23). Benny Goodman's Sensational Sextet. *Big Band Spotlight.* https://bigbandspotlight.wordpress.com/2011/10/23/benny-goodmans-sensational-sextet/. Accessed on July 16, 2023

Kirchner, B., Ed. (2005). *The Oxford companion To jazz.* Oxford University Press.

Stearns, M. (1958). *The story of jazz.* Oxford University Press.

Wikipedia. (2023). Miles Davis. https://en.wikipedia.org/wiki/Miles_Davis#1948-1950:_Miles_Davis_Nonet_and_Birth_of_the_Cool. Accessed on July 18, 2023

Credits

Fig. 11.1: William P. Gotlieb, "Minton's," https://commons.wikimedia.org/wiki/File:(Portrait_of_Thelonious_Monk,_Howard_McGhee,_Roy_Eldridge,_and_Teddy_Hill,_Minton%27s_Playhouse,_New_York,_N.Y.,_ca._Sept._1947)_(LOC)_(4843753254).jpg, 1947.

Fig. 11.2: New York Jazz Museum, https://commons.wikimedia.org/wiki/File:Poster-Jazz_Museum-Bird_%26_Diz-lge.jpg, 1973.

Fig. 11.3: William P. Gotlieb, "Miles Davis," https://commons.wikimedia.org/wiki/File:Miles_Davis,_(Gottlieb_06851)_(cropped).jpg, 1947.

Chapter 12

Rhythm and Blues/Country and Western/Rockabilly/Rock and Roll

What's in a Name?

Introduction

The former big band singers had a hold on the teenagers who grew up with the swing bands in the late 1930s and became adults through the next decade. But what about the generation of post-World War II baby boomers who became teenagers in the 1950s and wanted a new music to dance to and new stars to idolize?

Two older styles, **rhythm and blues** and **country and western** (called **hillbilly** at the time) had strong fan bases as far back as the 1930s in the Black community (R&B) and rural South and West (C&W). Bop jazz musicians tried to fill the void left by the swing bands. They had a brief flirtation with the rising generation, only to be rejected by them because the music was too complicated and undanceable.

Rhythm and blues, on the other hand, was the popular dance music of choice for many young Blacks and an increasing number of White kids from the mid-1940s on. In 1949, *Billboard* magazine renamed the category of race recordings rhythm and blues, while keeping the category strictly for music performed by Black musicians and recorded for mostly Black audiences (Starr & Waterman, 2018, p. 222). The musicians for rhythm and blues bands (also called jump bands) mostly came from the defunct big bands. One example is Louis Jordan, who is one of the founders of rhythm and blues.

In the last chapter it was suggested that big band musicians had a number of career choices after the big band era folded. Two of the options were playing rhythm and blues or bop jazz. Many former big band musicians, like Louis Jordan and Johnny Otis, formed "jump bands," playing a style of blues-based piano music called **boogie-woogie,** reorchestrated for a small group of instruments that included

KEY TERMS

- Rhythm and blues
- Race records
- Country and western
- Rockabilly
- Rock and roll
- Boogie-woogie
- Jump bands
- Brill Building
- Crossover
- Shuffle
- Gospel
- The Million Dollar Quartet
- Sun Records
- Blue Yodel
- Appalachia
- Billboard top 100
- Charts
- American Bandstand
- Rock and Roll Hall of Fame

guitar, piano, drums, bass, trumpet, saxophone, and singers (they were basically scaled down big bands). Boogie-woogie had been popular with African Americans since the 1930s, but under the new name of rhythm and blues it had a resurgence of fan interest at the end of the big band era. It was considerably easier to play than bop (mostly based on standard blues chord progressions, a shuffle beat, and blues melody), much more popular (it was the dance music which younger fans craved since the heyday of the big bands), and lucrative for the musicians (Breckenridge, 2012, p. 234).

Eventually rhythm and blues assumed prominence as ***the*** Black popular music, and modern jazz went in another, less lucrative, direction (Deveaux & Giddins, 2015, p. 370).

In rural southern and southwestern parts of the nation, **country and western** (first known as **hillbilly** music) appealed to those "whose way of life was being radically transformed by the mechanization of agriculture and changes in the American economy and migrants who left home behind to find jobs ... in the city" (Starr & Waterman, 2018, p. 146). The pioneers of country (hillbilly) music are The Carter Family Singers and Jimmy Rodgers.

The blending of rhythm and blues with country and western (hillbilly) became known as **rockabilly**— the immediate forerunner of rock and roll. White performers like Elvis Presley, Jerry Lee Lewis, and Bill Haley and the Comets were at first categorized as rockabilly because their music combined hillbilly and rhythm and blues elements. Each started out as a rockabilly act, but as they gained popularity their music became more associated with rhythm and blues with sanitized lyrics and more emphasis on the guitar as the background chord and solo instrument.

Rock and Roll (What's in a Name)

There was no separate and distinct category of new popular music called rock and roll. Even the name derives from a rhythm and blues song, "Sixty Minute Man," of which part of the lyrics are:

> "I rock 'em 'n roll 'em all night long ... I'm a sixty-minute man."

The term was first used by a disc jockey, the infamous Allen Freed, to attract an ever-growing White, teenaged audience to the rhythm and blues music he played on his nightly radio show. Record companies quickly adopted this brilliant marketing strategy, and the rock and roll era was born. It is interesting to note that rock and roll owes the use of the guitar as the featured chord and solo instrument to country and western more than to rhythm and blues.

Purpose

This chapter will familiarize the reader with the time period (circa 1950) after the failure of bop jazz to attract a significant national audience. The development of rhythm and blues, country and western, rockabilly, and rock and roll as the dominant popular music styles in the United States will be discussed in detail. The reader will learn that some record companies and DJs at the time presented rock and roll as a new and distinct style of music. This chapter will attempt to clarify that the foundation of rock and roll (and rockabilly) is rhythm and blues and country and western. Many of the performers highlighted in this chapter are not household names, but they are the unsung, iconic musicians, generally forgotten in the history books, who led the way for others. Sister Rosetta Tharpe, Carl Perkins, and Louis Jordan are three such performers you will meet in this chapter.

Outcomes

- Students will become familiar with and be able to discuss the major performers in rhythm and blues, country and western, rockabilly, and early rock and roll (1954–1958).
- Students will memorize and be able to explain the key terms used in this chapter.
- Students will be able to discuss and write about the development of each style.
- Students will be able to articulate the importance of each style in the ongoing development of American popular music.

The Role of Country and Western in Setting Up the Rock and Roll Era

Country and western today is a multifaceted set of music styles that could be considered the closest contemporary popular music style to the original traditional folk music brought to North America by English, Scottish, and Irish settlers. Just as African folk music provided the building blocks of music and culture for the slaves, the folk music of England, Ireland, and Scotland provided the framework, structure, and content for the first White settlers on the East Coast of America. Their music eventually was known as hillbilly or country music (Breckenridge, 2012, p. 157).

The role of country music in establishing the guitar as the central instrument of rock and roll is not often considered by scholars of American popular music. The common notion is that rock and roll is rhythm and blues performed mostly by Whites (A classic example of Black invention, White appropriation). However, White musicians tended to favor the guitar for accompaniment and solos, while Blacks more often preferred jazz era instruments like piano and saxophone.

The preferences derived from previous styles; country music was commonly associated with Whites and featured the guitar as the accompaniment and lead instrument. By contrast, jazz, out of which came rhythm and blues, was primarily performed by Blacks, and almost always relied on the piano for chordal backgrounds and saxophone and trumpet for solos. So the major White influence on rock and roll (by way of rockabilly) was the country usage of the guitar (although by the 1950s the guitar was electrified and much louder than the acoustic guitar). There are a few exceptions, notably Jerry Lee Lewis, who was a skilled piano player.

The piano and saxophone were played more often among Black musicians of rhythm and blues. In addition, while Black musicians tended to perform their music at moderate tempos, White rock and rollers used faster tempos for both original songs and the many covers of rhythm and blues songs released during the early 1950s.

The first country music styles (forerunners of today's pop and rock influenced country style), appeared almost as soon as the settlers set down roots. There are two seminal styles to know about and listen to—hillbilly and bluegrass. In addition, we will consider here the contributions of Jimmy Rodgers, who popularized yodeling during his brief career.

Hillbilly (The Original Name for Country and Western)

Hillbilly music stems from the English ballad folk song singing styles of the inhabitants of the Appalachian region (often referred to as "mountain people"). Later on, Scotch–Irish immigrant music became a part of the activities as early as the 18th century. People in rural areas gathered and sang songs and listened to or played fiddle music for pleasure and amusement. The style, known as "hillbilly," references the people who lived in the Appalachian Mountains and sang folk songs. "It is important to note that its designation as Country Music was not made until the 1940s, when the recording industry was looking for a broader, less explicitly rural stylistic category for the term *hillbilly*" (157).

The first country music recordings were made in 1923 by Ralph Peer, who recorded "Little Old Log Cabin In The Lane" (by Fiddlin' John Carson) for Victrola Records. He is also credited with discovering the two most celebrated and influential early country performers: **The Carter Family** and **Jimmy Rodgers** (157).

The Carter Family was discovered by Peer in 1927. "Their success is predominantly due to A. P. Carter's desire to perform and record songs, with his wife Sarah and her cousin, Maybelle, that were exactly like those sung by the mountain people of their home state of Virginia. They were the first vocal group to become Country music stars. A. P. Carter collected (recorded or wrote down) these songs while traveling through the mountain regions of Appalachia. Sarah and Maybelle played guitar and accompanied the songs, which were simple harmonically and often sung in primitive, two-part hymn style harmony. Some of them have become classics of the folk/country repertoire like 'Faded Flowers' and 'This Is Like Heaven To Me' (158).

Listen to The Carter Family sing "Faded Flowers":

Listen at: Listen at: https://www.youtube.com/watch?v=W9bwSUT2po4

Jimmie Rodgers and the Blue Yodel Style

Jimmie Rodgers's career lasted only six years due to his battle with tuberculosis. In that short time, he made 120 recordings of many of our most beloved early American songs. Rogers is often recognized as one of the first to record and popularize the **blue yodel** singing style.

Jimmie was born in Pine Springs, Mississippi, in 1897 and learned to play banjo and guitar early in his life. He became familiar with the styles of music and entertainment popular in the South during his formative years. Vaudeville, hobo, railroad songs, and **string band** music (string bands consisted of fiddle, 5-string banjo, acoustic guitar, and an upright bass), all folded into his on the job education in music and performance. He went to work for the railroad, and when that was cut short by tuberculosis, he became a musician. He was playing in a string band in Ashville, North Carolina, when he responded to Ralph Peer's advertisement for performers to audition for Victor Records. They were interested in recording authentic hillbilly music in Bristol, Tennessee, the same recording sessions which "discovered" The Carter Family. In 1927, he recorded "Sleep Baby, Sleep," and "The Soldier's Sweetheart," the first recordings of his truncated career. He went on to record some of the classics of early country, including a million-selling disc called "T for Texas" (one of his blue yodel songs).

Listen to Jimmy Rodgers sing "Blue Yodel No. 1" ("T is for Texas"):

Listen at: https://www.youtube.com/watch?v=qEIBmGZxAhg&t=3sBluegrass

He was a master of the style of country music called **yodeling**, and he is credited as being one of the first to accompany his singing on the guitar. His **blue yodel** style endeared him to the mountain people, and he became a model for the singing style of early country music. It was copied by a whole generation of western cowboy singers such as Gene Autry and Roy Rogers and an entire first generation of country and western singers, including Merle Haggard, Bonnie Raitt, Hank Williams, and Doc Watson (who is also noted for adopting the finger-picking guitar style of Sarah Carter (162–163).

Bluegrass

Bluegrass can be identified specifically by its inventor, Bill Monroe—the Father of Bluegrass (a rarity in American popular music). He was born in 1911 and grew up on a farm in rural Kentucky where he learned to sing and play music from his mother and other family relatives. He played for dances, church gatherings, and picnics. At age 10, he met Black fiddler and guitarist Arnold Schultz, from whom he learned, and was inspired by, the syncopated rhythms of ragtime and the vocal inferences of blues. He incorporated these stylistic qualities in his songs such as "Rotation Blues," "Lonesome Truck Drivers Blues" and "White House Blues." These were the qualities that infused Bluegrass with its energy and visceral appeal.

Once he moved to Chicago to join his brothers' band, he gained experience performing on radio and in live venues. Around 1945, the group he formed, Bill Monroe and the Bluegrass Boys, produced a string of recordings that define the bluegrass style, instrumentation, and even the name. The group became known for the remarkable technical ability of its members, especially Monroe on mandolin, Lester Flatt on guitar, and Earl Scruggs on banjo (164–165). In terms of its technical demand, rapid tempos, and inventiveness of soloists, the style is the equal of bop jazz.

Listen to Bill Monroe and the Bluegrass Boys play "It's Mighty Dark to Travel":

Listen at: https://www.youtube.com/watch?v=-MEw8tuhWZ4&t=50s

Typical Instrumentation for a Bluegrass Band

Violin (fiddle)
Banjo
Mandolin
Guitar
Upright bass

Note the absence of drums, although in recent years some bluegrass bands have added a drummer. Some if not all of the players also sing lead and or backup vocals.

Bluegrass has enjoyed periods of moderate popularity since the mid-1940s, but competition from other, more popular, styles from 1954 on, has kept it a niche music right up to today. There is a sizeable fan base for Bluegrass—listeners who buy recordings and attend concerts and "bluegrass conventions" such as the Old Fiddler's Convention in Galax, Virginia. Many contemporary country performers, notably Allison Kraus, Taylor Swift, and Dolly Parton incorporate bluegrass songs and style into their repertoire.

Leading Musicians of the Rhythm and Blues/Rockabilly/Early Rock and Roll Era

The performers profiled in this section created the foundation for rhythm and blues, rockabilly, and then early rock and roll. We will look at the life and work of Louis Jordan, Sister Rosetta Tharpe, Big Joe Turner, and Big Mama Thornton.

Louis Jordan

Born in Arkansas in 1908, Louis Jordan, saxophonist, singer, and songwriter, led one of the first rhythm and blues bands, Louis Jordan and His Tympany Five. His is credited with being, the "Father of Rhythm and Blues." He had almost 60 songs hit the charts, some at Number 1 or 2, between 1942 and 1951. Some even crossed over to the White pop charts. Songs like "Choo Choo Ch'Boogie," "Caldonia" *and* "Let the Good Times Roll" became classic jump or rhythm and blues standards, covered by bands all over the country (Breckenridge, 2012, p. 237–238).

Listen to Louis Jordan and his Tympany Five play "Choo Choo Ch'Boogie":

Listen at: https://www.youtube.com/watch?v=c8uxrypkqv4

Originally, Jordan played tenor saxophone with the Chick Webb Band, where he also worked with and for Ella Fitzgerald. When Chick Webb passed away, Ella assumed leadership of the band for a few years, but by 1942 she was out on her own and the band broke up (Deveaux & Giddins, 2015, p. 370–371).

This was the opportunity for Jordan to form the first rhythm and blues band, The Tympany Five. His drummer used a "tympani" with his drum set, so Jordan used it also in the group's name.

The band actually had seven members, plus a singer. With the success of this band and his catchy, fun-to-dance-to songs, Jordan skillfully managed to put rhythm and blues on the road to popular music dominance. His career slowed down after 1951 due to illness, but his influence continued on in the music of Chuck Berry, T-Bone Walker, Bill Haley, B. B. King, and Ray Charles (371).

Sister Rosetta Tharpe

FIGURE 12.1 Publicity photo of American musician Sister Rosetta Tharpe posed with a guitar in 1938.

Sister Rosetta Tharpe, born March 20, 1915 and died October 9, 1973, was an American singer, songwriter, guitarist, and recording artist considered a pioneer of 20th-century popular music. Tharpe attained great popularity in the 1930s and 1940s with her gospel recordings that were a mixture of spiritual lyrics and early rock and roll style guitar accompaniment. Some sources report that she sang exclusively gospel songs, whether she was working in a sacred or secular setting. But at least three sources consulted for this section suggest that she sang secular tunes with the big band of Lucky Millinder in the 1940s (Simon, 1971, p. 509). Most of what we know about her career comes from reports about her extensive background in gospel and her catalogue of gospel song recordings. However, it seems clear that she sang some secular songs as part of her repertoire.

As the first recording artist to impact the music charts with spiritual recordings, she became the first superstar of gospel music and was known as "the original soul sister." She was an early influence, both as a singer and guitarist, on iconic figures such as Elvis Presley, Jerry Lee Lewis, Little Richard, Chuck Berry, and Johnny Cash.

She was willing to cross the line between sacred and secular by performing her "music of light" in the darkness of nightclubs and concert halls. Whether she sang and played with big rhythm and blues bands behind her or in a sanctified church setting, Tharpe's witty, idiosyncratic style left a lasting mark on gospel and popular music. She offended some conservative churchgoers with her bluesy guitar solos and forays into the world of pop music, but she never abandoned her preference for gospel music.

Tharpe's 1944 hit "Down By The Riverside" was selected for the American Library of Congress National Recording Registry in 2004, with the citation stating that it captured her "spirited guitar playing" and "unique vocal style" which were an influence on early rhythm and blues performers, as well as gospel, jazz, and rock artists. She is considered the godmother of rock and roll.

On December 13, 2017, she was posthumously elected to the Rock and Roll Hall of Fame as an early influence (Wikipedia, 2023, Sister Rosetta Tharpe).

Listen to Sister Rosetta Tharpe with the Chicago Blues All-Stars:

Listen at: https://www.youtube.com/watch?v=1__zadGXR3A

Listen to The original version of "Shake, Rattle and Roll":

Listen at: https://www.youtube.com/watch?v=YhELpSeeipg&t=2s

Big Joe Turner

Big Joe Turner's greatest fame was due to his rock and roll recordings in the 1950s, particularly "Shake, Rattle and Roll," which rose to number one on the rhythm and blues charts. He enjoyed a career that lasted from the 1920s into the 1980s. Songwriter Doc Pomus opined that, "Rock and roll would have never happened without him" (Wikipedia, 2023, Big Joe Turner).

His style, along with that of other black vocalists of the period, is called **urban rhythm and blues**. Turner, along with Dinah Washington, Ruth Brown, and Big Mama Thornton were strictly singers in the blues tradition, and they created a new approach to rhythm and blues with the blending of blues, gospel, and vocal jazz styles (Breckenridge, 2012, p. 237). Turner was often referred to as a "**Blues Shouter**." Although primarily known for singing rhythm and blues, he started out in the 1930s singing boogie-woogie style jump music, and he even sang with the Count Basie Band at the Apollo Theatre and toured Europe with Basie. He was posthumously inducted into the Rock and Roll Hall of Fame in 1987 (Wikipedia, 2023, Big Joe Turner).

Big Mama Thornton

The first recording of "You Ain't Nothin' But a Hound Dog" is by the great rhythm and blues singer Big Mama Thornton. The song, however, was written in 1952 by Jerry Lieber and Mike Stoller, "a song-writing team in the Tin Pan Alley mold" (Crawford & Hamberlin, 2001, p. 451). They churned out dozens of hit songs for various artists. Young and college educated, they specialized in writing rhythm and blues and soul songs for Black performers, despite being White. They were part of the "corporate" music production and recording world, centered in the Brill Building in New York City.

"Hound Dog" was one of the best-selling hits on the R&B charts in 1953, staying at Number 1 on the charts for seven weeks (Starr & Waterman, 2018, p. 253). Along with Elvis Presley's cover version, recorded three years later, the original "Hound Dog" is considered one of the seminal rhythm and blues/rock and roll songs that ushered in the rock and roll era.

Born in Montgomery, Alabama, in 1926, Willie Mae Thornton, more well-known as Big Mama Thornton, was the daughter of a Baptist minister. She had a professional career as a singer, drummer, harmonica player, and comic on the Black vaudeville circuit, later settling in Houston, Texas, to work as a singer in Black nightclubs. Her imposing physique and occasionally malevolent personality helped to ensure her survival in the rough and tumble world of con artists and gangsters.

After her move to Los Angeles, she was introduced to Lieber and Stoller, who were so impressed with her powerful singing that they quickly composed "You Ain't Nothin' But a Hound Dog," which they felt complimented her rough and bluesy style (233). In total, she wrote and recorded over 20 blues songs,

Her long and successful career was marred in later years by severe alcoholism from which she died in 1984. She never received recognition for her important contributions to the blues, rock and roll, and soul music. She was Janis Joplin's idol and mentor, and Joplin worked hard to uplift Thornton's image, especially after Joplin had a big hit with Thornton's "*Ball n' Chain*" (Wikipedia, 2023, Big Mama Thornton).

Early Rock and Roll

Musically, early rock and roll was ostensibly rhythm and blues in "whiteface" (Breckenridge, 2012, p. 248). Consider the difference between the lyrics of the original version of "Shake, Rattle and Roll" by Big Joe Turner, and the cover version by Bill Haley and the Comets, released while the original was still Number 1 on the rhythm and blues chart. The Bill Haley cover is a lyrically sanitized version of the bawdy lyrics sung by Turner. Rhythm and blues lyrics were often vulgar and denigrating toward women. White record company executives mandated that any cover record of a rhythm and blues song by a White group had to be sanitized for white teenage fan consumption.

As you peruse the lyrics of both versions, note how many words and implied meanings are changed from overtly sexual in the Turner version to a more innocent, and less misogynistic, meaning in the Bill Haley version.

Big Joe Turner's version of "Shake, Rattle and Roll"

Listen to the YouTube recording below under the section on Big Joe Turner, while you read the lyrics from this site:

Read at: https://wmich.edu/mus-gened/mus152/lyrics/shakera.html

Bill Haley's version of "Shake, Rattle and Roll"

Listen to the YouTube recording below under the section on Bill Haley and the Comets, while you read the words:

Read at: https://wmich.edu/mus-gened/mus152/lyrics/hshakera.html

Bill Haley and the Comets

"Rock and roll, as first realized by Bill Haley, was a combination of Rhythm & Blues, Country and Western, and Pop. Bill Haley always insisted that though **Alan Freed** may have baptized the new music as rock and roll, and was the first to promote it, that it was he, Haley, who was its founding father. Haley developed some of the distinctive features of early rock from rhythm and blues" (Ewen, 1977, p. 555).

Those "distinctive features" included the shuffle rhythm common in rhythm and blues, and the guitars and drums pounding over the melody. He shouted rather than sang his lyrics. His singing was more percussively instrumental than vocal and the guitar lead and solos were part of his country and western upbringing, as was the ballad tradition, the simplistic attitude towards melody, and the repetitious phrasing. He also lifted what was useful to him from pop music, mainly his preference for talking about dolls, angels, dreams, and the moonlight (Ewen, 1977, p. 555).

Bill Haley was born in Detroit in 1927 and grew up playing the guitar. By age 13, he was playing in clubs for $1 per night, and he appeared on a local radio show as the "Rambling Yodeler." When he moved to Pennsylvania, he formed a group called "The Flour Aces of Western Swing," a hillbilly group.

> By 1950, he was drawn to Rhythm and Blues, mainly because he had noticed the way it was beginning to appeal to young audiences. He changed the name of his group to Bill Haley and the Comets and adopted the beat and drive of Rhythm & Blues. The Comets now began making records of country music and Rhythm & Blues, but it was the Rhythm & Blues numbers that began to sell. "Crazy Man Crazy" made the national charts in 1953, and "Shake, Rattle and Roll" did even better in 1954. (Ewen, 1977, p. 555)

Haley recorded "Shake, Rattle and Roll" for Decca, which then issued "Dim, Dim the Lights," "See You Later, Alligator" and the anthem of the fledgling rock and roll movement, "Rock Around the Clock." "Rock Around the Clock" was the first rock and roll song to hit Number 1 on the charts in 1955 and became one of the largest selling singles ever released (Ewen, 1977, p. 555).

As the 1950s faded into the 1960s, Haley and his band, like most of the other early rock and roll groups, lost much of their fan base. The early rock and roll style became yet another niche music, catering to the small, but loyal group who had aged out of their teenage years. Even today, doo-wop, rockabilly, early rock and roll, and rhythm and blues groups from the 1950s travel the country playing shows that attract a loyal but diminishing coterie of fans. The generation that grew up with 1950s popular music is proof that the concept of niche music is alive and well.

Carl Perkins

Carl Lee Perkins is the forgotten man of early rock and roll. Perkins. was born in 1932 and died in 1998. He richly deserves the title, **the "King of Rockabilly**." He recorded most notably at the **Sun Records** Studio in Memphis, Tennessee, beginning in 1954. His best-known song is "Blue Suede Shoes."

Click on the YouTube link to listen to "Shake Rattle and Roll" by Bill Haley and the Comets.

Liste at: https://www.youtube.com/watch?v=8B7xr_EjbzE

Perkins successfully auditioned for Sam Phillips at Sun Records in early October 1954. "Movie Magg" and "Turn Around" were released on the Phillips-owned Flip Records label on March 19, 1955, with "Turn Around" becoming a regional success. With the song getting airplay across the South and Southwest, Perkins was booked to appear along with Elvis Presley at theaters in Marianna and West Memphis, Arkansas. Commenting on the audience reaction to both Presley and him, Perkins said, "When I'd jump around they'd scream some, but they were gettin ready for him. It was like TNT, man, it just exploded. All of a sudden, the world was wrapped up in rock" (Wikipedia, 2023, Carl Perkins).

Perkin's biggest hit, "Blue Suede Shoes," rose to Number 2 on the pop chart, and was a hit on all three charts. It was the first million-selling record for Sun Studios, but shortly after, Perkins was hurt in an auto accident and could not appear live to promote the record for months.

According to Charlie Daniels, "Carl Perkins' songs personified the rockabilly era, and Carl Perkins' sound personifies the rockabilly sound more so than anybody involved in it, because he never changed." Perkins's songs were recorded by artists (and friends) as influential as Elvis Presley, the Beatles, Jimi Hendrix, and Johnny Cash, which further cemented his place in the history of popular music. Paul McCartney even claimed that "if there were no Carl Perkins, there would be no Beatles" (Wikipedia, 2023, Carl Perkins). As a tribute to Perkins, George Harrison went by the stage name Carl Harrison before the Beatles were famous (Covach & Flory, 2023, p. 102). Called "the King of Rockabilly," he was inducted into Rock and Roll, the Rockabilly, and the Nashville Songwriters Halls of Fame and received a Grammy Hall of Fame Award (Wikipedia, 2023, Carl Perkins).

FIGURE 12.2 Elvis Presley in 1957

Elvis Presley

Elvis Aaron Presley was born in Tupelo, Mississippi, on January 8, 1935, and he died on August 16, 1977. He was a singer, musician, and actor and one of the most significant cultural icons of the 20th century. He is often referred to as the "King of Rock and Roll," or simply, "the King."

The Presley family moved to Memphis, Tennessee, when Elvis was 13 years old. His music career began there in 1954, when he was discovered by Sam Phillips, the owner of Sun Records

Click on the YouTube link to listen to Elvis's version of "You Ain't Nothin' But a Hound Dog" on the Ed Sullivan Show, Sept. 9, 1956.

Listen at: https://www.youtube.com/watch?v=Lrn8nTMcv_k&t=2s

and Colonel Tom Parker, who became Elvis's manager. The story goes that Elvis went to Sun Records hoping to make a recording of some songs to present to his mother on her birthday. After this session, which seemed promising but went nowhere, he made two more sets of recordings before Philips heard him in a late-night session with a bass and guitar player (who eventually became Elvis's backup band). Phillips was impressed enough that he signed Presley to a recording contract. Tutored and accompanied by guitarist Scotty Moore and bassist Bill Black, Presley was first an early popularizer of rockabilly, an up-tempo, backbeat-driven fusion of country music and rhythm and blues (Ewen, 1977, p. 557).

RCA Victor acquired his contract for $35,000 in a deal arranged by Colonel Tom Parker, who was to manage the singer for more than two decades. Presley's first RCA single, "Heartbreak Hotel," released in January 1956, was a Number 1 hit in the U.S. He became the leading figure of rock and roll after a series of network television appearances and chart-topping records. His energized interpretations of songs and sexually provocative performance style, combined with a singularly potent mix of influences across color lines that coincided with the dawn of the civil rights movement, made him enormously popular and controversial (especially with the parents of his young teenage fans).

In November 1956, he made his film debut in *Love Me Tender*. In 1958, he was drafted into military service. His absence from the music business for his two-year military commitment, along with the plane crash that killed Buddy Holly, The Big Bopper, and Ritchie Valens in 1959, created a huge void in the music business that lasted until the British invasion breathed new life into popular music in 1964.

Elvis resumed his recording career in 1960, producing some of his most commercially successful work before devoting much of the 1960s to making Hollywood movies and their accompanying soundtrack albums—most of which were critically derided. In 1968, following a 7-year break from live performances, he returned to the stage in the acclaimed televised comeback special, *Elvis,* which led to an extended Las Vegas concert residency and a string of highly profitable tours. In 1973, Presley was featured in the first globally broadcast concert via satellite, *Aloha from Hawaii*. Several years of prescription drug abuse severely deteriorated his health, and he died in 1977 at the age of 42.

Commercially successful in many genres, including pop, blues, and gospel, he is one of the best-selling solo artists in the history of recorded music. He was nominated for 14 Grammys and won three, receiving the Grammy Lifetime Achievement Award at age 36. He was inducted into multiple music halls of fame (Wikipedia, 2023, Elvis Presley).

Jerry Lee Lewis

Click on the YouTube link to listen to Jerry Lee Lewis sing "Great Balls of Fire."

Listen at: https://www.youtube.com/watch?v=7IjgZGhHrYY

Though he had only three top ten hits in the first, purely rock and roll phase of his career, many believe Jerry Lee Lewis (a.k.a. "The Killer") was as talented a 1950s rocker as Sun label-mate Elvis Presley. Some also believe he could have made it just as big commercially if his piano-slamming style was not so relentlessly wild, his persona not so threateningly hard-edged.

His first musical influences were eclectic. His parents, who were poor, played swing and Al Jolson records on the Victrola. But his earliest big influence was country star Jimmie Rodgers. In his early teens he absorbed both the softer country style of Gene Autry and the more rocking music of local Black groups, along with the gospel hymns of the local Assembly of God church. Lewis first played his aunt's piano at age 8 and made his public debut in 1949 at age 14, sitting in with a local country and western band. When he was 15, Lewis went to a fundamentalist Bible school in Waxahachie, Texas, from which he was soon expelled. He has often said that rock and roll is the Devil's music.

In 1956, Lewis auditioned for Sam Phillips's Sun Records. Phillips's assistant, Jack Clement, was impressed with Lewis's piano style but suggested he play more rock and roll in a style similar to Elvis Presley's (Presley had recently switched from Sun to RCA). Lewis's debut single, "Crazy Arms" (previously a country hit for Ray Price) did well regionally, but it was the follow-up 1957's "Whole Lotta Shakin' Going On" that finally broke through at Number 3. "Great Balls of Fire" (Number 2 in 1957) sold more than 5 million copies and was followed by more than a half million in sales for "Breathless" (Number 7 in 1958) and "High School Confidential" (Number 21 in 1958), which was the title theme of a movie Lewis also appeared in.

Lewis's high school nickname was "The Killer," and it stuck with him as he established a reputation as a tough, rowdy performer with a flamboyant piano style. He assaulted the piano, using careening glissandos, pounding chords, and bench-toppling acrobatics. More than once, he set a piano on fire during a performance.

His career screeched to a halt though after he married his 13-year-old cousin, Myra Gale Brown, in December 1957. (She was his third wife since age 16. He had wed a 17-year-old, and soon after that ended, he got caught in a shotgun marriage.) The marriage lasted 13 years, but at the time Lewis was condemned by the church in the U.S. and hounded by the British press on a 1958 overseas tour. His career ran dry for nearly a decade. He had a modest hit in 1961 with "What'd I Say." He toured relentlessly, playing clubs, billing his act as "the greatest show on earth." Remarkably, he lived to the ripe old age of 87, performing well into the 2000s before his death in 2022 (Wikipedia, 2023, Jerry lee Lewis).

Little Richard

Richard Wayne Penniman, aka, Little Richard is considered one of the first African American rhythm and blues performers to "**crossover**" into rock and roll hit territory. He was known as "**The Architect of Rock & Roll**." Born on Christmas Day, 1935, in Macon, Georgia (Ewen, 1977, p. 544), he influenced popular music performers from Elvis Presley and Jerry Lee Lewis to the Beatles and the Rolling Stones. Besides Chuck Berry, no one was more influential in every aspect of popular music, from his pompadour hair style to his shouting, bluesy singing and his, "frenetic piano exhibitionism", than Little Richard (Ewen, 1977, p. 544).

His first music experiences were as a gospel singer at age 14, and by 1951, he had a recording contract that eventually led to his first big hit, "Tutti Frutti" in 1952. (Pat Boone had a more successful recording of the song on the Dot label.) His most successful songs, such as "Long Tall Sally," and "Lucille," were recorded between 1956 and 1958, when he left show business to devote himself to the gospel. By the early 1960s, he was again making records and performing live, almost until his death in May of 2020 (Ewen, 1977, p. 544–545). He was influential in popular music and culture for seven decades. Among his many honors, Little Richard was inducted into the first class of the Rock and Roll Hall of Fame, as well as the Rhythm and Blues, Blues and Songwriter's Halls of Fame.

Chuck Berry

Charles Edward "Chuck" Berry was born into a middle-class black family in 1926 and raised in St. Louis, Missouri. As with Little Richard, he is considered one of the founding fathers of rock and roll. His musical upbringing included playing guitar, piano, and saxophone, singing in his church choir, and playing around St. Louis with his first band.

When Berry moved to Chicago, the great blues guitarist Muddy Waters heard him and thought highly enough of his blues writing and guitar playing that he helped him get a recording contract with Chess Records. Berry brought them "Ida Red," an old-time blues/country-tinged song, which eventually was renamed and recorded as "Maybelline." Alan Freed, who supposedly co-wrote the song, plugged it on his radio show and it moved up the rhythm and blues charts to Number 1. Thanks to Alan Freed and his renaming of rhythm and blues to rock and roll, Chuck Berry's many hits are icons of early rock and roll. Songs made famous by him, and covered by three generations of his followers include "Johnny B. Goode," 'Roll Over Beethoven," "Rock and Roll Music," and "School Day" (543).

Click on the YouTube link to listen to Little Richard sing "Long, Tall Sally."

Listen at: https://www.youtube.com/watch?v=p_kTSQ40V1k

His music was not only important for its timely influence on the change from rhythm and blues to rock and roll, but it introduced lyrical content focusing on teen life and consumerism, which appealed to both Black and White teenagers. Berry's career spanned most of his adult life, from the early 1950s until his death in 2017.

Along with Little Richard, Chuck Berry was in the first class of inductees into the **Rock and Roll Hall of Fame** in 1986. He received a Grammy Lifetime Achievement Award in 1984 and was a Kennedy Center Honoree in 2000. *Rolling Stone* magazine placed him among the 100 greatest artists of all time, and rock critic Robert Christgau considers Berry "the greatest of the rock and rollers" (Wikipedia, 2023, Chuck Berry).

Other Early Rock and Roll Performers

The Big Bopper
Bo Diddley
Teresa Brewer
Buddy Holly and the Crickets
Johnny Cash
Eddie Cochran
Fats Domino
The Everly Brothers
Wanda Jackson
Brenda Lee
Ricky Nelson
Roy Orbison
Ritchie Valens (The first Latino Rock & Roll performer)
Gene Vincent

Payola and Disc Jockeys

It's a curious part of the history of American popular music that men (mostly) who never played a musical instrument or sang in a group could have such a powerful, controlling impact on the music industry and the men and women who made and recorded the music. Disc jockeys simply played records on radio or hosted live television broadcasts. The two most well-known personalities, Alan Freed and Dick Clark, had a profound impact on their teenage fans and paved the way for the success of rock and roll. One managed the payola scandal well, while the other was destroyed by it.

Payola

Payola was the practice of record companies bribing disc jockeys to play certain recording artists' recordings more often during a radio show than others. It was patently illegal, and DJs who were caught and convicted served jail time and or paid significant fines. The most well-known DJ to be charged with taking payola was Alan Freed. His career was destroyed in the early 1960s by the scandal and the U.S. Senate hearings into payola, where he was uncooperative. Dick Clark, the other major spokesman for broadcasters to be called before the committee, was not charged with taking bribes, mostly because he divested himself beforehand of his financial holdings with record producers and other music industry entities.

Alan Freed

Albert James "Alan" Freed was an American disc jockey who spun records on radio and produced and promoted traveling concerts of both Black and White performers. He helped to spread the importance of rock and roll music throughout North America. He was born in 1921 and died as a result of chronic alcoholism in 1965.

Freed is important in American popular music history as the first radio disc jockey and concert producer who frequently played and promoted rock and roll; he popularized the phrase *rock and roll* on mainstream radio in the early 1950s. The term already existed and had been used by Billboard as early as 1946, but it was little used until Freed promoted the phrase on his radio show **"The Moondog House"** in Cleveland).

Several sources suggest that he first discovered the term on the record, *Sixty Minute Man* by Billy Ward and his Dominoes. The lyrics include the line, "I rock 'em, n' roll 'em, all night long." Freed did not accept that inspiration (or that lewd meaning of the expression) in interviews.

He helped bridge the gap of segregation between young White and African American teenagers by presenting music by Black artists (rather than cover versions by White artists) on his radio programs in both Cleveland and at WINS in New York City. He also promoted live concerts attended by racially mixed audiences.

In the early 1960s, Freed was blackballed by the music industry, and his career was destroyed for his role in the payola scandal that hit the broadcasting industry. In addition, he was accused of taking credit for songs he did not write, and his chronic alcoholism led to his untimely death in 1965 (Starr & Waterman, 2018, p. 250).

In 1986, Freed was posthumously inducted into the first class of the Rock and Roll Hall of Fame. His "role in breaking down racial barriers in U.S. pop culture in the 1950s, by leading white and black kids to listen to the same music, put the radio personality 'at the vanguard' and made him 'a really important figure.' " Freed was honored with a star on the Hollywood Walk of Fame in 1991 (Wikipedia, 2023, Alan Freed).

Dick Clark

Richard Augustus Wagstaff "Dick" Clark Jr. was born in 1929 and died in 2012. An American radio and television personality and cultural icon, he is best known for hosting **American Bandstand** from 1957 to 1987. He also hosted for two decades Dick Clark's New Year's Rockin' Eve, as part of Times Square's New Year's Eve celebrations.

As host of American Bandstand, Clark introduced rock and roll to many American teenagers and their parents. The show gave many new performers their first exposure to a national audience—Ike and Tina Turner, Smokey Robinson and the Miracles, Stevie Wonder, Talking Heads, and Simon & Garfunkel had their first nationally televised debuts on "Bandstand." Clark's broadcasts were among the first where Blacks and Whites performed on the same stage. Singer Paul Anka claimed that Bandstand was responsible for creating a "youth culture." Due to his perennial youthful appearance, Clark was often referred to as "America's oldest teenager."

During an interview with Clark by Henry Schipper of *Rolling Stone* magazine in 1990, it was noted that "over two-thirds of the people who've been initiated into the Rock and Roll Hall of Fame had their television debuts on American Bandstand. During the show's lifetime, it featured over 10,000 live performances, many by artists who would have been unable to appear anywhere else on TV, as the variety shows during much of this period were "anti-rock."

Clark knew he was the object of ridicule by much of the "old guard" of the music performance community. In addition, parents of his young audience hated rock and roll and severely criticized Clark for promoting what Jerry Lee Lewis called "the Devil's music." The Senate hearings into the payola scandal were seen by some as an opportunity for elected officials to "respond to the pressures they were getting from parents and publishing companies and people who were being driven out of business [by rock]. ... It hit a responsive chord with the electorate, the older people. ... they full-out hated the music. But it stayed alive. It could've been nipped in the bud because they could've stopped it from being on television and radio" (Wikipedia, 2023, Dick Clark).

Looking Ahead

At the beginning of Chapter 13, we will take a brief look at the period from 1958–1963 to assess the state of American popular music at that time. The remainder of the chapter will focus on **how the Beatles changed the world,** which details their meteoric rise and seven-year reign over the music industry, their music, their influence on social and political issues, and the remarkable innovations they fostered that continue to influence American popular music today.

Key Takeaways

- Every generation creates a new niche music, which continues to recycle through succeeding musical eras.
- The decline of the big bands helped to usher in new and very different styles of music from 1946 through the 1960s.
- Along with the reduction in the size of bands after the big band era came a profound change in the use of instruments—a reduction in the number and use of wind instruments and a change to primarily electric instruments, including electric guitar, electric bass guitar, and electric piano, all played through amplifiers.
- The emphasis on the use of guitar as the main chordal, melodic, and solo instrument in rock and roll comes from the guitar-centric tradition of hillbilly and country and western music.
- Rock and roll was simply a renaming of rhythm and blues and rockabilly to attract a new, young generation of fans to a music they could call their own.

Review Questions

Directions: Refer to what you learned in this chapter to help you respond completely and correctly to the questions and prompts below.

1. Describe the rise of rhythm and blues during the post-big band period of 1945–1950.
2. Name and briefly discuss four performers of the early rock and roll period from 1954 to 1958.

3. What styles do you associate with each of the following musicians:
    a. Bill Haley and the Comets
    b. Louis Jordan
    c. Big Mama Thornton
    d. Sister Rosetta Tharpe
4. What instrument(s) did each of the following play?
    a. Elvis Presley
    b. Jerry Lee Lewis
    c. Louis Jordan
    d. Carl Perkins
    e. Bill Monroe
5. Describe payola and discuss its impact on the recording industry during the 1950s.

Class or Individual Project

Write a multipage comparison of the stylistic differences between Black rhythm and blues and White covers of rhythm and blues songs, using the song "Shake, Rattle and Roll." Refer to the recordings and lyrics presented in this chapter.

References

Breckenridge, S. L. (2012). *Popular music in America.* Kendall Hunt.

Burns, K., & Ward, J. C. (2000). *Jazz: A history of America's music.* Alfred A. Knopf.

Covach, J., & Flory, A. (2023). *What's that sound?* W. W. Norton & Company.

Crawford, R., & Hamberlin, L. (2001). *An introduction to America's music.* W. W. Norton and Co.

Deveaux, S., & Giddins, G. (2015). *Jazz.* W. W. Norton & Company.

Ewen, D. (1977). *All the years of American popular music.* Prentice Hall, Inc.

Simon, G. T. (1971). *The big bands.* The Macmillan Company.

Starr, L., & Waterman, C. (2018). *American popular music.* (5th ed.). Oxford University Press.

Stearns, M. (1958). *The story of jazz.* Oxford University Press.

Wikipedia. (2023). Dick Clark. https://en.wikipedia.org/wiki/Dick_Clark. Accessed July 28, 2023

Wikipedia. (2023). Alan Freed. https://en.wikipedia.org/wiki/Alan_Freed. Accessed July 28, 2023

Wikipedia. (2023). Jerry Lee Lewis. https://en.wikipedia.org/wiki/Jerry_Lee_Lewis. Accessed July 28, 2023

Wikipedia. (2023). Carl Perkins. https://en. wikipedia.org/wiki/Carl Perkins. Accessed July 24, 2023

Wikipedia. (2023). Elvis Presley. https://en.wikipedia.org/wiki/Elvis_Presley. Accessed July 28, 2023

Wikipedia. (2023). Sister Rosetta Tharpe. https://en.wikipedia.org/wiki/Sister_Rosetta_Tharpe. Accessed July 22, 2023

Wikipedia. (2023). Big Mama Thornton. https://en.wikipedia.org/wiki/Big_Mama_Thornton. Accessed July 28, 2023

Wikipedia. (2023). Big Joe Turner. https://en.wikipedia.org/wiki/Big_Joe_Turner, Accessed July 29, 2023

Credits

Fig. 12.1: James J. Kriegsmann, "Sister Rosetta Tharpe," https://commons.wikimedia.org/wiki/File:Sister_Rosetta_Tharpe_(1938_publicity_photo_-_headshot).jpg, 1938.

Fig. 12.2: Metro-Goldwyn-Mayer, Inc., "Elvis Presley," https://commons.wikimedia.org/wiki/File:Elvis_Presley_promoting_Jailhouse_Rock.jpg, 1956.

Chapter 13

Between Early Rock and Roll and the Beatles

How the Beatles Changed the World (They Really Did!)

Introduction

The unusual events in American popular music in 1958–59 set in motion changes that affected much of the music industry until the rise of the Beatles in 1963–64. Elvis enlisted in the Army for two years, a horrible plane crash killed three rising rock and roll stars, and the fallout from the payola scandal caused a crisis in popular music broadcasting. All of this caused a downturn in interest on the part of fans. This chapter will begin with an examination of the transition years 1958–1963, followed by an examination of how the **Beatles** and the **British Invasion** reinvigorated American popular music (more appropriately world music) and changed the world. Along the way, you will see a significant stylistic change from rhythm and blues

KEY TERMS

Beatlemania
The British Invasion
Rock
Brill Building
Pop music
The Boomerang Effect
South Philadelphia
Burtonwood Air Force Base
Liverpool
The Twist
A & R Reps.
Skiffle
Fab Four
World's greatest rock and roll band

FIGURE 13.1

based rock and roll to the more agreeable (to parents) **pop** music, and the rise of professional songwriters who targeted the youth market with slick songs about teen relationships based on simple melodies and chords.

Purpose

Chapter 13 introduces the reader to the transition period in American popular music between 1958 and 1963. During that period rock and pop music transitioned first from early rock and roll to a period when vapid and mediocre Elvis lookalikes (selected by the record producers to maintain Elvis's image and sound) did not measure up to their media hype. Other styles of pop music filled the void until the Beatles completed their apprenticeship in Germany and the U.K. and took Europe and the United States by storm.

Outcomes

After reading Chapter 13, the student will have a thorough understanding of the following concepts and terms:

- What the British Invasion meant to popular music in the United States
- The phenomenon known as Beatlemania
- How the events in 1958–59 reshaped American popular music for the next decade
- How songwriters, movie producers, and record companies targeted teenage consumers (who had plenty of disposable income) with visually appealing "boy next door" type singers and actors
- How the influence of the Beatles, and the other British Invasion bands was felt worldwide both in music and the social and cultural attitudes of young people

Looking for Another Elvis

Between 1958 and 1960 a significant number of the rock and roll "first wave" performers and innovators were either out of the music business, temporarily indisposed, or dead.

Out Or Temporarily Indisposed

- Elvis joined the Army.
- Jerry Lee Lewis lost most of his fans when he married his 13-year-old cousin, Myra Gale Brown.
- Little Richard decided to dedicate his life "to the Lord."
- Alan Freed was ruined by the payola scandal.
- Buddy Holly, The Big Bopper, and Ritchie Valens died in a plane crash.
- Gene Vincent and Eddie Cochran suffered untimely deaths.

All this "dampened the momentum of rock and roll. The final straw was probably Chuck Berry's two-year jail sentence for a violation of the Mann Act"—transporting an underage girl across state lines (Breckenridge, 2012, p. 254).

Early rock and roll developed a bad reputation with the parents of teens and old-line record executives who saw the new music as a challenge to the status quo—morally and economically. Many parents felt that the sexualized lyrics and dance moves of rock and roll performers like Elvis caused inappropriate behavior and contributed to the decline of American teenagers. Some of this was precipitated by the burgeoning number of White teens who (mostly thanks to Alan Freed) were buying into (and buying up) the rhythm and blues recordings of Black performers like Chuck Berry, Bo Diddley, and Little Richard (254).

Record companies were frantically trying to replace Elvis with an Elvis clone. The long line of young men put forward had the look but not the charisma needed to perpetuate the Elvis mystique. At the same time, the record company executives tried to move music away from explicit lyrics and suggestive dance moves by performers. The notion was that **pop** (popular) music, with less offensive lyrics, sung by handsome Elvis lookalikes would appeal to both parents and White teenagers.

> It was another indication of how poorly regarded rock and roll was within the music business that record companies figured anybody could be a rock singer; if the songs were written by pros and the backing music was played by experienced studio musicians, all that was needed was somebody who could carry a tune or be coached to do so. The crucial thing was that these teen idols look and act the part effectively (Covach & Flory, 2023, p. 116).

After Elvis's death in 1977, a large cadre of Elvis impersonators sprang up all over the world. Today, there are still hundreds of such Elvis clones—Shawn Klush is one example—who make their living as Elvis "tribute artists."

The Twist

"Good rock is largely a matter of production and publicity" (Christgau, 2000, p. 38). When he wrote this, Robert Christgau was referring to the music of the Monkees and the fact that they were a made-for-television group who could barely play or sing, chosen from a field of 437 who auditioned for the parts (2000, p. 38). The Monkees, however, did have a brilliant songwriting team and production/recording staff. Sadly, Christgau's statement can be made about much of the pop music landscape between the late 1950s and the advent of the British Invasion (mid-1960s). One classic example is **The Twist** phenomenon.

The Twist became for the 1960s what the Charleston was for the 1920s, the signature dance of its generation. The song was originally written in 1958 by Hank Ballard. Chubby Checker recorded it in 1961 for Cameo Parkway, and it became a runaway best seller. Checker was a 20-year-old singer and dancer from South Philadelphia whose name originally was Ernest Evans. He admired Fats Domino, whom he resembled physically, and

See Chubby Checker sing and dance "The Twist"

Watch at: https://www.youtube.com/watch?v=-CCgDvUM4TM

that admiration led him to assume his stage name, Chubby, rather than Fats, and Checker, rather than Domino.

"The Twist," both the song and the dance, made Chubby Checker an international celebrity. On The Ed Sullivan Show, Checker performed a solo dance as he sang "The Twist," which started a nationwide, then worldwide, craze for the twist. Everybody was doing the twist, not just the young, but older folks as well. For Cameo Parkway, Chubby Checker recorded "Let's Twist Again," which received a Grammy as the year's best rock recording. Elvis Presley sang "Rocka Hula Baby," a twist number in the movie *Blue Hawaii.* Other popular twist numbers were "Twist and Shout," which was eventually recorded by The Beatles, "Twistin' The Night Away," sung by Sam Cooke, "The Peppermint Twist," and "Twist, Twist Señora" [yes, really!].

The twist became big business. There was the revenue earned from the sale of records, live and broadcast performances, and that earned in the night spots and ballrooms where the twist was the predominant attraction. The twist was exploited in a number of movies, including *Twist Around the Clock*, starring Chubby Checker. Then there was money to be made manufacturing Chubby Checker T-shirts, jeans, and dolls, along with twist skirts, twist raincoats, and twist nighties (Ewen, 1977, p. 631–632).

More Pop Singers of the Late 50s and Early 60s

Paul Anka
Frankie Avalon
Freddy Cannon
Bobby Darin
Connie Francis
Fabian Forte
Annette Funicello
Brenda Lee
Ricky Nelson
Bobby Rydell
Neil Sedaka
Bobby Vee
Bobby Vinton

Could (Did) Anyone Take the King's Place?

When Elvis enlisted in the Army in 1958, record company executives dispatched artists and repertoire personnel to seek out and recruit handsome young men to replace Elvis in the hearts and minds of America's teens. Some had experience as actors, singers, and performers, and others not so much. Some had long and successful careers while others were one or two hit wonders. None would rise to the level of Elvis's popularity and cult status, and the music industry would not experience another success of the proportion of Elvis until 1964 when Beatlemania overwhelmed much of the world.

The poster child for the Elvis replacement effort was **Fabian (Forte)**. He was among a group of young men, some discovered in **South Philadelphia** and surrounding areas, who

FIGURES 13.2a, 13.2b, 13.2c Fabian Forte, Bobby Rydell, Frankie Avalon—Teen Idols

had the look that was supposed to make teen girls swoon and spend their parents' money on recordings, movies, and concert appearances—and forget about Elvis. Other popular Elvis replacement hopefuls included Frankie Avalon, Bobby Rydell, and Paul Anka, who all tried to win the King's crown but fell short to one degree or another. Frankie Avalon and Bobby Rydell, while very popular and successful as singers and movie stars for the first part of the 1960s, faded into niche music obscurity after the Beatles and other British bands became popular. Paul Anka, Bobby Darin, and Neil Sedaka, initially teen idols, became successful songwriters and appealed to a broader audience of older teens and young adults.

Fabian, by his own admission, could not sing even after months of lessons and felt "like a fish out of water" (Wikipedia, 2023, Fabian Forte). He was about 15 when he was discovered in a South Philadelphia neighborhood, oddly enough by a record company executive who was visiting a next-door neighbor. Fabian's father was having a heart attack and was taken to the hospital by an ambulance. The record executive, who was watching the scenario unfold, took one look at Fabian, a 15-year-old very handsome Elvis look-alike, and offered to help him break into the music business. Fabian eventually acquiesced, and, after some singing and stage presence lessons, he was booked for appearances on American Bandstand and Ed Sullivan's variety show. He had a few successful hit recordings and roles in a short list of movies where he portrayed the "good boy" who would make an ideal boyfriend—similar to the other 1960s teen idols (Wikipedia, 2023, Fabian Forte).

See Fabian sing "Turn Me Loose"

Watch at: https://www.youtube.com/watch?v=EPI4fA5chzw

What Set Up The Beatles for Success?

In his book, *How to Hide an Empire*, Daniel Immerwahr presents a little-known side story to the success of the Beatles and other **British Invasion** groups. Most discussions of this period in British history do not address any of this information. Immerwahr suggests that the American military bases in England during and after WWII, and the thousands of U.S. troops stationed there, brought American culture, values, and money to a nation trying to rebuild after the devastation of the War. He points to Liverpool and the nearby Burtonwood U.S. Air Force Base (the largest in Europe), as one of the epicenters of American influence over Britain's new generation of teens and their parents in the early 1950s.

> There has to be some reason, wrote The Beatles manager George Martin, that Liverpool, of all British cities, actually had a vibrant teenage culture centered around pop music in the 1950s ... the answer was to be found ... in that ... Liverpool was a base city ... 15 miles West of Burtonwood, the largest US Air Force base in Europe.
>
> [Burtonwood] was the gateway to Europe, where transatlantic military flights landed. ... The thousands of US servicemen who came through were like millionaires. Teenage girls charged at them at the train station ... Burtonwood plowed more than $75,000 into the local economy per day. Musicians did especially well. They could get gigs on the base, or they could catch the troops whose pockets, bulging with dollars, made their way to the Merseyside nightclubs at night.
>
> The servicemen ... brought their culture and their favorite records. Plugging both directly into the mainstream of Liverpool life, the men dispensed nylon stockings, chocolate, money and records ...
>
> Young men got caught in this magnetic field too ... especially Ringo. His stepfather, worked on the base and fed Ringo a steady diet of comic books and records from the United States. John's mother, Julia managed to accumulate an admirably large and up-to-date record collection, which John and Paul eagerly raided. George got his records by stealing them from Brian Epstein's shop, brimming with the latest music from across the Atlantic. Epstein later became The Beatles' manager.
>
> The youth of Liverpool had records, particularly those featuring African American artists that no one else in the UK had access to, and they had strong financial incentives to master the songs emanating from the United States. Their music scene exploded. The Liverpool groups were essentially cover bands.
>
> The first side that John, Paul and George recorded, in 1958, was, *That'll Be The Day,* by Buddy Holly. It was performed with remarkable fidelity to the original. They weren't trying to dislodge Holly, just to establish themselves as recording artists in his style. There was only one copy pressed, which the bandmates passed around. Today, it's the most valuable record in existence. (Immerwahr, 2019, p. 357–359)

In the 60s, the British Invasion reversed the cultural flow of Rock music. The author of this book refers to this as **The Boomerang Effect.** British musicians, who had mastered early rock and roll, rockabilly and rhythm & blues, came to the U.S. in person and on recordings, easily displacing Elvis, Chuck Berry, Fabian, Frankie Avalon, etc. and dominating American record sales, top 100 charts, and concert ticket sales (358).

The Beatles

It can be safely said that the Beatles changed the world.

> Just as Elvis Presley dominated rock in the 50s, and was largely responsible for the character it assumed, so the propelling force of rock in the 60s was The Beatles. This foursome from England not only revolutionized the structure, style and techniques of rock, but they became a social force and the most profitable commodity the rock market had so far known. (Ewen, 1977, p. 612)

Assuming that Immerwahr's assessment of their early influences is correct, it's no wonder that the Beatles and other British groups were so accurate and faithful in copying the style of early and mid-1950s rhythm and blues, rock and roll, and rockabilly. They had the original recordings and an incentive to (cover) recreate them in live performance.

"The Beatles first attracted attention at The Cavern, a jazz club in Liverpool, England. They appeared there almost 300 times between December of 1960 and February of 1962 and built up a dedicated following. In the summer of 1961, a local disc jockey wrote in a Liverpool Beat journal, 'Why do you think The Beatles are so popular? They resurrected rock and roll, the origins of which are to be found in American Negro singers' " (Ewen, 1977, p. 612).

John Lennon was the group's accepted leader. He had taken music lessons from his aunt and learned to play piano, guitar, and harmonica. His intense interest in music was motivated by Elvis Presley records. In 1958, with his friend Paul McCartney, he formed the Nerk Twins, sometimes called the British Everly Brothers. George Harrison, guitar, and Peter Best, drums, joined them, and they became the Quarrymen, and then in rapid succession the Moondogs, Moonshiners, Silver Beatles, and ultimately, in 1960 at Litherland Town Hall, The Beatles. A fifth member, Stuart Sutcliffe, joined them on bass guitar, and they began playing gigs not just at clubs in Liverpool, but also in Hamburg, Germany, and Scotland. The quintet also made some recordings while in Germany (Ewen, 1977, p. 612).

Skiffle

Not too many Americans are familiar with the style of music known as skiffle because it was a popular music distinct to Britain in the late 1950s and early 1960s. **Lonnie Donegan** (and his band) was the most important performer in the style, which was a blend of American folk music with a traditional New Orleans jazz beat. Skiffle songs were simple and catchy, so many U.K. teenagers, including the future Beatles, learned to play and perform skiffle. Other bands that started out with skiffle include Gerry and the Pacemakers, The Animals, and the Searchers (Breckenridge, 2012, p. 262).

Back in Liverpool, Brian Epstein became their manager and immediately gave them a more presentable, polished image, including a new wardrobe, long but neat hairdos, and a more controlled presence on stage. He upgraded their bookings in Germany and England, arranged for their London television debut in 1962, and their first recordings for EMI: "Love Me Do" and "P.S. I love You." Stu Sutcliffe left the group, and Peter Best was replaced by Richard Starkey, known to all as Ringo Starr. The Beatles were now formalized as the group that would conquer and change the world of popular music (Ewen, 1977, p. 613).

After two failed attempts in 1963 to gain a foothold in America with albums on the Vee-Jay and Swan labels, Brian Epstein brought the **Fab Four** to the U.S. for three consecutive appearances on the Ed Sullivan show starting on February 9, 1964. This started the firestorm of Beatlemania in the U.S. (already in full force in Europe), which did not let up until their much-publicized breakup in 1970. In the interim, The Beatles phenomenal success around the world saw them break every record and ceiling in popular music.

They were the first European group to top Billboard's pop charts. During the week of April 4, 1964, they held the top five spots on the Billboard Top 100 with the following songs:

1. *Can't Buy Me Love*
2. *Twist and Shout*
3. *She Loves You*
4. *I Want to Hold Your Hand*
5. *Please Please Me*

The Beatles were the first rock band to sell out major sports arenas, and just as important because of their intersection with the civil rights movement, they would not play any American venue without a guarantee that tickets would be sold to people of all races. They played their last large venue live performance in 1966 at San Francisco's Candlestick Park (Breckenridge, 2012, p. 264–265). From this point on, they solely produced and recorded studio albums so they could concentrate on more complex material, innovative studio recording techniques, and effects that at the time could not be duplicated in live performance.

Between 1965 and 1969, the Beatles produced what may be considered their finest material, including the innovative and widely influential albums *Rubber Soul* (1965), *Revolver* (1966), *Sgt. Pepper's Lonely Hearts Club Band* (1967), *The Beatles* (commonly known as the *White Album*, 1968) and *Abbey Road* (1969).

After their breakup in 1970, they each enjoyed successful musical careers of varying lengths. McCartney and Starr, the surviving members, remain musically active. Lennon was shot and killed in December 1980 outside his New York City apartment, and Harrison died of lung cancer in November 2001.

In What Ways Did the Beatles Change the World?

As songwriters—Lennon and McCartney (and Harrison and Starr) continually developed more innovative approaches to song composition, using ever more complex harmonies, rhythms, and styles (including baroque and classical music, which had never been used in popular music up to that point). "Here are opened up not only new vistas for Rock music, but also for Rock lyrics which achieve the symbolic, the allegorical, the mystic and the Dadaistic ... *Sergeant Pepper* ... is a song cycle, the first in rock" (Ewen, 1977, p. 616–617). In fact, it is the first album of its kind, conceived as a whole, rather than as a collection of songs, and in that way similar to the great classical and romantic symphonies. None of the pieces on *Sgt. Pepper's Lonely Hearts Club Band* was released as a single.

As instrumentalists—Each musician became a master of their primary instruments and branched out to learn new instruments, for example the Indian instruments the sitar and tabla and electronic keyboards. They used traditional instruments in novel ways, modifying sound electronically and manipulating and shaping sound to fit particular moments in their compositions.

As arrangers and composers—They introduced non-rock instruments and ensembles on their recordings, utilizing brass ensembles, solo strings, string quartets, harp, and solo trumpet. "She's Leaving Home" opens with a harp ostinato, while "Penny Lane" has a piccolo trumpet solo. All of which gave their studio albums a unique power, substance, and depth far beyond anything happening in Rock at the time.

As social commentators and leaders of the youth counterculture—The Beatles made no apologies for their advocacy of recreational drugs. From the beginning they were open about their habitual use of pot, and experimentation with a range of drugs, including cocaine and LSD. They used psychedelic musical themes, such as the distorted voices in "Lucy in the Sky with Diamonds." John Lennon insisted that the song was inspired by a picture, drawn by his young son, who called it, Lucy in the sky with diamonds. Lennon denied any connection between the song and drugs (Schloss, 2012, p. 142). Visually, the use of psychedelic art on the album cover of *Sgt. Pepper's Lonely Hearts Club Band* and later album covers, sent unequivocal signals to their fans that recreational drug use was a personal choice, which tacitly gave permission to young people to engage in and experiment with drugs.

The Beatles traveled to India to study with Maharishi Mahesh Yogi, adopting his Transcendental Meditation techniques and simultaneously giving up LSD. Again, the Beatles started a trend that became common among musicians and some followers, seeking enlightenment through spiritualism and inner reflection, rather than mind-altering chemicals. For the Beatles, it seemed to work. Their success during the year of their study with the Maharishi was highly productive, resulting in 16 new songs in six months. The made for TV film, *Magical Mystery Tour*, was released, and they won two Grammys (Ewen, 1977, p. 615–61).

The Beatles advocacy for positive social justice issues in the areas of racism, sexism, political corruption, and even teenage runaways ("She's Leaving Home"), comes through in a powerful way. For example they, "promoted peace and love among all people with songs like, 'All You

The Beatles's recording of *Sgt. Pepper's Lonely Hearts Club Band*

Watch at: https://www.youtube.com/watch?v=xwwABrNLvFs&t=21s

Need Is Love,' 'Revolution' ... and 'Let It Be'" (Breckenridge, 2012, p. 265). Their worldwide influence on millions of fans can be seen as an extension of the socially conscious lyrics of Bob Dylan, who they admired. Dylan encouraged Lennon and McCartney to move beyond teenage love songs and write more substantive lyrics (Covach & Flory, 2023, p. 171).

With eclecticism—After the Beatles and the other British Invasion bands, no one could go back to the same old rock and roll! Any group that wanted to appeal to a mass audience had to follow in the footsteps of the Beatles, the Rolling Stones, The Who, Emerson, Lake, and Palmer, Pink Floyd, and others who drew on many diverse musical sources for their sound and style. Folk, classical, Indian, and other world music, as well as the blues and country and western, were used to create eclectic, multifaceted pieces that were as much art music as pop music.

A Short List of Representative Recordings of the Beatles

All My Lovin'
All You Need Is love
A Day in a Life
Eleanor Rigby (Grammy for best Rock vocal)
For The Benefit of Mr. Kite
I Saw Her Standing There
I Want to Hold Your Hand
Let It Be
Michelle (Grammy for Best Song of the Year)
Nowhere Man
Penny Lane
Revolution No. 9
She's Leaving Home
Twist and Shout
Yesterday

The Rolling Stones

No discussion of the British Invasion is complete without a section on the Rolling Stones, the **world's greatest rock and roll band.** (They were introduced as the greatest rock and roll band in the world throughout their 1969 tour, and it has stuck with them to this day). Just consider that as this chapter is written in August 2023, they are still together as a band after 61 years. They continue to tour, make recordings, and stay relevant in the rapidly changing world of popular music. Two of the original five members are still with the group: Mick Jagger and Keith Richards. Bill Wyman, their original bass guitarist from 1962–1963, still occasionally plays with them. Brian Jones, the original rhythm guitarist, died in 1969 and was replaced by Mick Taylor, who was in turn replaced by Ronnie Wood. Sadly, their original drummer, Charlie Watts, one of the greatest of all rock drummers, died in 2021 at age 80. He was quickly replaced by Steve Jordan on their No Filter tour, and he was also in the drum chair for their 2022 tour.

At one point early on in his career, Mike Jagger told an interviewer that his goal in music was to be the world's greatest blues singer. The "Stones" initially covered songs originally done by Black Chicago style rhythm and blues bands. They even derived their name from a

Muddy Waters's song "Rollin' Stone." What distinguished the Rolling Stones from the Beatles was the hard-edged, almost menacing approach they took to performing, as opposed to the Beatles cute, boy-next-door image. The contrast between the two bands was intentional and good for both.

The five members of the group came from working-class roots and met at the Marquee Club in London where they frequently went to listen to bands. They formed a band in 1962 and played their first gig at the Crawdaddy Club in Richmond, Surrey. After a year there, they were signed to a recording contract by British Decca. Andrew Long, originally a playing member of the band, became their manager and helped them to cultivate their disagreeable and disreputable bad boy image, which would carry them to international fame.

Mick Jagger, singer and front man, took on the mantle of the trickster persona from African Folk mythology. "*Time* magazine called him 'the king bitch of Rock' and possibly the supreme sexual object in modern Western culture" (Ewen, 1977, p. 617–618). His antics on stage, his outlandish costumes, and his unique singing style set the tone for rock front men for the rest of the century.

The Rolling Stones made three highly successful tours to the U.S.—1964, 1965, and 1966—before they were arrested and charged with drug possession and abuse in the U.K. They were out of commission for about one year, after which they regrouped and recorded *Beggar's Banquet* in 1968 and *Through the Past Darkly* in 1969. Both became gold records. *Beggar's Banquet,* included the provocative, "Sympathy for the Devil."

Despite achieving the peak of their fame and popularity in the late 1960s and early 1970s, there were some dark moments, especially on their American tour in 1969 when they performed a free concert at the Altamont Speedway near San Francisco. The Hells Angels motorcycle gang was hired to protect the Rolling Stones, but instead of keeping order, they ran amok through the crowd on their motorcycles, beating, stabbing, and even killing one person during the rampage. Violence at other Stones concerts made it clear that the Stones would not be welcome in the U.S. for an extended period. They did not perform again on American soil for almost two years.

> Between 1971 and 1981, all eight of the Stones studio albums reached the top of the American charts. In 1986 the group achieved a top ten hit with Harlem Shuffle, their faithful remake of a neglected American Rhythm & Blues hit from 1964. ... However, while both their new releases and back catalog continued to sell well in the age of the digital download, The Rolling Stones remain, first and foremost, a live band. The album *Steel Wheels* reached number three on the charts, but the record was far overshadowed in economic terms by its supporting tour, which grossed over $140 million and set a new watershed for box office records. The huge concert earnings that have been generated by the Stones over the last two decades are an indication of the increasing importance of live performance revenues over sales of recordings, and attendance at a Rolling Stones concert today remains a badge of honor from many rock fans.

The Rolling Stones perform "Sympathy for the Devil"

Watch at: https://www.youtube.com/watch?v=Jwtyn-L-2gQ

The International A Bigger Bang Tour of 2005 through 2007 was the highest grossing rock tour of its time, generating well over half a billion dollars in receipts. In 2016, the group toured Latin America, including an historic performance in Havana, Cuba, and returned to their roots with *Blue and Lonesome*, their first album devoted entirely to cover versions of Blues songs, which debuted at #4 on the pop album charts. This meant that The Rolling Stones had scored a record 37 top ten albums in the course of their career, an accomplishment unequaled by any other artists in popular music history (Starr & Waterman, 2018, p. 364).

The Rolling Stones must certainly be considered the most celebrated and enduring rock and roll band in popular music history.

Other Rolling Stones Songs

Brown Sugar
Coming Down Again
Harlem Shuffle
Honky Tonk Women
Jumpin' Jack Flash
Living in a Ghost Town
Miss You
Satisfaction
Start Me Up
Street Fighting Man
You Can't Always Get What You Want

Other British Invasion Groups

The Animals
Blind Faith
Cream
The Dave Clark Five
Emerson, Lake and Palmer
Pink Floyd
Gerry and the Pacemakers
Herman's Hermits
Slade
Jethro Tull
The Yardbirds
The Who
Led Zeppelin
The Zombies

British Singers/Guitarists and Songwriters

Long John Baldry
Jeff Beck
Eric Clapton
Petula Clark
Jimi Hendrix (American guitarist who immigrated to the U.K.)
Elton John
Tom Jones
John Mayall
Jimmy Page (as soloist and with Led Zeppelin)
Robert Plant (as soloist and front man of Led Zeppelin)

Looking Ahead

In the final chapter of this book, we will take a cursory look, decade by decade, at popular music after the Beatles. The goal is to cover the major styles and developments in American popular music, but not provide extensive detail about any style or performer. Styles covered will include disco, urban folk, funk, soul, rap and hip-hop, pop, punk, alternative, reggae, Latin, house, EDM, and other contemporary forms. Thus, an overview of the last 50 years of American popular music will round out this text.

Key Takeaways

- After the first phase of rock and roll from 1954–1958, there was a period of stagnation in American popular music.
- The Beatles and other British Invasion groups reinvigorated American popular music with the boomerang effect, reflecting early rhythm and blues and rock and roll back to America via recordings, television appearances, and concert tours.
- The Beatles changed the world in socially and culturally significant ways that continue to have an effect on society.
- The Beatles eclectic style influenced all pop music to grow and mature toward more artistic musical goals.

Review Questions

Directions: Refer to what you learned in this chapter to help you respond completely and correctly to the questions and prompts below.

1. Name five British Invasion bands.
2. Discuss four ways in which the Beatles changed the world.
3. Were any of the post-1958 "Elvis replacements" suitable substitutes for "The King"? Explain your answer in a one paragraph discussion.
4. Name the most important influences on the British Invasion bands.
5. Why did Liverpool stand out as one of the leading cities in the U.K. for producing successful rock bands?

Class or Individual Project

In a short one-page essay, compare and contrast the lyrics of an early Beatles song with one written after they stopped performing live. Consider the subject matter of each song and how the lyrics may have changed between the early and later samples.

References

Breckenridge, S. L. (2012). *Popular music in America.* Kendall Hunt.

Christgau, R. (2000). *Any old way you choose it: Rock and other pop music, 1967–73.* Cooper Square Press.

Covach, J., & Flory, A. (2023). *What's that sound?* W. W. Norton & Company.

Crawford, R., & Hamberlin, L. (2001). *An introduction to America's music.* W.W. Norton and Co.

Ewen, D. (1977). *All the years of American popular music.* Prentice Hall, Inc.

Immerwahr, D. (2019). *How to hide an empire.* Farrar, Straus and Giroux.

Schloss J., Starr, L., & Waterman, C. (2012). *Rock music, culture and business.* Oxford University Press.

Starr, L., & Waterman, C. (2018). *American popular music.* (5th ed.). Oxford University Press.

Wikipedia. (2023). Fabian Forte. https://en.wikipedia.org/wiki/Fabian_Forte. Accessed on August 6, 23

Credits

Fig. 13.1: Henry Grossman, "The Beatles," https://commons.wikimedia.org/wiki/File:Beatles_ad_1965_just_the_beatles_crop.jpg, 1967.

Fig. 13.2a: Am-Par Record Corporation, "Fabian Forte," https://commons.wikimedia.org/wiki/File:Fabulous!_Fabian_Billboard_1959.jpg, 1959.

Fig. 13.2b: James Kriegsmann, "Bobby Rydelll," https://commons.wikimedia.org/wiki/File:Bobby_Rydell_1960.JPG, 1960.

Fig. 13.2c: ABC Television, "Frankie Avalon," https://commons.wikimedia.org/wiki/File:Frankie_Avalon_1959.jpg, 1960.

Chapter 14

Pop Music After the Beatles

Introduction

In this chapter, you will first meet important groups and solo performers who were contemporaries of the Beatles in the 1960s—and in competition with them. Next, we identify important styles, in 5-to-10-year intervals, that followed the denouement of the British Invasion and established a place in pop history. We will proceed decade by decade from the 1970s through the 2000s to meet and discuss the prominent innovators and hit makers of each decade.

It is important to restate that the purpose of this book is to identify, as much as possible, the originators and innovators of a style or trend in popular music. We focus on the Beatles because they are icons who stand the test of time, top the charts repeatedly, receive important accolades from their peers and fans, and set the example for all who follow.

Artists such as Bob Dylan, Carlos Santana, Dave Grohl, Dave Matthews, Michael Jackson, The Beach Boys, Aretha Franklin, Taylor Swift, and many others are the originators and performers of the highest caliber who others imitate. They are the people we will highlight in this final chapter. Please don't be offended if your favorite performer or style is not mentioned; there just is not room for everyone who may deserve a mention in this chapter.

The List of icons of Popular Music you will find in the appendix includes many more performers, from all eras of American popular music, than are mentioned in this text. Look it over to see if your favorite performer is listed. If not, ask yourself why and what does it take to achieve icon status in American popular music?

KEY TERMS

Urban folk music
Folk rock
Soul
Funk
Soul brother
The Memphis Sound
The Detroit Sound
The California Sound
The Disco Sound
Grand Ole Opry
Honky Tonk
Reggae
Ska
Fillmore West (and East)
Guitar hero
Rap
Hip-hop
Blue language
Glam rock
Shock rock
Psychedelic (acid) rock
Grunge
Indie rock
Punk
Heavy metal
A cappella

Purpose

The purpose of this final chapter is to provide the reader with a chronological outline of the most relevant styles of popular music from the late 1960s to the first two decades of the 2000s. No one genre or style is treated in depth, and only a few representative performers from each decade are featured. The goal of the chapter is to provide an overview of the last 60 years in popular music that will allow the reader to discover people and styles of interest for possible further research and listening.

Outcomes

After reading Chapter 14, the student will have a thorough understanding of the following concepts and terms:

- The reader will be able to define and discuss the key terms.
- The reader will understand the progression of events in popular music from the late 1960s to the 2000s.
- The reader will be able to name and discuss the prominent performers from each decade.
- The reader will be able to write about and discuss the expanding involvement of popular musicians in sociopolitical advocacy from the late 1960s on.

The 1960s (There Were Other Groups Besides the Beatles)

The Beatles were one among a large number of pop music groups and styles during the 1960s. Urban folk music, country and western, soul music, and San Francisco rock were all part of the scene. Leading popular musicians included Bob Dylan, The Beach Boys, James Brown, Aretha Franklin, and Carlos Santana. Let's consider the 1960s in more detail.

Urban Folk Music

Folk music has been an important part of the fabric of American music since the first European settlers arrived in North America. In its purist form, folk music is the expression of the culture and character of a group of people. We have seen how European and African folk music blended together in the Western hemisphere over four centuries to become one American popular music. We have also seen that European folk music served as the impetus for hillbilly and western styles eventually known as country and western.

At some point in the evolution of any music style it ceases to be pure folk music and becomes a form of entertainment. In music in modern America, that change generally coincides with the style becoming popular with large a number of people and the performers involved receiving money to perform concerts, make recordings, and develop a fan base. This is what occurred in the folk music movement over many years to move it from a small community of amateur folk singers to the very successful and popular style called urban folk music.

The 1960s was a decade of upheaval and mistrust in America, especially among the youth and young adults who witnessed the Bay of Pigs Invasion, the assassination of President John F. Kennedy, the Vietnam War, and the civil rights struggle. Young Americans had a crisis of confidence in their government and military institutions, and it was manifested in the rise of protest songs intended to rally young people to action against "the establishment." The songs and the singers Bob Dylan, Peter, Paul and Mary, Joan Baez, Judy Collins (and many others) were antiestablishment, anti-war (Vietnam in particular), anti-affluence, anti-race discrimination, pro-pot and other recreational drugs, and anti-big business. Much of the music was newly written to express those themes, but protest songs by older folk singers/songwriters like Woody Guthrie and Pete Seeger were resurrected as well.

Some urban folk singers and groups like the Kingston Trio, The Limeliters, the Smothers Brothers, and Gordon Lightfoot, sang both traditional folk song material and new songs in the traditional style, but tread lightly on controversial topics like the war and the establishment. Some became big musical acts, drawing thousands of fans to concerts and folk festivals and selling millions of recordings. As we have often seen with other music styles, folk music became big business for much of the 1960s. Even though the Beatles were the most notable performers in popular music, urban folk had a sizable fan base. It was not unusual for young people to follow and enjoy folk and rock and pop music styles simultaneously.

An intersection of the folk and rock idioms, called folk-rock, emerged in the mid-1960s with The Byrds (following in the footsteps of Bob Dylan's conversion to electric instruments and more rock oriented material), Simon & Garfunkel, Joni Mitchell, and Cat Stevens.

Bob Dylan

Of all of the singer/songwriters in any pop music style, Bob Dylan, (born Robert Allen Zimmerman in 1941) is considered the most influential and enduring. He has been at the forefront of popular music and culture (including visual arts) for more than six decades. His most celebrated songs and recordings came out of the 1960s when his lyrics chronicled social unrest, racism, war, and the other issues described above. Dylan never agreed that he was a spokesman for his generation, even though his most influential early songs such as "Blowin' in the Wind" and "The Times They Are a-Changin'" became synonymous with the civil rights and anti-war movements. In 1965, he radically changed his style, based in the American folk music revival to reflect the reality of the Beatle's overwhelming success in America. His 6-minute single "Like a Rolling Stone" altered the range of popular music with the use of an all-electric, rock-style backup band (to the dismay of many in the traditional folk movement).

FIGURE 14.1 Bob Dylan and Joan Baez at a civil rights march in Washington, D.C. in 1963

See Bob Dylan sing "Like a Rolling Stone"

Watch at: https://www.youtube.com/watch?v=a6Kv0vF41Bc

Dylan plays guitar, keyboard, harmonica, and generally sings lead or solo on most songs, especially his own. He tours constantly on what is called the Never Ending Tour. Beginning in 1994, he published six books of drawings and paintings, and his work has been exhibited in major art galleries throughout the world.

One of the best-selling artists of all time, he has sold more than 100 million records, and he has received every important award for music and literary excellence, including multiple Grammys, a Golden Globe, and an Academy Award. He was inducted into the Rock and Roll Hall of Fame, Minnesota Music Hall of Fame, Nashville Songwriters Hall of Fame, and Songwriters Hall of Fame. In 1997, Dylan was a Kennedy Center Honoree. The Pulitzer Prize jury in 2008 awarded him a special citation for "his profound impact on popular music and American culture, marked by lyrical compositions of extraordinary poetic power." In May 2012, Dylan received the Presidential Medal of Freedom from Barack Obama. Bob Dylan is the only musician to be awarded the Nobel Prize in Literature.

At 81 years old, he ranks with a handful of icons from the 1960s as pop music superstars who are still with us: Paul McCartney, Ringo Starr, Elton John, Mick Jagger, Keith Richards, Stevie Wonder, Eric Clapton, Diana Ross, Paul Simon, Cher, and a few others. As a musician, recording artist, and performer, he had, and continues to have, immeasurable influence on the music world, but most would agree that his greatest contribution is his songwriting.

Other Folk Singers and Folk Groups of the 1960s

Joan Baez (the queen of folk singers)
Buffy Sainte-Marie
The Byrds (folk rock)
Judy Collins
Janis Ian
The Kingston Trio
The Limeliters
Phil Ochs
Peter, Paul and Mary
Pete Seeger
Paul Simon (single and with Simon & Garfunkel)
The Smothers Brothers

Country and Western

The discussion of the advent of country and western music centers around its transition from a true American Folk music (think hillbilly and bluegrass) to a rock and roll and pop influenced hybrid. The first steps in that process occurred with the first **Grand Ole Opry** radio broadcasts in 1925 and the development in the late 1940s of the **honky tonk** country style of Merle Travis and Ernest Tubb. Both hastened the fall of hillbilly/country as a pure (noncommercial) folk music and accelerated its acceptance as a commercial music genre.

By the late 1960s, Nashville, Tennessee, was the undisputed epicenter of Country music, and it supported a $250 million a year industry. As the greatest single production center for music in the U.S., it supported over 400 country genre performers and 900 songwriters, according to the American Federation of Musicians (the musician's union). There were 60 recording studios, 400 members of the Nashville Song Writers Association, and 300 music publishers (Ewen, 1971, p. 658). By the time Opryland U.S.A. opened in Nashville in 1974, the $15-million-dollar concert hall that would house the Grand Ole Opry had broadcasts being beamed to over 1,000 radio stations in the U.S., as well as a national television network (Ewen. 1971, p. 658). Country music had arrived as a dominant force in the music industry.

All these forces combined to create, promote, and distribute country music. At that time, more than half of all music created in the United States originated in Nashville.

Notable Country and Western Performers

Gene Autry
Glen Campbell
Johnny Cash
Roy Clark
Bobby Gentry
Merle Haggard
Wanda Jackson
Olivia Newton John (one of the first crossover country–pop performers)
George Jones
Kris Kristofferson (also a noted actor)
Loretta Lynn
Reba McEntire
Buck Owens
Dolly Parton
Ray Price
Charlie Pride (one of a handful of Black country performers)
Tex Ritter (The Singing Cowboy)
Kitty Wells
Hank Williams, Sr.
Hank Williams, Jr.
Bob Wills

The Beach Boys

Formed in Hawthorne, California, in 1961, The Beach Boys are one of the most critically acclaimed and commercially successful bands of all time, selling over 100 million records worldwide. They have remained together, despite significant personnel changes, for as long as the Rolling Stones, and recently they celebrated 60 years together. They helped legitimize popular music as a recognized art form and influenced the development of music genres and movements such as psychedelia, power pop, progressive rock, punk, alternative, and lo-fi.

Originally, The Beach Boys consisted of brothers Brian, Dennis, and Carl Wilson, their cousin Mike Love, and friend Al Jardine. Their adolescent-themed lyrics, which at first focused on the Southern California sun, surf, and hot cars lifestyle, were a breath of fresh air for teen-agers, especially on the East Coast, that were stuck in the post-Elvis musical doldrums of the early 1960s. They were musically ingenuous and one of the most influential acts of the rock era. They drew on the sound of older pop vocal groups like The Letterman and The Four Freshman, 1950s rock and roll, and Black R&B to create their unique sound. Under Brian's leadership they often incorporated classical or jazz elements and unconventional recording techniques in innovative ways.

In 1963, they scored their first national hit with "Surfin' U.S.A.," beginning a string of top 10 singles that reflected a Southern California youth culture of surfing, cars, and romance, which was dubbed the **California Sound**. They were one of the few American rock bands to sustain their commercial success during the British Invasion.

In 1965, they abandoned beachgoing themes for more personal lyrics and ambitious orchestrations, even recording **a cappella** songs like the haunting "In My Room." In 1966, the *Pet Sounds* album and "Good Vibrations" single raised the group's prestige as rock innovators.

In the mid-1970s, they experienced a comeback: their concerts drew larger audiences and the band transitioned into an oldies act (the very definition of a niche music group). Mike Love obtained legal rights to tour under the group's name. In the early 2010s, the original members briefly reunited for the band's 50th anniversary.

Between the 1960s and 2020s, the group had 37 songs reach the U.S. Top 40 (the most by any American band), with four topping the Billboard Hot 100. In 2004, they were ranked number 12 on Rolling Stone's list of the greatest artists of all time. The founding members (the Wilson brothers, Love, and Jardine) were inducted into the Rock and Roll Hall of Fame in 1988. They were selected for the Vocal Group Hall of Fame 10 years later. In 2004, the album *Pet Sounds* was preserved in the National Recording Registry by the Library of Congress for being "culturally, historically, and aesthetically significant." Their recordings of "In My Room," "Good Vibrations," "California Girls," and the entire *Pet Sounds* album have been inducted into the Grammy Hall of Fame.

As of 2022, Brian and Jardine do not perform with Love's edition of The Beach Boys, but they remain official members of the band (Wikipedia, 2023, The Beach Boys).

Soul

At the same moment in time that Beatlemania and the British Invasion were overwhelming most U.S. pop music markets, a resurgence of rhythm and blues and gospel, now called soul, took off in African American sections of the nation, especially in cities like Memphis, Chicago, and Oakland, California. Thanks to the civil rights advances of the 1960s, Black entrepreneurs, songwriters, record producers, and record company owners saw the way forward, using "idiomatic techniques and methods basic to rhythm and blues" (Ewen, 1971, p. 676) to reinvigorate Black music for a younger generation of African American youth. Black bands and singer/song writers emerged who could communicate the "soulfulness of the Negro people," or put more simply, "Soul is Rhythm & Blues with the religious fervor of Gospel" (Ewen, 1971, p. 678).

The Beach Boys perform "I Get Around" on the Ed Sullivan Show.

Watch at: https://www.youtube.com/watch?v=ruKCw797JM4

The Memphis Sound

One of the defining sounds of soul came out of Stax Records in Memphis, Tennessee. Starting out in an abandoned movie theater converted to a recording studio with Booker T and The MGS and Otis Redding as the main talent, Stax eventually became a multimillion-dollar enterprise, with Number 1 records from superstars of Soul like Redding, Issac Hayes, Jimmy Floyd, Carla Thomas, and Al Green. Redding died in a plane crash at age 29, just two months after being named foremost male vocalist in the world by the British publication, *Melody Maker* magazine (683).

The Memphis sound was unique for two reasons: First, both the recording artists, and the backup musicians stayed consistent over many years. In the video *Soul Comes Home*, Carla Thomas describes the feeling of family she felt every time she walked into the Stax building to record. Secondly, the recording process never included written out music, which was referred to by musicians as "charts."

Issac Hayes conducts and sings the theme from the movie *Shaft* at the Soul Comes Home celebration of the opening of the Stax Museum in Memphis in 2003.

Watch at: https://www.youtube.com/watch?v=12NQZWz0HKg

> Al Bell, executive at Stax Records, told how the Memphis sound came to be. "... we like for the artists to be able to feel what's in the lyrics of a song, to live with them, and to interpret them in their own fashion. Here, when we get a group of musicians together in a studio, there are no written arrangements. The song has been sketched out by the writer or producer, and the musicians go over it and over it, adding their own ideas, working it over until everybody begins to feel it, then they begin recording it, and it's the spontaneity of the whole thing that brings about the Memphis Sound ..." (683)

The Detroit (Motown) Sound

The other powerhouse of soul in the 1960s was Berry Gordy's Motown Record Corporation in Detroit, Michigan. They were for a time the largest Black owned and operated recording company in the nation. Gordy was a part-time songwriter who started a recording company in 1959 to produce and record Smokey Robinson and the Miracles. After forming Motown records and Tamla, he added the Marvelettes, Mary Wells, The Contours, Martha and the Vandellas, The Supremes, the Four Tops, and 12-year-old little Stevie Wonder, who became one of the great icons of Black music.

The Detroit/Motown Sound envisioned by Gordy and three of his house songwriters was the antithesis of the Memphis Sound. The concept involved discipline and control over all aspects of the writing, arranging, and recording process, which resulted in a more subtle and softer style of soul, more palatable to White teenagers and young adults. The foundational rhythm instruments, bass and percussion, laid down a strong, basic beat with an incessant tambourine in the background hinting at gospel influences (691).

The Motown vision helped propel some great musicians into the spotlight. In 1974, Wonder earned four Grammys, including best album of the year. *Newsweek* called Stevie Wonder, the, "most creative, and popular pop musician of his generation ..." (690). Both Stevie Wonder and Diana Ross (lead singer of the Supremes) have enjoyed 60-year long, immensely successful careers. They continue to receive national and international acclaim for their music and humanitarian outreach.

James Brown and The Famous Flames in 1964.

Watch at: https://www.youtube.com/watch?v=2MRN3GrWHos

James Brown

Number 1 soul brother, the hardest working man in show business, and Mr. Dynamite—James Brown was all of these descriptors and more. From his debut single "Try Me" in 1956, he created rhythmically powerful, intensely personal songs that captured the essence of Black pride and helped him to become one of the most powerful and exciting Black performers in the music business. He was an inspiration to the British Invasion bands. His on-stage persona and delivery were electric—a combination of a Southern Black preacher and the great blues shouters of the 1940s. Among his many accolades, *Look* magazine featured him in a cover story in 1969 (679).

Aretha Franklin

Aretha Franklin, known around the world as "The High Priestess of Soul," was one of the most significant singers, recording artists, and performers in the history of American popular music. She stands with a small number of Black, female singers who define African American popular music, including Mahalia Jackson, Bessie Smith, Ma Rainey, and Ella Fitzgerald and Billie Holiday. She was born in Memphis, Tennessee, in 1942 and grew up in her father's Baptist church in Detroit where he was pastor.

She studied music with Reverend James Cleveland and formed a gospel group with her sister and some friends to sing at local churches. Her father's church was a gathering place for many famous gospel singers, including Mahalia Jackson, but she learned most of her prodigious singing style from her father.

In 1960, She moved to New York, and one year later she signed a contract with Columbia Records, for which she recorded nine albums of popular standards, jazz, and novelty tunes. Her recordings were well received by the critics but had only moderate sales. Her first big break came in 1963 when she performed for the Newport Jazz Festival. Her first Gold record was *I Never Loved a Man*, recorded in 1967 for Atlantic Records. It stayed in at the top of the rhythm and blues charts for seven weeks. From this point on, the succession of successful hits, Gold records, and Grammy awards came rapidly and often (Ewen, 1971, p. 683–684).

Her most well-known song, "Respect," was recorded in 1967 and earned her the first of multiple Grammy Awards, including a Grammy Lifetime Achievement Award. She received hundreds of accolades and awards, including a star on the Hollywood Walk of Fame. The Rock and Roll Hall of Fame named her as the first woman inductee in 1987, she was a Kennedy Center Honoree in 1994, and President Obama awarded her the Presidential Medal of Freedom in 2005.

Aretha Franklin died of pancreatic cancer on August 16, 2018, at age 76. But her music and legacy continues.

San Francisco Rock

San Francisco in the late 1960s had a vibrant youth culture centered on the Haight-Ashbury section of the city where thousands of young people flocked from all over the nation to join the hippie movement. Drugs of all kinds, especially psychedelic varieties like LSD, were popular and easy to acquire. It was also home to an alternative rock music culture inspired by the experimentation of the Beatles and other British bands earlier in the decade.

The many start-up bands and places for them to play sparked interest from local entrepreneurs and promotors like Bill Graham. He capitalized on the popular "psychedelic events" (evenings mixing LSD with rock music) by opening the soon to be legendary **Fillmore West** in an old skating rink. Shows featuring local bands like Jefferson Airplane and the Grateful Dead (a full-on psychedelic band) sold out the Fillmore night after night, and the popularity of the style multiplied exponentially until the music became nationally popular and the bands (mentioned below) had the usual success with recording contracts, concerts, and tours across the country. Of all the groups listed below, only Tower of Power is still together and performing on a consistent basis.

Carlos Santana

Born in 1947, Carlos Santana is a Mexican American guitarist who rose to fame in the late 1960s with his band Santana. A virtuoso guitarist and prolific composer, he emerged from the San Francisco Bay area and pioneered a fusion of psychedelic rock and roll and Latin American jazz. Its sound featured his melodic, blues-based lines set against Latin and African rhythms played on percussion instruments such as timbales and congas, which were not generally heard in rock. Santana's inspired performance at Woodstock in 1969 was a highlight of the festival.

Santana continued to work in these forms over the decades that followed. He experienced a resurgence of popularity and critical acclaim in the late 1990s. In 2015, *Rolling Stone* magazine listed Santana at Number 20 on their list of the 100 greatest guitarists. He has won 10 Grammy Awards and three Latin Grammy Awards. In 1998, he and his band Santana were inducted into the Rock and Roll Hall of Fame. Santana is considered one of the first generation of **guitar heros,** along with Jimi Hendrix, Eric Clapton, and Jimmy Page.

Santana was the poster child of the 1970s for multiculturalism and social justice for minorities. His music and his message of love and peace resonated with his audiences and continues to inspire millions of his fans today. Well into his 70s, he continues to perform and is certainly one of the great icons of American popular music.

Carlos Santana and his band Santana play "Oye Como Va"

Watch at: https://www.youtube.com/watch?v=DolqXz2AIFs

Important Bands of the San Francisco Scene

Country Joe and the Fish
Creedence Clearwater Revival
The Grateful Dead
Janis Joplin with Big Brother and The Holding Company
Jefferson Airplane
Quicksilver Messenger Service
Tower of Power (soul and funk)

Grace Slick and Jefferson Airplane perform "White Rabbit" at Woodstock in 1969

Watch at: https://www.youtube.com/watch?v=Vl89g2SwMh4&t=1s

The 1970s

As you can discern from the above, the 1960s was a decade of unprecedented change and upheaval in American society. By the turn to the new decade, the teenagers who grew up with the Beatles and the British Invasion bands were young adults and ready to move on with their tastes in music. At the same time a new decade brought a new crop of emerging teenagers for the music industry to market to.

Thanks to the immeasurable musical contributions of the Beatles, the Rolling Stones, The Beach Boys, The Who, and so many other bands of the 1960s, popular music was now more eclectic, integrated, and varied than ever. There were so many genres and styles from which to choose, and most were performed by highly skilled professional musicians and singers. The metamorphosis of one musical style into another, for example experimental rock into punk and alternative, shows the expanding creativity of the music community and the acceptance of the style by a large cohort of young people. The common themes that resonate with teenagers—rebellion, denial of adult values, disdain for convention, etc.—fueled the market for groups like the Doors, Alice Cooper, and Black Sabbath.

Disco

Disco is a genre of dance music containing elements of rhythm and blues, funk, soul, pop, and salsa. It rose to popularity from the early-1970s to the early 1980s. Its initial audiences were club-goers from the gay, African American, Italian American, Latino, and psychedelic communities in Philadelphia during the late 1960s and early 1970s.

Disco was a reaction against both the domination of rock music and the stigmatization of dance music by the counterculture during this period. It was a reaction to the progression of rock and roll from danceable, simple tunes to complex, artistic, thought-provoking music.

The disco sound has soaring vocals over a steady 4/4 bass drumbeat, an eighth note or 16th note hi-hat pattern with an open hi-hat on the off-beat, and a prominent, syncopated electric bass line. Many disco recordings feature string sections, brass and saxophones, electric piano, synthesizers, and electric rhythm guitars to create a lush background sound. Instruments such as the flute are often used for solo melodies. Notably, guitar is less frequently used in disco as a lead or solo instrument than at any time since before the early rock and roll era.

While performers and singers garnered the most public attention, record producers working behind the scenes played an important role in developing the disco sound. Improving technology allowed arrangers and producers to incorporate electronic synthesizers, echo effects, and sound layering. Films such as *Saturday Night Fever* (1977) and *Thank God It's Friday* (1978) contributed to disco's rise in mainstream popularity, and many non-disco artists recorded disco tracks at the height of its popularity.

Donna Summer sings an extended version of "Last Dance"

Watch at: https://www.youtube.com/watch?v=v22YbORzDD0&t=7s

Popular dances included The Hustle, a sexually suggestive dance. Discotheque-goers often wore expensive, extravagant, and sexy fashions. There was also a thriving drug subculture in the disco scene, particularly for drugs that would enhance the experience of dancing to loud music and flashing lights, such as cocaine. Disco was the last major popular music movement that was driven by the Baby Boom Generation. For most of the 1970s it was a worldwide phenomenon, but its popularity drastically declined in the United States in 1979 and 1980, and disco was no longer popular in the U.S. by 1981. Disco Demolition Night, an anti-disco protest held in Chicago in July 1979, was likely a factor in disco's fast and drastic decline (Wikipedia, 2023, Disco).

Well-Known Late 1960s and 1970s Disco Performers

The Bee Gees
Chic
Gloria Gaynor
KC and the Sunshine Band
Van McCoy
Walter Murphy (*A Fifth of Beethoven*)
Donna Summer
The Trammps
Village People
Barry White (and The Love Unlimited Orchestra)

Watch at: https://www.youtube.com/watch?v=haGWi5lTibI

Hip-Hop and Rap

As a preface to this discussion of **rap** and **hip-hop,** it is important for the reader to go back to Chapter 1 to view and listen again to the videos in the following textbox.

The first video is an example of African poetry and rhythm. It is indicative of the rich heritage of African folk music and its connection to the rap music of today.

The second video is another example of the same heritage being passed down to current African villagers. Start the

Watch at: https://www.youtube.com/watch?v=lVPLIuBy-9CY&list=RDrrEqNTyMF_A&index=3

video at 4'40" to hear an indigenous African drum ensemble accompany a vocalist who is "rapping" about the king's desire to have rice with his beans.

The point, to be made here again, is that rap and hip-hop are as old as indigenous African folk music and culture. The 20th and 21st century manifestations that are now called rap and hip-hop have been percolating in the African and African American cultural stream for thousands of years. This rich cultural heritage is manifested today in rap and hip-hop, one of the most successful, commercial popular musics in American popular music history.

The terms *rap* and *hip-hop* are so intertwined that many use the two interchangeably. Rap is the primary musical and lyrical element in hip-hop, one of the most significant cultural umbrellas in African American life.

The story of modern rap and hip-hop begins exactly 50 years ago. Just by coincidence, this chapter is being written during the same week in August (2023) that DJ Kool Herc (Clive Campbell) and his sister hosted a house party, a back-to-school jam, at their apartment house in the Bronx, New York, on August 11, 1973. Clive worked with two turntables, "alternating between the two to isolate and extend the drum breaks ..." to allow the dancers more time to dance (George, 2023, p. 46). He also was fond of driving around the Bronx in his Pontiac Bonneville convertible, blasting out tunes to the neighborhood from two huge speakers protruding from his back seat. This was a common sight in his home country of Jamaica, where a "sound system man" drove from village to village playing the latest American rhythm and blues tunes from a huge speaker system mounted on a truck (Covach & Flory, 2023, p. 353).

In the 50-year time span of hip-hop it has become a cultural touchstone of Black life in America, but it is now entrenched in almost every society around the world. Those who attack hip-hop and rap lyrics for the raw, often vulgar, language, don't recognize the honesty of expression that finds favor with Black and White youth. It is not just current Black music styles that use vulgar curse words and sexual innuendo in the lyrics; much of the youth music, Black and White, from the 1950s on uses subtle (sometimes explicit) vulgarities and sexual innuendo in song lyrics.

The following documentary video was made to focus attention on Kool Herc and his pioneering work on, and probable invention of, hip-hop.

Watch at: https://www.youtube.com/watch?v=Qjnc-X-Vfyg

The modern era of popular music, 1954 to the present, represented by primarily Black music styles performed by Blacks and Black music appropriated and performed by Whites, is peppered with lyrics that were considered "unspeakable in polite society" until the youth counterculture movement of the 1960s. Once the music and entertainment industries saw a market for comedians who use **blue** language in their acts (Lenny Bruce, Richard Pryor, George Carlin, Eddie Murphy), and rock and roll groups that sing vulgar, suggestive lyrics (Sid Vicious, Korn, Green Day), the shock value of those lyrics wore off and people became accustomed to hearing them in progressive styles of popular music.

The first collaboration of a White rock band and a Black rap group was between Aerosmith (who recorded the original song in 1975) and Run DMC. "Walk This Way" helped rap cross over to the [White] rock audience in the mid-1980s (Covach & Flory, p. 309). Meanwhile, the East-West rivalry between New York (Biggie) and L.A. (Tupac Shakur) hip-hop styles, which emerged in the 1990s, unfortunately became associated with violence, ending in the murders of Tupac Shakur and Biggie Smalls.

Run-DMC and Aerosmith Perform "Walk This Way"

Watch at: https://www.youtube.com/watch?v=4B_UYYPb-Gk

In the late 20th century and into the 21st century, hip-hop culture encompassed music styles, fashion, television, Broadway, movies, and sports. Jay-Z, Rihanna, Sean Combs, and many other hip-hop luminaries are among the wealthiest people in show business. Perhaps most important is the recognition that rap and hip-hop received from the music industry. As of 2022, there are 10 rappers in the Rock and Roll Hall of Fame. They include the following:

Beastie Boys
Eminem
Grandmaster Flash and the Furious Five
Jay-Z
LL Cool J
The Notorious B.I.G
N.W.A.
Public Enemy
Run-DMC
Tupac Shakur

Many naysayers in the music world thought hip-hop and rap would die out within a few years. It seems that the general public and people who write, produce, and perform the style have proven them wrong. It's safe to say that rap and hip-hop will be around and popular with a wide segment of the world's population for years to come.

Rap and Hip-Hop Groups and Solo Acts Through the Years

Beastie Boys
Mary J. Blige
DJ Jazzy Jeff & the Fresh Prince (Will Smith)
Kurtis Blow
Eminem
Grandmaster Flash
Lauryn Hill
Ice Cube
Jay-Z
Kendrick Lamar
LL Cool J.
MC Hammer
The Notorious B.I.G.
N.W.A.
Public Enemy
Queen Latifah
Run-DMC
Tupac Shakur
Will Smith
Kanye West

Reggae and Ska

In 1974, English rock and blues guitar virtuoso Eric Clapton released a single titled, "I Shot the Sheriff" which became a best-selling song in the U.S. It was a cover of an original reggae song by Bob Marley. This jump-started the popularity of reggae in both the U.S. and the U.K. Reggae developed out of the original Jamaican **ska** style in the 1960s. It had a unique rhythm pattern that emphasized the syncopated "and" of the beat in 4/4 time.

Marley and his band, the Wailers, were popular among reggae fans, but their music and the style remained underground until the mid-1970s when a movie about a fictional Jamaican singer became a cult hit in the U.S., and a soundtrack of the album featuring Jamaican star Jimmy Cliff was released at the same time. These events, and the Clapton single, spurred a reggae craze in both the U.S. and England.

Bob Marley's work became increasingly prominent, and he developed a well-deserved reputation as an advocate for social and political justice in Jamaica and other third-world countries. His death in 1981 at age 36 from cancer was mourned all over the world. His legacy and music have risen to cult status. Reggae remains a very strong niche music in the U.S. and is still popular throughout much of the world (353–357).

More Pop Singers and Groups of the 1970s

Aerosmith
The Allman Brothers Band
Blood Sweat & Tears
David Bowie
Chicago
Alice Cooper
Steely Dan
The Eagles
Earth, Wind and Fire
Fleetwood Mac
Genesis
Grand Funk Railroad
The Jackson Five
Billy Joel
Elton John
Carole King
KISS
Joni Mitchell
Queen
Carly Simon
Steppenwolf
James Taylor
Stevie Wonder
ZZ Top

The 1980s

The number of different pop music genres, styles, and offshoots continued to expand through the 1970s and into the 1980s. One of the drivers of this diversity was the rise of visual media, especially MTV. It debuted on August 1, 1981, and MTV's influence grew throughout the decade, challenging radio as the most prominent way to distribute new music and build performers' careers. With its roots in cable TV, teen-oriented movies, and broadcast television, it served an ever-expanding line up of music styles and catered to a wider age range than had radio and television in previous decades. It became a significant and easy way for audiences to access their favorite stars and audition newcomers.

Along with the impact of MTV, the 1980s fostered the notion of the rock star as artist, an increasing reliance on multimillion dollar album sales, and international concert tours (Schloss, et al., 2012, p. 279). The most impactful performers of the decade were almost all superstars by the end of the decade: Michael Jackson, Madonna, Prince, and Bruce Springsteen. There were many others, but this short list is representative of the best that the 1980s offered up.

An additional group, Swans, is discussed as a seminal group in the growing experimental/punk/extreme metal styles. Their influence across the years from the New York New Wave Movement to death metal is significant.

Michael Jackson

Michael Jackson was arguably the biggest star in popular music in the 1980s, earning the title "The King of Pop," and at least approaching, if not exceeding, the popularity of Elvis from 1955 through the mid-1960s. As a singer, dancer, and actor (his music videos are as much theatre as they are music and dance), he set the standard for every other performer of the decade.

Michael Jackson left Motown and the Jackson Five in 1975 to become a solo performer. His new recording company Epic Records paired him with the great producer/arranger Quincy Jones. They collaborated on two successful albums, *Off the Wall* in 1979 and *Thriller* in 1982. Thanks to the three music videos of *Thriller* in particular, the album had seven top 10 singles. *Thriller* set the industry standard for production, creativity, and cost, and elevated the video medium to the status of the most important way of promoting popular music (Schloss et al., 2012, p. 252). *Thriller* is still the top selling album in music business history, with sales of over 100 million copies. His string of successful albums and singles continued throughout the decade because of his strong choreography and visual presence (406–409).

Sadly, Jackson was the target of critics who accused him of being an "Uncle Tom" or selling out his blackness because of his frequent crossover from Black to White music styles. Even sadder were the accusations of child abuse, and persecution for those accusations, which dogged him for much of his career. The whole world was shocked by his death from an overdose of propofol (an anesthetic drug he used to help him sleep), in 2009 at age 41.

Madonna

The Queen of Pop—The Material Girl—Madonna Ciccone could have had a stellar career as a professional dancer. Her early professional dance associations were with the Pearl Lang and Alvin Ailey dance companies. With her strong dance background, her performances depended as much on the visual as the musical. She was one of the earliest dance-oriented performers to appear frequently on MTV.

Her 1985 album, *Like a Virgin,* shot up the pop album charts, and four singles from it hit the top five, including "Like a Virgin" and "Material Girl." *True Blue* did even better, reaching Number

Michael Jackson sang "Thriller" live in Munich in 1997.

Watch at: https://www.youtube.com/watch?v=7DOzITFjq70

Madonna sang "Express Yourself" at the VMA Awards in 1989.

Watch at: https://www.youtube.com/watch?v=pehMBaHgpWE

1 on the pop album charts in 1986 and producing three Number 1 pop singles that same year—"Live to Tell," "Papa Don't Preach," and "Open Your Heart."

Madonna did not write or produce many of her early hits, but beginning with *True Blue* in 1986, she took a more active role in the creative aspects of her music, earning songwriter and production credits along the way. Madonna's albums and singles in the mid-1980s established her as one of the most important figures in pop music, and she remains among the most successful acts in the music business.

She has continually challenged aspects of what she perceives to be some of society's most troubling issues and practices. As an example, she explored sexuality, race, and the traditional and alternative roles of women and spirituality. While some thought her material was intentionally designed to shock and titillate her audiences for publicity, she fiercely maintained that these issues were important social issues to expose and debate (411–412).

Prince

Prince Rogers Nelson had a relatively normal upbringing in Minneapolis, Minnesota, in a middle-class neighborhood where he was exposed to an eclectic mix of cultures and music styles. He was one of the most creative and prolific performers of the 1980s, writing and producing hit after hit for himself and others like percussionist Shelia E. (Covach & Flory, p. 412).

His music spans a wide range of styles and influences from rhythm and blues, guitar centric rock and roll, urban blues and folk, new wave, jazz, and psychedelic rock. He consistently sought to exert and maintain tight control over the rights to his music and its marketing. In his Paisley Park Studio, he produced and played each instrument on his recordings and sought for years to have total control over his master tapes (Schloss, et al., 2012, p. 272–273).

With his third album, *Dirty Mind*, in 1980 he scored a commercial breakthrough when it climbed to Number 7 on the R&B album charts. His many hit singles and albums to follow were tainted by accusations from the Christian Right that his music was Satanic or pornographic, mostly due to "Darling Nikki," from the *Purple Rain* Album. That recording received a parental advisory warning from the Parents' Music Resource Center (Schloss, et al., 2012, p. 274).

Prince's most controversial episode, however, was not musical. It was his 1993 decision to change his name to "The Artist Formally Known As Prince," represented by the symbol for love. It was prompted by his frustration with Warner Brothers Records, which insisted that they owned the Prince name and all related music marketed under the Prince name (Schloss, et al., 2012, p. 274).

Throughout his career and up until his death Prince remained an enigma to his fans and the press: flower child or dictator, male chauvinist or women's rights advocate, intensely private person or shrewd self-promoter? Suffice it to say that he was a very complex and highly gifted musician and human being.

As with so many top stars of the pop music world, Prince died of opiate addiction and an accidental overdose of fentanyl on April 21, 2016, at age 57.

Prince and the Revolution perform "Let's Go Crazy" live in 1985.

Watch at: https://www.youtube.com/watch?v=svqYueRzAh0&t=1s

Bruce Springsteen

Bruce Springsteen and the E Street Band—one cannot think of one without the other. His peak popularity straddles the decades between the early 1970s and 1980s, and his career continues unabated to today. From the beginning of his success in 1975 with the album *Born to Run,* Springsteen and his band drew on older rock traditions from the 1950s and 1960s. His greatest success would come in the 1980s with his fifth album, *The River,* featuring the hit "Hungry Heart," and continuing with the more introspective and stripped-down album *Nebraska.* Springsteen's landmark release was 1984's *Born in the USA,* which topped the charts in both the United States and Britain and produced six Top 10 American hits, including "Glory Days" and "Born in the U.S.A." *Born in the U.S.A.* is widely considered the "rock anthem" of choice for patriotic men and women throughout the U.S.

> Springsteen's image relied on the idea that he was the voice of that average working-class guy, and his lyrics reflect on common emotional and social problems. *Born in the USA,* for instance, paints a vivid picture of the decay of American values in the industrial heartland, all seen from the perspective of someone who was powerless to affect change (Covach & Flory, p. 421).

For most of his career, Springsteen has promoted the image and persona of the early White rock and roll singer, even while his lyrics more closely align with those of Bob Dylan. Even his backup band, The E Street Band, harks back to the look and instrumentation of 1950's rock and roll bands like Bill Haley and the Comets. Until his death in 2011, Clarence Clemons's tenor saxophone was an indispensable part of that imagery and music style. Today, Springsteen is as relevant and popular with old and new fans as he was at the height of his commercial success.

Watch Bruce Springsteen sing "Dancing In The Dark"

Watch at: https://www.youtube.com/watch?v=129kuDCQtHs

Swans

One group that is not well-known but is considered highly innovative and influential is **Swans**, an American experimental rock band originally active from 1982 to 1997 and led by singer, songwriter, and multi-instrumentalist, Michael Gira. The band was one of the few groups to emerge from the early 1980s

Swans perform "The Glowing Man"

Watch at: https://www.youtube.com/watch?v=gTyzLI2laB4

New York new wave scene and stay intact into the next decade. Formed by Gira in 1982, Swans employed a shifting lineup of musicians until their dissolution in 1997. Besides Gira, the only other constant members were keyboardist/ vocalist/ songwriter Jarboe from 1984 to 1997 and semi-constant guitarist Norman Westberg. Best known for its experimental instrumentation and repetitive song structures. Swans' music has morphed greatly over the decades but is typically dark and apocalyptic, often focusing on themes of power, religion, sex, and death.

In 2010, Gira reformed Swans without Jarboe. They have been active off and on in recent years and produced a new album, *The Beggar*, in June 2023. Swans and Gira are credited with influencing a long list of rock and extreme metal groups, including Nirvana, Tool, and Neurosis (Wikipedia, 2023, Swans).

Prominent Pop Singers and Groups of the 1980s

AC/DC
Boston
David Bowie
Phil Collins and Genesis
Devo
Eurythmics
Boy George
Guns n' Roses
Van Halen
Hall & Oates
Whitney Houston
Janet Jackson
Bon Jovi
Cyndi Lauper
Metallica
Tom Petty and the Heartbreakers
The Police
Styx
Tina Turner
U2

The 1990s

At the end of the 1980s there was a sense of the growing historical importance of rock among both performers and fans, as a result of the first inductees into the Rock and Roll Hall of Fame in 1986 and the continued success of many groups and solo acts from previous decades. Alternative forms of rock and pop music continued to evolve and challenge the traditional elements of the music industry, pumping new blood and new ways of making music into the system.

The march of technology was a major theme in 1990s pop music. Computer-based technology drove economic and social issues, especially when the internet became widely accessible to the general public. When Napster was launched in 1999, it became almost instantaneously popular among young people who saw anything on the internet as fair game and for free, especially recorded music and other artistic entities. Napster allowed them to download and share copyrighted music content over the internet, cutting record companies and performers out of their share of revenue. Music industry group RIAA sued Napster and won, thus shutting them down. Even today the music industry struggles with copyright, file sharing, and intellectual property theft issues (Covach & Flory, p. 467–468).

Generation X (code for people born between 1965 and 1980) were raised on classic rock and punk, internalizing the music culture of their parents and eager to experiment with and define new styles. They were the first generation to grow up with MTV where a song/video was an instant hit across the country—or not. Those performers who were MTV friendly, such as Madonna, Prince, Michael Jackson, and metal/big hair bands saw MTV as a huge boost to their careers. Those who were not selected for MTV broadcast, or eschewed it for "artistic" reasons, alternative rock and hip-hop groups for instance, struggled to break through to the top levels of music and financial success.

A clear example of the fragmentation of discrete styles of rock into multiple versions of the style is alternative rock. It emerged from the indie and hard-core movements in the 1980s and was a reaction to the proliferation and commercialism of mainstream pop and rock in the 1980s. Nirvana, a Seattle based **grunge** band, launched the movement with *Nevermind* in 1991. Several bands, notably Korn and Rage Against the Machine, incorporated the punk aesthetic and developed extensions of metal with rap. Nine Inch Nails further dissected alternative elements into what they called "industrial music," blending noise and avant-garde approaches (Covach & Flory, p. 471).

Nirvana

When Nirvana's second album, *Nevermind*, was released in late 1991, it shot to the top of the pop charts in America and the U.K., mostly with the help of the single, "Smells Like Teen Spirit." Nirvana was the most significant grunge style band to come out of Seattle in the first half of the 1990s.

"The Grunge sound appealed to young white suburbanites (mostly males), who felt alienated from mainstream American values" (Covach & Flory, p. 471). Led by singer-songwriter, guitarist Kurt Cobain, they quickly attained stardom, despite Cobain's assertion that Nirvana's music rejected the rock star/show business imagery. Cobain, along with drummer Dave Grohl and bassist Krist Novoselic, "projected an image of amateurism, but Cobain was ... really a gifted songwriter and a tasteful guitarist" (Covach & Flory, p. 473). The two albums that followed *Nevermind* further cemented the band's status as one of the hottest acts in popular music. Their next two albums both rose to Number 1 in the United States and the U.K.

Nirvana plays "Smells Like Teen Spirit"

Watch at: https://www.youtube.com/watch?v=zucJHYwi2Uc

Cobain, guitarist and leader of the group, committed suicide in 1994 (Covach & Flory, p. 473), but his bandmate, drummer Dave Grohl, continued carrying the standard of alternative with a new group, Foo Fighters.

Dave Grohl

Drummer, guitarist, and vocalist Dave Grohl has carved out a career as one of the most thoughtful and artistic performers in the sphere of alternative rock. A multi-instrumentalist,

Dave Grohl and Foo Fighters perform "Times Like These"

Watch at: https://www.youtube.com/watch?v=rhzmNRtIp8k

songwriter, and producer, he started Foo Fighters in the mid-1990s as a "one man band," playing all of the instruments on his recordings, in the tradition of Prince. Shortly, he brought others onboard, and the group became one of the premier touring and recording bands in rock. With Foo Fighters he plays mostly guitar and fronts the group as lead singer. They are known as one of the most important advocates for modern rock since the new millennium (580).

Between Nirvana and Foo Fighters, Grohl played in the group Them Crooked Vultures, along with Josh Homme and former Led Zeppelin bass player John Paul Jones. Their self-titled album of 2009 won a Grammy for the song "New Fang."

Grohl is acknowledged as one of the most successful rock musicians at balancing his mainstream acceptance with the need to remain true to the heavy styles of the alternative rock sound (580). He continues to perform with Foo Fighters and as a solo guest performer. Among his accolades, he has appeared on a cover of *Rolling Stone* magazine.

Dave Matthews Band

Dave Matthews met his bandmates and formed The Dave Matthews Band while working at a bar in Charlottesville, Virginia, in the 1990s. He learned to play acoustic guitar at age 9 and is considered a virtuoso on the instrument. His band uses an uncommon instrumentation for what is essentially a rock jam band, drums, bass, saxophone, violin, and acoustic guitar. Equally as unorthodox is the mix of styles the band plays: jazz, funk, bluegrass, and original songs all used to create large scale, collective improvisation—thus the notion of a loose, free-wheeling jam band.

While in Charlottesville, they built a large regional following and gained national exposure with the release of *Under the Table and Dreaming*. They were the opening act for Phish on several concerts and then became a fixture on the Billboard charts with successful albums, *Crash*, *Before These Crowded Streets*, *Everyday*, and *Stand Up* (Covach & Flory, 2023, p. 502).

They have won two Grammy Awards and numerous other accolades.

Matthews is also a highly respected actor who has appeared in numerous movies, documentaries, and television shows. He is a generous donor to many political and social causes and well respected for his philanthropy with organizations like Farm-Aid. The Dave Matthews Band continues to perform in concerts through the world and record new music (Wikipedia, 2023, Dave Matthews).

The Dave Matthews Band play "What Would You Say"

Watch at: https://www.youtube.com/watch?v=pGRAG1xaSdg&t=1s

More Rock, Pop, and Country Singers and Groups of the 1990s

Back Street Boys	N.W.A.
Boy Matheney II Men	Sinead O'Connor
Dr. Dre	Pearl Jam Phish
Green Day	Public Enemy
Hootie & the Blowfish	Queen Latifah
Korn	Radiohead
Limp Bizkit	Rage Against the Machine
Lyle Lovett	Red Hot Chili Peppers
MC Hammer	Tupac Shakur
Alanis Morissette	Snoop Dogg
Nine Inch Nails	Britney Spears
NSYNC	Sting

The 2000s and Beyond (The Millennium)

With the advent of a new century came sweeping changes in technology that had profound effects on the music industry. One example among hundreds is the improvements in computerized and digital recording and playback systems that allowed live performance techniques not even imaginable when the Beatles recorded *Sgt. Pepper's Lonely Heart Club Band* in the 1960s. Digital recording, invented in the 1990s, made recording accessible and affordable for start-up as well as experienced groups. Digital tools like sampling and sequencing, as well as the ability to distribute music electronically over the internet greatly improved a musician's chance of producing and promoting a high-quality product.

Recorded media delivery systems changed radically from the 1960s to the 2000s. Consider that within a 50-year time span, recorded media went from vinyl long-play disks (for albums) and 45 RPM records (for singles), to 8-track tape cassettes (only albums) to cassette tapes (only albums), to CDs (only albums), to MP3s and digital file sharing (albums and singles), to the current format where media of all kinds is downloaded to personal devices like phones and PCs from streaming services like Apple Music. In the early 2000s, satellite radio platforms like Sirius became available to listeners, although at a monthly subscription cost for the service. For visual media, satellite and cable television services competed with and sometimes replaced broadcast television as the primary viewing medium in American homes.

Bear in mind that all of the above technologies (and others like reel-to-reel tape) are still available and in use by some listeners. Vinyl, in particular, is experiencing a comeback at present, while many continue to hold on to and enjoy their collection of CDs. Science and technology inevitably will develop more advances in recording and playback techniques and equipment, and manufacturers will offer the new latest technologies to the general public for mass consumption.

For the last section of this chapter, we will focus on the major trends in popular music over the past 20-plus years and highlight four of the hundreds of popular performers who have remained in the public's eyes and ears. We can safely say that almost all of the music styles that have been written and recorded since 1900 (plus or minus 10 years) have a niche music audience who listen to recordings, go to the concerts, and buy new recordings of their chosen performers. In the first two decades of the 2000s, a significant number of performers from the previous five decades—acts from the 1950s like Jerry Lee Lewis and Little Richard, from the 1960's, The Rolling Stones and Paul McCartney, from the 1970s, Earth, Wind and Fire and Chicago, (and so on)— continued to make recordings and perform in public. With that in mind, the four performers highlighted below represent both multi-decade popularity and exceptional artistry in music performance and composition across the first two decades of the 21st century.

Pat Metheny (Group)

You may question the inclusion of Pat Metheny on this very short list of performers from the first two decades of the 2000s. It's likely that you have not heard of him. If not, please take the time to listen to the YouTube recording below before you read this section. Also, read some of the comments below the video to understand the high regard for Metheny and his pianist/collaborator Lyle Mays (who wrote *The First Circle* and many of the group's signature pieces).

Pat Metheny is a virtuoso guitarist who has mastered virtually every style of popular music and incorporates an eclectic mix of styles in his compositions and performances. Although categorized mainly as a jazz guitarist in the 1970s, even today he continues to defy any singular stylistic definitions. He is often lumped in with a select group of eclectic jazz and pop musicians that include Chuck Mangione, Al Di Meola (another superb guitarist), Brecker Brothers, and bands like Yellowjackets.

Metheny was born into a musical family in Kansas City in 1954. He began trumpet lessons at age 8 and switched to guitar at age 12. By 15, he was working regularly with the best jazz musicians in Kansas City. With the release of his first album, *Bright Size Life,* in 1975, he reinvented the traditional "jazz guitar" sound for a new generation of players. Pat Metheny has continued to redefine and expand the jazz genre by utilizing new technology and working to evolve the improvisational and sonic potential of his instrument. His versatility and improvisational skills are without peer.

The Pat Metheny Group perform "The First Circle"

Watch at: https://www.youtube.com/watch?v=FTGgle6mxF0

His body of work includes compositions for solo guitar, small ensembles, electric and acoustic instruments, large orchestras, and ballet pieces, with settings ranging from modern jazz to rock to classical. This is where Metheny's range of musical acumen and compositional abilities sets him apart. He is certainly one of the great performers and composers in any music genre of the 20th and 21st centuries.

Metheny has been awarded three gold records for *Still Life (Talking)*, *Letter from Home*, and *Secret Story*. In addition, he has won countless polls for best jazz guitarist. He won 20 Grammy Awards in 12 different categories, including Best Rock

Instrumental, Best Contemporary Jazz Recording, Best Jazz Instrumental Solo, and Best Instrumental Composition. The Pat Metheny Group won an unprecedented seven consecutive Grammys for seven consecutive albums (Wikipedia, 2023, Pat Metheny).

Beyonce

Since the early 2000s, Beyonce (Knowles-Carter) has been one of the brightest and most versatile female singers, songwriters, dancers, and actresses in the music business. Her initial exposure to the public came as the lead singer of the group Destiny's Child. To millions of her fans, she represents female empowerment, financial independence, and the best qualities of a strong African American woman.

Her music style is a combination of rhythm and blues, hip-hop, and pop, and she consciously works to evoke the image and memory of female singers from the past: Diana Ross, Donna Summer, Tina Turner, and Etta James (who Beyonce portrayed in the 2008 movie *Cadillac Records*). It seems clear that she is working to establish a legacy, standing on the shoulders of the great female singers of the previous century (Starr & Waterman, 2018, p. 592).

Her marriage to Jay Z on April 4, 2008, created one of the most powerful show business "power couples" in history. As of April 2014, the couple had sold a combined 300 million records together (Wikipedia, 2023, Beyonce).

She is the most awarded female performer of all time. A partial list of her accolades and accomplishments include Super Bowl performances in 2013 and 2016, 32 Grammy awards in various categories—she shares with Adele the most Grammys awarded to a female vocalist in one night, six (Wikipedia, 2023, Beyonce).

Beyonce is still in the prime of her career and she already richly deserves her well-earned moniker, "Queen Bey."

Taylor Swift

Three of the four highlighted performers rely on visual as well as sonic imagery in their live performances. Taylor Swift's life and music are as much about her lifestyle as her onstage persona. She has hundreds of millions of followers on her Instagram account, and her whole life seems to be on display 24/7 on social media. That said, Taylor Swift is today one of the most important and iconic female performers in the world. Her most recent tour sold out every show, and fans spent thousands of dollars for tickets and Taylor Swift "merch."

Beyonce sing "Spirit"
(from *The Lion King*)

Watch at: https://www.youtube.com/watch?v=civgUOommC8

Taylor Swift was born in West Reading, Pennsylvania, in 1989. She was inspired to become a country music performer by listening to recordings of Shania Twain and Faith Hill. Before she was 15 years old, she and her family moved to the Nashville, Tennessee, area so that she could pursue a career in country music. While still a teen, she recorded her second album, *Fearless,* from which came 11 Hot 100 hit singles. It won Best Album view and hear Taylor Swift sing "Mean"

Watch at: https://www.youtube.com/watch?v=jYa1eI1hpDE

and Best Country Album in 2006 (Starr & Waterman, 2018, p. 541–542). From this point on, her albums have consistently topped the country and pop charts, although it appears that she has spent much of her career moving away from the country genre and toward the wider pop music market and fan base.

She is now considered a key performer in the larger pop music landscape and has captured a new generation of young, adoring fans. Swift made a conscious decision to embrace and remake herself in the image of Carole King and Joni Mitchell, the iconic singer-songwriters from the 1960s and 1970s. Her album, *1989,* recorded and released in 2015, was her official break from country music. Interestingly, on the last night of her recent concert tour, she announced that she was ready to reissue the *1989* album (Starr & Waterman, 2018, 594–595).

Like Beyonce, Taylor Swift is in the prime of her career, and fans and admirers can likely look forward to many more years as "Swiftys" (fans) of Taylor Swift's special brand of music and entertainment.

Lady Gaga

Of all of the women singers highlighted in this book, Lady Gaga may be the most uniquely gifted and eclectic performer in modern popular music history. She certainly is one of the most strikingly original singers and actors to emerge in the post-millennium era. Her original name, Stefani Germanotta, her Italian family background, and her New York upbringing evoke some comparisons with other great music icons—Frank Sinatra, Tony Bennett (with whom she became best friends), and Madonna (who Gaga credits as one of her main influences).

She has a strong academic pedigree to go along with her stunning abilities. She studied piano from age four and she performed in theatre through high school. She majored in music at NYU, where she studied songwriting but left in her sophomore year to pursue her career. She also studied acting with Lee Strasburg for 10 years. As an actress she starred in and wrote most of the music for a remake of *A Star Is Born* with Bradley Cooper. That performance garnered nominations for a Golden Globe and an Academy Award.

One of the most unique facets of her style and career is her kaleidoscopic persona and constantly changing visual image. Her "act" which is always much more than a concert of her songs, includes outrageous costumes and sets and large contingents of background singers and dancers. She has absorbed the grand tradition of excess in production values from predecessors like David Bowie, Madonna, and Michael Jackson (575).

In recent years, especially when performing with singers like Tony Bennett (with whom she toured and performed in a well-received television special), she has toned down her image, ostensibly to allow the music and her superb voice and delivery to shine through. The last video below is not only a wonderful example of Lady Gaga's musicianship, but also a fitting tribute to the recently deceased Tony Bennett, who Frank Sinatra called "The greatest singer in the world."

Like the other performers above, Lady Gaga has many more years of performance excellence and artistic growth to look forward to.

Lady Gaga and Tony Bennett sing "I've Got You Under My Skin"

Watch at: https://www.youtube.com/watch?v=xyTa_gJkYwI&t=4s

More Popular Singers and Groups of the 2000s

50 Cent
Adele
Black Eyed Peas
Mary J. Blige
Coldplay
Drake
Jay-Z
Toby Keith
Alicia Keys
Kendrick Lamar
Bruno Mars
Nicki Minaj
Brad Paisley
Linkin Park
Maroon 5
Radiohead
Rihanna
Shakira
Kanye West

Key Takeaways

- The number of different styles in American popular music increased exponentially from the 1960s to the 2000s.
- Most of the traditional rock and pop styles remained popular with their initial audiences as the years passed, and their music went from very popular to the niche music category.
- Some new music styles remained popular for a short period and then faded into obscurity, while others like rap and hip-hop gained strength, matured, and deepened in social and cultural importance.
- There is now a style or genre of popular music to satisfy every person's taste, no matter how jaded or unique.
- The only question now is what's the next big thing in American popular music?

Review Questions

Directions: Refer to what you learned in this chapter to help you respond completely and correctly to the questions and prompts below.

1. Explain the effect the introduction MTV had on the music business in 1981.
2. How did disco change the landscape of American popular music?
3. What aspects of music production and performance remained constant throughout the years from 1970 to 2020?
4. Write a list of reasons Michael Jackson and Madonna are considered the King and Queen of Pop.

5. What factors played into the increasing use of vulgar lyrics and extreme on-stage behaviors (shock rock) from the 1970s on?
6. In your opinion, what will American popular music look and sound like 10 years from now?

Class or Individual Project

In a two-page essay, compare a style or performer from the 1970s with one from the 2000s or later. Discuss influences, changes in singing style that you may hear in the videos, instrumentation, and visual/stage presentation.

References

Breckenridge, S. L. (2012). *Popular music in America.* Kendall Hunt.

Christgau, R. (2000). *Any old way you choose it: Rock and other pop music, 1967–73.* Cooper Square Press.

Covach, J., & Flory, A. (2023). *What's that Sound?* W. W. Norton & Company.

Crawford, R., & Hamberlin, L. (2001). *An Introduction* to *America's Music.* W. W. Norton and Co.

Ewen, D. (1977). *All the years of American popular music,* Prentice Hall, Inc.

George, N. (2023, June/July). 50 years of hip-hop. *AARP the Magazine.*

Immerwahr, D. (2019). *How to hide an empire.* Farrar, Straus and Giroux.

Schloss J., Starr, L., & Waterman, C. (2012). *Rock music, culture and business.* Oxford University Press.

Starr, L., & Waterman, C. (2018). *American popular music* (5th ed). Oxford University Press.

Wikipedia. (2023). The Beach Boys. https://en.wikipedia.org/wiki/The_Beach_Boys

Wikipedia. (2023). Beyonce. https://en.wikipedia.org/wiki/Beyoncé. Accessed August 16, 2023

Wikipedia. (2023). Disco. https://en.wikipedia.org/wiki/Disco. Accessed August 13, 2023

Wikipedia. (2023). Fabian Forte. https://en.wikipedia.org/wiki/Fabian_Forte. Accessed on August 6, 23

Wikipedia. (2023). Dave Matthews. https://en.wikipedia.org/wiki/Dave_Matthews. Accessed, August 15, 2023

Wikipedia. (2023). Pat Metheny. https://www.patmetheny.com/bio/. Accessed, August 16, 2023

Wikipedia. (2023). Swans. https://en.wikipedia.org/wiki/Swans_(band). Accessed, August 14, 2023

Credit

Fig. 14.1: Rowland Scherman, "Bob Dylan and Joan Baez," https://commons.wikimedia.org/wiki/File:Joan_Baez_and_Bob_Dylan.jpg, 1963.

Appendix A
Icons of American Popular Music, by Decade

A musical icon is someone who develops or radically changes a musical style, contributes original music of the highest quality over multiple decades, and receives accolades and awards from multiple organizations such as the Grammys, Oscars, and the Rock and Roll Hall of Fame.

This list includes some of the most iconic American Popular Music performers since the early years of American popular music. They are listed by the decade in which they began their career.

Pre-1900

Steven Foster
John Philip Sousa
Scott Joplin
Buddy Bolden
James A. Bland

1900–1920

Joe King Oliver
Louis Armstrong
Bessie Smith
Jelly Roll Morton
The Original Dixieland Jazz Band
Ma Rainey
W.C. Handy
Hoagy Carmichael
Leadbelly
George M. Cohan

1920–1930

Paul Whiteman
George Gershwin
Fletcher Henderson
Al Jolson
Irving Berlin
Cole Porter
Bing Crosby
Jerome Kern
Blind Lemon Jefferson
Robert Johnson

1930–1940

Jimmy Rogers
The Carter Family Singers
Woody Guthrie
Benny Goodman
Duke Ellington
Count Basie
Glenn Miller
Frank Sinatra
Ella Fitzgerald
Billie Holiday
Art Tatum
Tommy Dorsey
Jimmy Dorsey

1940–1950

Tony Bennett
Thelonious Monk
Charlie Parker
Dizzy Gillespie
Billy Holiday
Art Blakey
Kenny Clarke
Miles Davis
John Lewis
Sister Rosetta Tharpe

1950–1960

Buddy Holley
Carl Perkins
Chuck Berry
Bo Didley
The Everly Brothers
Bill Haley and the Comets
Little Richard
Jerry Lee Lewis
Elvis Presley
Carl Perkins
Johnny Cash
Les Paul and Mary Ford
Oscar Peterson
Maynard Ferguson
Buddy Rich
Herbie Hancock
Ray Charles
B.B. King
Dave Brubeck
Ray Charles

1960–1970

The Beatles
Paul McCartney
Ringo Starr
John Lennon
George Harrison
The Rolling Stones
The Beach Boys
Diana Ross and the Supremes
Stevie Wonder
Quincy Jones
Peter, Paul and Mary
The Kingston Trio
Bob Dylan
Joan Baez
Willie Nelson
Eric Clapton
Jimi Hendrix

Bob Marley
The Doors
The Grateful Dead
Janice Joplin
The Yardbirds
Jimmy Page
Aretha Franklin
Velvet Underground
Lou Reed
Dolly Parton
Frankie Valli and the Four Seasons
Barbara Streisand

1970–1980

Kool Herc
Steely Dan
Led Zepplin
Yes
Frank Zappa
Pink Floyd
Alice Cooper
Kiss
The Police; Sting
Black Sabbath
Carlos Santana and Santana
ZZ Top
Aerosmith
The Who
James Taylor
Carol King
Paul Simon
Elton John
The Eagles
Blood, Sweat and Tears
Chicago
David Bowie
Tower of Power
Earth, Wind and Fire
The Ramones
The New York Dolls

Bob Marley
Billy Joel
Lionel Richie
Stevie Wonder
Isaac Hayes
Bee Gees
Donna Summer
Rush
Queen
Pat Metheny

1980–1990

Michael Jackson
Madonna
Janet Jackson
Cyndi Lauper
Bruce Springsteen
Prince
U2
AC/DC
Tina Turner
Run-DMC
Ice-T
Queen Latifa
Public Enemy
Selena
Swans

1990s

Nirvana
Dave Grohl
Rage Against the Machine
Green Day
Nine Inch Nails
Dave Matthews
Sheryl Crow
Mary J. Blige
Eminen

2000s

Taylor Swift
Lady Gaga
Beyonce
Jay-Z
Usher
Kelly Clarkson
Coldplay
Alicia Keys
John Legend
Ed Sheeran

About the Author

Dr. Philip G. Simon, Associate Professor of Music Emeritus, is in his third year as an instructor with the Osher Life Long Learning Institute at Temple University. As an adjunct faculty at Wilkes University he currently teaches private lessons on string bass and tuba and serves on University Committees. He also teaches a hybrid class in American Popular Music at Temple's Ambler Campus. Dr. Simon was Director of Bands and Associate Professor of Music at Wilkes University for 19 years. He taught high school instrumental music in Maryland and Virginia for 29 years, including 16 years as the Director of Bands at the Thomas Jefferson High School for Science and Technology in Fairfax County, Virginia.

Dr. Simon continues to perform, guest conduct, and give back to the music education community as an adjudicator, clinician, and consultant. He has conducted professional, collegiate, and high school bands and orchestras in Pennsylvania, Texas, Kansas, Florida, Massachusetts, Virginia, Washington, D.C., California, Maryland, and the United Kingdom. He is a contributing author to the popular music education series, *Teaching Music Through Performance In Band,* published by GIA. His DMA dissertation is published by VDM Publications. He performs in the Northeastern Pennsylvania region on tuba, string bass, and bass guitar. Dr. Simon earned degrees from Boston University, the University of Maryland, and his DMA in Wind Conducting is from the University of North Texas.

Dr. Simon recently was appointed an Alumni Ambassador for the Boston Youth Symphony Orchestra, and he is listed in the most recent editions of *Marquis Who's Who in America* and *Who's Who In American Education.* In fall 2012, he was awarded the Multiculturalism Award by Wilkes University for excellence in teaching multiculturalism in the classroom. He received The Pennsylvania Music Educators Association District 9 Citation of Excellence Award for 2007, and he has been honored with three Citations of Excellence from the National Band Association.

Dr. Simon served in the First US Army Band as principal tubist from 1969 to 1971. He and his wife Lucinda live in Drums, PA. They have three grown children and seven grandchildren.

Printed in the USA
CPSIA information can be obtained
at www.ICGtesting.com
LVHW060508200824
788703LV00013B/59

9 781793 516848